CENTRE FOR CO-OPERATION WITH NON-MEMBERS (CCNM)

OECD ECONOMIC SURVEYS

1999-2000

THE BALTIC STATES

A *Regional Economic Assessment*

ORGANISATION FOR ECONOMIC CO-OPERATION AND DEVELOPMENT

ORGANISATION FOR ECONOMIC CO-OPERATION AND DEVELOPMENT

Pursuant to Article 1 of the Convention signed in Paris on 14th December 1960, and which came into force on 30th September 1961, the Organisation for Economic Co-operation and Development (OECD) shall promote policies designed:

- to achieve the highest sustainable economic growth and employment and a rising standard of living in Member countries, while maintaining financial stability, and thus to contribute to the development of the world economy;
- to contribute to sound economic expansion in Member as well as non-Member countries in the process of economic development; and
- to contribute to the expansion of world trade on a multilateral, non-discriminatory basis in accordance with international obligations.

The original Member countries of the OECD are Austria, Belgium, Canada, Denmark, France, Germany, Greece, Iceland, Ireland, Italy, Luxembourg, the Netherlands, Norway, Portugal, Spain, Sweden, Switzerland, Turkey, the United Kingdom and the United States. The following countries became Members subsequently through accession at the dates indicated hereafter: Japan (28th April 1964), Finland (28th January 1969), Australia (7th June 1971), New Zealand (29th May 1973), Mexico (18th May 1994), the Czech Republic (21st December 1995), Hungary (7th May 1996), Poland (22nd November 1996) and Korea (12th December 1996). The Commission of the European Communities takes part in the work of the OECD (Article 13 of the OECD Convention).

OECD CENTRE FOR CO-OPERATION WITH NON-MEMBERS

The OECD Centre for Co-operation with Non-Members (CCNM) promotes and co-ordinates OECD's policy dialogue and co-operation with economies outside the OECD area. The OECD currently maintains policy co-operation with approximately 70 non-Member economies.

The essence of CCNM co-operative programmes with non-Members is to make the rich and varied assets of the OECD available beyond its current Membership to interested non-Members. For example, the OECD's unique co-operative working methods that have been developed over many years; a stock of best practices across all areas of public policy experiences among Members; on-going policy dialogue among senior representatives from capitals, reinforced by reciprocal peer pressure; and the capacity to address interdisciplinary issues. All of this is supported by a rich historical database and strong analytical capacity within the Secretariat. Likewise, Member countries benefit from the exchange of experience with experts and officials from non-Member economies.

The CCNM's programmes cover the major policy areas of OECD expertise that are of mutual interest to non-Members. These include: economic monitoring, structural adjustment through sectoral policies, trade policy, international investment, financial sector reform, international taxation, environment, agriculture, labour market, education and social policy, as well as innovation and technological policy development.

Table of contents

Policy insights from a decade of Baltic transition   9

I.   Overview of the transition process   21

    Context, and structure of the study   21
    The Soviet period and the similar starting point of transition   24
    Management of the transition: different paths during 1990-98   29
    Developments and problems in the real economy   38

II.   Monetary developments and policy   57

    Background: institutional parallels and similar policy choices   57
    First steps towards monetary stabilisation   58
    Securing stabilisation and building monetary credibility   62
    Sustainability of the monetary framework   74

III.   Comparison of developments in fiscal policy   81

    Fiscal policy at the centre of macroeconomic policy making   81
    Reform of the tax system   85
    Management of expenditure   90
    The Russian crisis: a source of divergence   97
    Policy challenges ahead   100

IV.   Banking and financial sector reform   103

    Initial explosion in the number of banks   104
    ... but, weak supervision invited banking crises   104
    Faster international integration and financial deepening followed financial
      crisis   108
    Testing the new financial structures: the Asian and Russian crises   112
    Further bank consolidation and financial deepening is needed   115

V.   Enterprise reform and economic restructuring   119

    A comparison of the privatisation process in the Baltics   119
    Establishing the links between privatisation and corporate governance   132
    Regional and sectoral dimensions of enterprise restructuring   140

VI.   Labour market and social policy developments   151

    A tremendous transition shock   151
    The worst hardships have been overcome, but moderate poverty persists   152

VII. Integration in the world economy and regional co-operation   179

    Trade liberalisation has led sectoral adjustment   179
    Economic integration of the Baltic countries   184
    Foreign investment liberalisation should be pursued further   192

Notes   195

Bibliography   207

Annexes

  I.   Agriculture in Estonia, Latvia and Lithuania: developments and policies   215
  II. Statistical Annex   233

●●●●●

Boxes

1.   National Account Systems in the Baltics: comparability and progress   47
2.   Overview of tax reform   84
3.   Case study: the informal sector in Latvia   90
4.   The Estonian Stabilisation Reserve Fund (SRF)   99
5.   Organisation of a financial supervisory authority   110
6.   Principles of corporate governance: developments in the Baltics   133
7.   Issues in education policy   162
8.   Reform of pension systems   174
9.   Institution of political co-operation between Baltic countries   185
10. Cases of trade dispute resolution mechanisms within the Baltics   188
11. The institutional framework for co-operation with Nordic countries   189
12. International investment: the OECD's rules of the game   193

Tables

1.   Change in the ethnic composition of the Baltic States, 20th century   22
2.   Quality of life: some indicators, 1991-97   25
3.   Structure of gross domestic product in 1989   27
4.   Structure of industrial production in 1989   28
5.   A different management of the transition process, 1990-98   30
6.   Key macroeconomic indicators, 1991-99   34
7.   Monetary policy strategies, instruments and procedures   77
8.   Government expenditure by type, 1995-99   93
9.   Scope of the national budget   94
10. Shares in selected government expenditure by tier, 1996   94
11. Some financial sector indicators, 1995-99   105
12. Loan classification and provisions, 1995-99   109
13. Top regional banks, ranked by assets end-1998   116
14a. An overview of the privatisation process, 1989-98   120
14b. Different types of privatisation of large enterprises, end-1998   127
15. Role of foreign investors in large privatisation, 1998   130

16.   Some observations of efficiency by ownership group   137
17.   Results on the relation between type of ownership and performance   138
18.   Personal incomes: key amounts per month   153
19.   Food shares in household consumption expenditure   154
20.   Income distribution by deciles, 1998   155
21.   Employed persons by type of activity, 1998   157
22.   Labour force participation, employment and unemployment by gender
        and age, 1998   160
23.   Labour force participation, employment and unemployment rates:
        international comparison, 1998   161
24.   Unemployed persons, 1998   163
25.   Unemployment rates by ethnic group, 1998   164
26.   Working time   164
27.   Industrial relations   165
28.   Average pre-tax wage, 1998   166
29.   Public expenditures on social programmes   172
30.   Comparison of trade structure   180
31a. Estonia: net job creation and destruction by enterprise size, 1994-97   181
31b. Latvia: net job creation and destruction by enterprise size, 1995-98   182
31c. Lithuania: net job creation and destruction by enterprise size, 1995-97   183
32.   Trade structure by partner country   186
33.   FDI stocks by country of origin, 1998   190

Annexes

A1.   Gross agricultural output, total, crops and livestock   218
A2.   Share of agriculture and food products in total trade   220
A3.   Agricultural and food exports by destination, 1993-98   221
A4.   Agricultural and food imports by source, 1993-98   222
A5.   Estimates of support to agriculture by country, 1996-98   226
A6.   Indicators of living standards   234
A7.   Employment by main sector   236
A8.   Employment in industry by sector   237
A9.   Labour force developments in Estonia, 1989-98   238
A10. Labour force participation, employment and unemployment   239
A11. Employment and educational attainment   240
A12. Wage characteristics   241
A13. Relative wages by sector   241
A14. Consumption expenditure in rural versus urban households   242
A15. Regional disparities   243
A16. Internal and external mobility   245
A17. Balance of payments: Estonia   246
A18. Balance of payments: Latvia   247
A19. Balance of payments: Lithuania   248
A20. GDP by expenditure: Estonia   249
A21. GDP by expenditure: Latvia   250
A22. GDP by expenditure: Lithuania   251
A23. Employment, output and productivity growth, 1994-97: Estonia   252
A24. Employment, output and productivity growth, 1995-98: Latvia   253
A25. Employment, output and productivity growth, 1995-97: Lithuania   254
A26. Trade structure: Estonia   255

A27.   Trade structure: Latvia   256
A28.   Trade structure: Lithuania   257
A29.   Consolidated general government operations, 1994-99: Estonia   258
A30.   Consolidated general government operations, 1994-99: Latvia   259
A31.   Consolidated general government operations, 1994-99: Lithuania   260
A32.   Composition of consolidated bank balance sheets: assets   261
A33.   Composition of consolidated bank balance sheets: liabilities   262
A34.   Monetary survey of Estonia   263
A35.   Monetary survey of Latvia   264
A36.   Monetary survey of Lithuania   265

Figures

1.   Output decline and recovery in transition countries   39
2.   Output decline and recovery, Baltics and Russian Federation   41
3.   GDP recovery and trade trends   42
4a.   Contributions to GDP growth in Estonia   44
4b.   Contributions to GDP growth in Latvia   45
4c.   Contributions to GDP growth in Lithuania   46
5a.   Sustainability of the current account   49
5b.   Sustainability of the current account net of FDI flows   50
6.   Recent trends in industrial production   52
7.   Recent trends in retail sales   52
8.   Recent trends in credit growth   53
9.   Recent trends in registered unemployment   54
10.   Recent trends in bilateral exchange rates   55
11.   Monthly inflation, 1991-94   59
12.   Roubles per unit of local currency   61
13.   Nominal effective exchange rates   62
14.   Annual CPI inflation   63
15.   Real effective exchange rates   64
16.   Official reserves and money aggregates   66
17.   Broad money as share of GDP   67
18.   Monetisation ratio relative to GDP per capita, 1997   67
19.   Developments in deposit and currency holdings   68
20.   Recent growth rates in money aggregates   70
21.   Interest rate developments   72
22.   Interbank market average interest rates   73
23.   Real interest rates on local currency deposits   74
24.   General government balance, 1993-98   83
25.   General government revenues, 1993-98   83
26.   Composition of revenues, 1998   86
27.   Payroll taxes and social security contributions, 1999   88
28.   Shares in government expenditure, 1993-98   92
29.   Gross stocks of public debt, 1998   95
30.   General government balance by quarter   98
31.   Russian and Baltic States stock market indices   113
32.   Activity as share of GDP   142
33a.   Regions and major cities in Estonia   143
33b.   Regions and major cities in Latvia   143

33c. Regions and major cities in Lithuania 144
34. Real wages 156
35. Employment 156
36. Population 158
37. Educational attainment of the labour force 161
38. Average wages after tax by gender and type of enterprise 167

Annexes

A1. Share of agriculture in GDP 216
A2. Share of agriculture in employment 217

The draft document on which this Survey is based was prepared by Joaquim Oliveira Martins and Tristan Price, under the supervision of Silvana Malle. Substantive contributions were made by Maitland MacFarlan (Chapter II) and Anders Reutersward, OECD/DEELSA (Chapter VI).

Consultancy support was provided by Niels Mygind, Inna Steinbucka, Andres Sutt and Nijolé Zambaité. Additional material was provided by OECD/DAFFE and OECD/SIGMA, and Annex I was prepared by OECD/AGR. Seija Lainela and Christian Lövgren also participated in the preparation of the Study. Technical assistance was provided by Anne Legendre and Azita Kolster, secretarial assistance by Hazel Rhodes and Anne Prioul. The Survey was carried out in the context of the CCNM Baltic programme and was presented at a special meeting of the Economic and Development Review Committee on 8 November 1999.

This Survey is published under the responsibility of the Secretary-General of the OECD.

Policy insights from a decade of Baltic transition

From Soviet Republics to integration with Europe

Following their renewed independence in the early 1990s, the Baltic countries have achieved impressive progress over a decade of transition. They have liberalised and opened their economies to the international market, and have implemented a significant number of difficult and complex market-oriented structural reforms. The tremendous output fall of the early nineties reflected the extent of the economic distortions existing before transition and the degree of restructuring required. By 1994-95 positive growth had resurfaced, and by 1997 growth in the Baltics was amongst the fastest in transition economies. The Russian crisis of mid-1998 brought a halt to fast growth, but did not reverse the trend. The Baltic countries are on the track to sustainable growth, although the deterioration of macroeconomic indicators has raised concerns and suggests that the transformation process, even if relatively advanced, is not yet over.

The Baltic countries had similar starting points, but adopted a different management of the transition. This created some divergence in the economic situations up to the mid-1990s. But the prospects of EU enlargement stimulated convergence, and even emulation, across the three countries by creating a common policy framework and goals. Facilitated by the cyclical upswing there was convergence in macroeconomic policies and in some important areas of structural reform. However, the impact of the Russian crisis on these economies brought back into focus the differing pace of structural adjustment that the apparent convergence had obscured. In this regard, the way each Baltic economy reacted to the Russian crisis has been revealing.

This Study is a regional economic assessment, focusing on the process of transformation in the Baltic area as a whole, rather than a sequence of country-by-country developments. Within this context, the different approaches to reform adopted in the first decade of transition in Estonia, Latvia and Lithuania have provided a real policy experiment. Some relevant insights can be drawn on the basis of this comparison of policies, and their outcomes.

Transition is a package of interdependent reforms

Like other transition countries, the Baltics were offered roughly the same "policy package" in the early 1990s: a liberal approach towards economic policy under a rigorous macroeconomic framework. Drawing the lessons from a decade of transition, the initial recommendations of this package need to be fine-tuned in several areas. Not only does each country face specific conditions that need to be taken into account, but also the process of transition itself has been quite unique. The OECD's policy recommendations towards transition countries have aimed precisely at designing coherent macroeconomic stabilisation and structural reform packages tailored to each country's needs. In retrospect, the critical advantage of a liberal policy package is its strong internal coherence. Indeed, most policy prescriptions are targeted towards the same aim: the use of market mechanisms to obtain the best possible allocation of resources, which in turn creates the conditions for sustainable growth and an improvement of living standards. This truly makes the management of the transition a package of interdependent reforms. The experience of the Baltic countries confirms this insight: in practice, the difficulty of managing a transition process is about the need to set up a coherent policy framework for mutually supportive macroeconomic policies and structural reforms, encompassing a vision of the dynamics.

Many examples of these policy links can be found. The observation of a decade of transition in the Baltics and in other transition countries reported in several OECD Surveys provides solid evidence that macroeconomic stabilisation is not an end in itself. It is a necessary condition to start the reform process. But stabilisation can only be sustained and lead to economic recovery if significant and steady progress is achieved in the area of structural reform. In turn, all structural reforms have to be adequately co-ordinated. For example, even the best-laid plans for large enterprise restructuring cannot bear their full fruits if the banking sector is not behaving according to appropriate market incentives ensuring financial discipline. Likewise, if banks have been restructured but bankruptcy proceedings are not effective, banks cannot both provide credits and impose financial discipline. Fiscal discipline cannot be sustained if the sector of the large state-owned enterprises remains unrestructured. It is hard to attract foreign capital when privatisation lacks momentum or insiders are privileged.

In the Baltic countries, differences in the management of transition have been concentrated in the approach to structural reform, both in terms of scope and timing. In most cases, transition countries need not only to solve the problems of *stocks* related to legacies of the previous regime, such as bad debts and unrestructured firms, but also to ensure that policies get the *flows* right, namely exit and entry of firms, new financing and investment. When the flow problems have not been solved, the stock problems tend to re-emerge, sometimes making their solution even more costly. The direction of causality is often difficult to disentangle. Given that all the variables are interdependent there is in principle no optimal sequencing of policies; reforms have to take place in parallel. Where it is not possible, for whatever reason, actually to implement a well-focused and comprehensive liberal reform package, a second-best approach is to identify and prioritise the bottlenecks in the adjustment process. But policy-makers need to tread carefully. If the policy links are not in place, there is an increased risk that isolated policy initiatives may inadvertently lead to crisis situations, with all the social and political consequences they may entail.

Insufficient emphasis has been put on the time needed for institution building

Successfully making use of market mechanisms requires Baltic countries to develop new institutions, without which transitional reforms will be delayed or frustrated. They are needed for macroeconomic management and structural policy, but go wider than economic management to include an effective and transparent system of civil justice and achieving a clear set of working relationships between central government and local authorities. In many cases commentators have underestimated the time and effort needed to develop the human capital to operate new institutions, and the bureaucratic complexities in getting them established. Good policy choices minimise the time taken to build institutions needed for a market economy, but there is a limit below which this time cannot be compressed.

Institutions that can be created quite quickly include establishing a two-tier banking system and setting out new tax structures. This is not enough on its own. Authorities are needed to ensure adequate banking supervision and collect taxes that are due. Bureaucrats and entrepreneurs need to be trained. Even with good banking supervision, medium-term health in the industrial sector depends on developing transparent and accountable governance from within, and imposing effective competition policy from without. This includes developing corporate governance structures. Many of these institutions derive their authority from government legislation, and their actions must be based in law. To be effective they must operate in an environment where there is open and speedy civil justice. But it takes time to train judges, and for them to build up experience of dealing with complex civil cases.

A given exchange rate regime is unlikely to be a permanent policy choice

Exchange rate pegs in the Baltics have provided currency stability and significant progress with disinflation. Overall, governments have embraced the constraints that this choice imposed, leading to convergence of fiscal policies. But existing exchange rate regimes should not be considered permanent policy choices. Choosing between a fixed or a flexible regime depends on the economic environment at a particular time and the nature of expected economic developments. A credible fixed rate clearly increases confidence in the quality of the domestic currency. This effect produced good results in the case of the Baltic currencies and fitted well with the need to establish institutions and improve their credibility.

However, where the exchange rate is fixed, the burden of adjustment in response to external shocks, or shifts in relative competitiveness, falls elsewhere in the economy. To the extent that prices or wages are not flexible enough, the real economy has to adjust. In a world where both fixed and flexible exchange rates co-exist, a fixed rate regime can actually induce large variation in relative prices among trading partners. So far, the Baltics, as other transition countries, have benefited from comparatively lower unit labour costs and average wages. Owing to incomplete price liberalisation, they still benefit from lower utility costs. It is likely, nevertheless, that further wage and price adjustment will start eroding these initial advantages over the medium-term. To compensate for this, the supply-side will need to become more diversified and less price-sensitive. Some time will be needed for these conditions to emerge, as it requires development of private entrepreneurship with much higher rates of firm creation and survival. Therefore, balancing the risks and advantages of a fixed versus a flexible exchange rate regime will ultimately need to be a fine policy judgement. So far, the Baltic governments are committed to maintain their exchange rate arrangements. Some flexibility in the exchange rate could be a way to absorb external shocks or pressures, such as a tendency to high import growth, but excessive flexibility could jeopardise stabilisation and the restructuring effort by artificially sustaining unrestructured industries or complicating long-term investment plans.

Better control of public expenditure requires prioritisation

The Baltic countries all adopted a tight fiscal stance to support their fixed exchange rate regimes. This led to a substantial reduction in their budget deficits, though the heart of this lay in maintaining, and indeed increasing, revenue collection. Fiscal prudence was severely tested in the wake of the Russian economic crisis that began in August 1998. Growth slowed in all the Baltic countries, fiscal positions deteriorated and the process of further fiscal reform has had to contend with a less favourable environment. The Russian crisis revealed the different degree of progress made in the three countries. In two cases, public expenditure increased significantly in relation to GDP, calling into question the sustainability of the macroeconomic framework.

Governments have had to work hard to restore fiscal credibility. All Baltic countries are implementing improved expenditure monitoring and budget management. The most important element in setting credible fiscal plans is for the budget process to make transparent choices about expenditure priorities, and then to monitor that expenditure is distributed as has been agreed, and has achieved the intended objectives. Progress in meeting these aims is made difficult by the presence of significant off-budget funds and an unclear financial relationship between central government and local authorities or state-owned enterprises. It is also complicated by the presence of significant one-off revenues from privatisation. The need to make important and sustainable policy choices will only increase as the Baltic countries seek to reform currently unaffordable public pensions systems. Public trust depends on difficult decisions being made transparently.

Banking supervision is central to releasing entrepreneurial energy

The banking sector is central to transition. Access to finance is an important constraint on many entrepreneurs, and the nature of the links between banks and industry are a powerful determinant of speed and outcome of industrial restructuring. Privatising the banking sector is a first step, but more is needed to provide a durable solution. Experience in the Baltic banking sector underlines the importance of co-ordinating reform policies. Rapid capital account liberalisation and relaxation of the rules on establishing new banks culminated, in the absence of adequate banking supervision, in a financial crisis in all three Baltic countries. This followed an explosion, in the early 1990s, in the number of undercapitalised and weakly managed banks that lacked even basic credit controls or systems for managing financial risk. In the event this had a cleansing effect. National authorities tightened supervision and there was a wave of consolidation in the sector. But it has taken some time to rebuild public confidence, and the impact of any future crisis would be much greater as there has been considerable financial deepening in the intervening period.

The response to banking crises in the Baltics has been to encourage prudent behaviour by tightening capital standards and preventing a recurrence of unsustainable growth in the number of banks. The constraint of currency board arrangements has further underpinned governments' insistence that they would not intervene to rescue troubled banks. Prudent lending policy has to be tempered by the need to compete for capital and customers if it is not to discourage dynamic entrepreneurs from capitalising on restructuring by making it difficult for them to gain access to loans. There is also a danger that too much concentration, especially if accompanied by a bar on foreign ownership, damages competition. It is vital that the banking system collects and allocates credit efficiently. Good supervision ensures that the right incentives are in place. But it goes wider than just eliminating moral hazard by enforcing tough bankruptcy rules on banks and financial institutions; supervision has to mature to cope adequately with systemic risks and to support other reforms in the transition process.

Dispersed ownership does not favour industrial restructuring

The three Baltic countries initially adopted very different approaches to managing the transition of their state-owned industrial sectors. Finally, however, they all adopted the "Treuhand" model of privatisation, by which enterprises are generally sold by international tender to a strategic investor. Interestingly, where firms started with wide employee ownership this is now giving way to more concentrated manager-ownership. Indeed, the most important change in the dynamics of ownership in the Baltics has been the taking over by managers of employee-owned firms, especially in small and medium sized enterprises. Consequently, a strong element of insider ownership will prevail in the foreseeable future.

Diffuse ownership resulting from voucher-based investment funds was also unhelpful in promoting necessary restructuring. However, a useful insight that emerges from the comparison of Baltic experience with privatisation is that the disadvantages of voucher privatisation can be circumvented if the voucher market is open for outsiders, notably foreign investors. Concentrating ownership through the accumulation of vouchers in investment funds has turned out to be a less favourable option, as these funds often do not have the means to exercise efficient control over their investments, further weakening corporate governance.

Foreign ownership can be a way to circumvent weak corporate governance structures

Comparison of relative enterprise performance in the Baltic countries suggests that foreign companies tend to implement active restructuring, whereas insider owned enterprises tend to restructure in a more defensive manner. Thus, the challenge is not only to develop further co-operation with foreign investors, but also to improve the conditions for the domestically owned enterprises to match the advantages and standards provided by foreign ownership, such as access to capital, management training or building networks for exports. Certainly, the development of domestic businesses would be stimulated by the development of financial markets, which in turn, benefit from the openness of the economy. Also the development of institutions for management training and consulting, and international networking for SMEs could be an important elements in restructuring the Baltic economies. Employee-owned enterprises also have the chance to develop in certain cases, if firmly profit-oriented. A competitive environment enhances motivation and aligns the interests of owners and employees.

In order to improve domestic corporate governance structures, the Baltic countries have achieved substantial progress in enacting essential economic legislation during a relatively short time-span. But important work remains to be done. There are several areas in which further efforts are likely to be required. Notably, the institutional capacity of the regulatory and judicial authorities to implement legislation and enforce property rights needs to be enhanced. Encouraging the emergence of a set of intermediary market institutions, such as brokerages and custodians would also help keep shareholders informed and assist them in exercising their rights of control. Finally, by improving the capacity of the accounting, audit, and legal professions through appropriate education and training.

Labour markets have adjusted flexibly, but social policies need better targeting to support economic restructuring

Increasing wage dispersion is evidence of labour market adjustment, as are the job loss figures by industry sector, and the growth of the service sector. Labour has not been a constraint on restructuring or growth potential, though until now transitional adjustment has led to only a partial recovery in living standards. The prospects for further improvement are good in the medium term, as restructuring permits the largely well educated labour forces to become more profitably employed. However, for the time being large parts of the three countries' populations still suffer some degree of deprivation. Pensions and other public income transfers are often too low to bring the recipients above conventional poverty limits. For many low-income households actual living standards depend significantly on home-produced food and various informal economic activities. While such alternatives may have helped many to endure the transition period they seem to be associated with low mobility among the unemployed, weakening their chances of finding more productive work in the formal economy.

In this situation, any large increase in social spending financed by taxes or compulsory contributions would be potentially counter-productive, as it would further reduce the financial incentive for individuals to work in the formal compared with the informal economy. Some increase in unemployment benefits may nevertheless be warranted, where they are currently very low, as a means to facilitate public acceptance of economic adjustments in enterprises that lead to job cuts. This could also be useful as an incentive for jobless individuals to keep contact with the public employment service, which can help make their job search more effective. Job search in the Baltic countries has to become nation-wide to overcome the constraints of relatively small local labour markets.

In the long run, minimum pensions and means-tested social-assistance benefits should be gradually increased up to the level of an objectively defined poverty line. But this can only be done in line with economic progress so as not to prejudice growth potential. Transition countries in particular depend on rapid modernisation and growth in the whole economy to reduce poverty. While extreme hardship has generally been overcome, many inhabitants in these countries still suffer moderate degrees of poverty, because much of the economic restructuring has yet to be accomplished.

Fifty years of central planning have not altered Baltic comparative advantage

Adopting free trade policies has led to dramatic geographical and sectoral shifts in the pattern of Baltic trade. While some pre-transition trade links have remained, in 1998 the EU countries accounted for between 38 and 57 per cent of the exports of the Baltic countries and between 50 and 60 per cent of their imports. Trade liberalisation has interacted strongly with inter-sectoral adjustment and economic restructuring. Employment and revealed comparative advantages have decreased in most heavy or capital-intensive industries, such as machinery, textile fabrics or electronics, whereas the light industry and sectors in line with Baltic resource endowments, such as wood and wood manufactures and clothing have re-surfaced. In other words, trade structures have partly reverted to the pattern observed at the time of Baltic independence before World War II. It will take time to create new dynamic comparative advantages on the basis of new investments, creation of new enterprises and diversification of output. It is worth noting that new industries that have been emerging in terms of trade specialisation, such as telecommunication equipment or furniture, are largely connected with foreign direct investments. Notwithstanding the impact of these new influences, the Baltic experience is a powerful practical expression of the law of comparative advantage, and demonstrates how resilient its effects have been to fifty years of central planning.

Regional integration has helped Baltic transition

The Baltic economies have traditionally played the role of East-West gateway. However, hopes in the region that the Russian economy will recover quickly and provide a boost to production, trade and services may have to be reconsidered given the uncertainty of political and economic developments in the Russian Federation. Neither should the Baltic role as an intermediary for eastern commercial flows be taken for granted. The prospect of accession to the EU and possible benefits from access to a larger market should not overshadow the challenges posed to comparatively weaker production structures. These include, on the one hand, aggressive and competitive businesses in Western Europe, and, on the other hand, the costs of the EU regulatory framework.

The Baltic Sea Rim can provide an intermediate level of integration where many economic synergies can be exploited. In this regard, the Baltic cities enjoy advantageous locations and have benefited from significant inflows of foreign direct investments, notably from their Nordic neighbours. FDI has brought in its wake new management and technical skills releasing the potential of a well educated labour force, and has opened up wider markets for products made in the Baltics. These conditions favour network externalities in production, and vertical specialisation that can be an important source of both static and dynamic efficiency gains. Together with a continuous regional inter-governmental co-operation, this relationship has proved a useful way to support the Baltics in their progression to European integration.

I. Overview of the transition process

Context, and structure of the study

The Baltic region: a mosaic of small European nations

The Baltic region includes three small countries, Estonia, Latvia and Lithuania and appears like a small-scale model of the European nations' mosaic. From a broad geographical perspective it makes sense to include these countries in one group, the *Baltics* or *Balticum*. However, in spite of the geographical proximity of the three countries, it is difficult to overlook the region's remarkable historical, ethnic, cultural and social differences. To some extent, these differences were reinforced both under the Soviet rule and after the re-establishment of each country's statehood in the early 1990s (March 1990 for Lithuania, August 1991 for Estonia and Latvia), as each of the Baltic States sought to reassert its own identity.

Lithuania has a long tradition of independence and is the biggest of the three Baltic States with a population of 3.7 million. At the outset of the transition, Lithuania, unlike Estonia and Latvia, had a fairly homogenous population (see Table 1) an outcome resulting from the Second World War and less immigration of Russians during the Soviet rule. Under these conditions, the integration of minorities has posed few problems compared with the other Baltics. The vast majority of Lithuanians are Roman Catholic, a legacy reflecting its close historic ties with Poland. Together with Latvian, Lithuanian forms a specific branch of the Indo-European language group, although the two languages are quite different. Again, Lithuania, unlike Estonia and Latvia, has had few contacts with the Nordic countries being mainly influenced by Poland and Germany, indeed until 1918 Lithuania's third largest city Kleipeda in the coastal area was part of Germany itself.

While Lithuania was comparatively sheltered from the mass migration of industrial workers from Russia, this movement dramatically shaped the ethnic composition of populations in the other Baltic countries. *Latvia* with its population of 2.7 million people in 1990 had the largest immigration. The share of Eastern Slavs (mainly Russians) more than tripled after the end of World War II. At the end

Table 1. **Change in the ethnic composition of the Baltic States, 20th century**

	Estonia		Latvia		Lithuania	
	1934-35	1989	1934-35	1989	1923	1989
Native	88	62	77	52	69	80
Eastern Slav	8	35	12	42	3	12
Poles	0	0	2	2	15	7
Others	4	3	9	4	13	1

Source: Norgaard (1996), p. 172.

of the 1980s, native Latvians were less than 40 per cent of the population in the capital, Riga. Situated between Estonia and Lithuania, Latvia was open to cultural influences from Nordic countries as well as from Germany and Poland. Ethnic Latvians are either Protestants (Lutherans) or Roman Catholics, while Slavs, as a rule, adhere to the Russian Orthodox Church.

In *Estonia*, the share of Eastern Slavs grew more than fourfold during the Soviet period. By the end of the 1980s, out of a total population of 1.6 million, more than 550 000 were Slavs (mainly Russians). Estonia has strong historic ties with the Nordic countries, in particular Sweden and Finland, although both Latvia and Estonia were under German influence through the Middle Ages and up until the First World War. Ethnic Estonians are predominantly Protestants (Lutherans). Unlike Latvian and Lithuanian, the Estonian language is close to Finnish and belongs to the Finno-Ugric group.

A certain regional identity

While differences exist, there is a Baltic regional identity.[1] In medieval times, much remembered, there was an intensive trade relationship among Baltic cities through a confederation of city-states, the Hanseatic League. This brought prosperity to the region in the late Middle Ages and signs of this period are still visible in the Baltic capitals. In the XXth century, during the short spell of independence that lasted from 1918 until 1940, a sense of regional identity emerged in a number of political initiatives in each country. These included support for the creation of a Baltic Union (together with Finland and Poland), and the formation of a customs union between Estonia and Latvia. Under Soviet rule, economic planning took into account the similarities among the Baltics. They were the most developed areas of the FSU and were generally treated as a single economic zone, which in the CMEA[2] division of labour specialised in the production of industrial products and some more sophisticated consumer goods.

After the start of the transition, a number of political initiatives aimed to reinforce regional integration. In 1991, the Baltic Assembly was created, followed in 1993 by the Baltic Council of Ministers. A Baltic Free Trade Agreement came into force on 1 April 1994, which was completed by a Free Trade Agreement in Agricultural Products on January 1997. Other initiatives have been pursued on sectoral basis. These include the highway project across the three Baltic countries (so-called *Via Baltica*) and co-operation in the energy sector with the recent creation of the Baltic Gas Association.

Despite these efforts towards economic integration, the interplay of economic similarities and perceived national interests has also created divergent forces. Indeed, having broadly comparable endowments in capital and labour, producing roughly the same type of goods and competing in the same external markets, the expected gains from intra-Baltic trade are not very large. This may explain why trade linkages across the Baltic States are actually quite modest (see Chapter VII). Worthy of mention is that bureaucratic and custom delays still hinder the movement of people and goods across the Baltic borders. A reaction to the Russian crisis was a rise in protectionist pressures in each Baltic State.

A broader view of Baltic economic integration

Against this background, which contrasts well-defined national identities with regional legacies and policies, the view adopted in this Study is that in order to be analytically relevant, the Baltic region needs to be placed into a broader context. On the one hand, the Baltics have traditionally played the role of East-West gateway, giving rise to large growth potential from the associated trade and business links. But, given the difficult economic situation in the Russian Federation, this potential has not yet been realised.

On the other hand, most economic policies in the Baltics are now geared towards the goal of EU membership. This process will create access to a large market where, despite similar endowments, even small countries can specialise in a wide range of product and service niches. Yet, diversification of output will also take time, since it requires, amongst other things, a rapidly growing number of insightful and motivated entrepreneurs. Looking ahead to full integration with the EU, the Baltic Sea Rim can provide an intermediate level of integration where many economic synergies can be exploited. In this regard, the Baltic cities enjoy advantageous locations and have benefited from significant inflows of foreign direct investments, notably from their Nordic neighbours. These conditions favour network externalities in production, and vertical specialisation can be an important source of both static and dynamic efficiency gains.

Structure of the study

Within this context, this study also aims to highlight the origin and possible consequences of the different policies adopted in the first decade of transition in Estonia, Latvia and Lithuania. This comparison provides an interesting laboratory for the evaluation of transition economic policies and their potential impact for sustainable growth. The following sections of Chapter I set the scene in terms of the similar positions from which the Baltic countries started the transition and their different approaches to its management. In this respect, the experience of the Baltics suggests that the linkages between reforms in different areas and macroeconomic policies are more important than individual policy choices. These policy differences were highlighted by the impact of the Russian financial crisis, which severely affected the Baltic economies. Being small economies that adopted liberal trade policies, this study focuses on the role of trade and the sustainability of external deficits in analysing the process of output decline and recovery in the Baltics.

Following this overview, the most relevant policy areas are analysed in more detail. The choice of monetary and exchange rate regimes (Chapter II) has had strong implications on the developments of fiscal policies (Chapter III). Similarly, the reform of the banking sector (Chapter IV) is closely interrelated with enterprise and economic restructuring (Chapter V). Progress in these areas determines to what extent the labour market has to bear the burden of the adjustment, with all the implications this has for social welfare (Chapter VI). Finally, the study concludes with a review of how far trade specialisation and structural change in the Baltics has evolved (Chapter VII) and, looking forward, on the institutional changes needed to ensure their successful integration with the European and world economy.

The Soviet period and the similar starting point of transition

Relatively advanced social conditions

During the inter-war period, Estonia had the highest living standard among the Baltic States, comparable to that of Finland at that time. During the Soviet period, living standards in the Baltics significantly exceeded the average in the Soviet Union, with Estonia ranked at the top. In 1989, national income as measured by the net material product (NMP)[3] per capita was 22 per cent higher in Estonia than the Soviet average. In Latvia and Lithuania, NMP per capita was above the Soviet average by respectively 16 and 6 per cent (Van Arkadie and Karlsson, 1992). These comparisons, however, are subject to some uncertainty. Nevertheless, by 1997, income in terms of GDP per capita still shows Estonia ahead (Table 2).

Table 2. **Quality of life: some indicators, 1991-97**

	Estonia		Latvia		Lithuania		Belarus		Russian Federation		Ukraine		Poland		Finland		Sweden	
	1991	1997	1991	1997	1991	1997	1991	1997	1991	1997	1991	1997	1991	1997	1991	1997	1991	1997
Immunisation, DPT (% of children under 12 months)	75	85	83	71	73	90	86	97	59	87[1]	82	:	94	:	95	100[1]	99	:
Immunisation, measles (% of children under 12 months)	78	88	96	94	86	96	95	98	79	95[1]	89	:	94	:	97	98[1]	95	:
Life expectancy at birth, total (years)	69	70	69	70	71	71	70	68	69	67	69	67	71	73	75	77	:	79
Mortality rate, infant (per 1 000 live births)	13	10	16	15	14	10	12	12	18	17	14	14	18	10	6	4	6	4
Passenger cars (per 1 000 people)	167	293	124	176	142	238	64	110	65	120	69	96	160	221	381	379	420	418
Personal computers (per 1 000 people)	:	15	:	:	:	:	:	:	4	32	:	:	10	36	113	311	128	350
Telephone mainlines (per 1 000 people)	212	321	254	314	217	283	163	227	150	183	141	186	93	194	540	556	691	679
Television sets (per 1 000 people)	350	479	379	592[1]	378	337[1]	268	314	368	390	329	493	270	413	497	534	468	531
Internet hosts (per 10 000 people)	:	45	:	21	:	8	:	0.4	:	6	:	2	:	11	:	654	:	322
Energy use per capita kg	:	3 834	:	1 674	:	2 414	:	2 386	:	4 169	:	3 012	:	2 807	:	6 143	:	5 944
Memorandum items:																		
GDP per capita, PPP[2] in 1997 US$	7 537		5 631		6 223		5 868		6 950		3 300		6 883		20 031		20 082	
Population, total in millions	1.6	1.5	2.7	2.5	3.7	3.7	10.3	10.3	148.6	147.3	52.0	50.7	38.2	38.7	5.0	5.1	8.6	8.8

1. 1996.
2. Source: OECD/STD.
Source: World Development Indicators (1999), World Bank.

Urbanisation increased rapidly during the Soviet period together with large-scale industrialisation. By 1990, the percentage of population living in the cities was 71 per cent in Estonia and 69 and 68 per cent respectively in Latvia and Lithuania. As in more advanced economies, the birth rate was low in Estonia and Latvia and among the lowest in Europe. Life expectancy at birth was longest in Lithuania with 71 years, followed by 69 years in Estonia and Latvia. After initially falling, by and large social indicators have improved since the beginning of the transition.

Broadly similar economic structures at the outset of the transition...

The present economic structure in the Baltic economies, and their common features, owe much to development under Soviet planning, whilst acknowledging more permanent features related to history and geography. Forestry is the most important natural endowment in all three Baltic countries. In Latvia, forests cover 43 per cent of land, in Estonia about 40 per cent and in Lithuania 28 per cent. Apart from that, Latvia and Lithuania have similar and limited raw materials resources, mostly building materials. Estonia has significant deposits of shale oil, which is still the primary source of energy in the country. In Latvia and Lithuania there are small deposits of oil and gas.

Certain aspects of the Baltic economies were already formed when they belonged to the Russian Empire around the turn of the century. A rapid industrialisation in Estonia and Latvia occurred during the domination by Tsarist Russia, with a few large industries, some employing thousands of workers, often financed by German capital. With a railway connection to Russia and a port, Latvia had already emerged at that time as a main transport hub for Russian foreign trade. Furthermore, the city of Riga developed into an important regional financial centre before the First World War (Norgaard, 1996).

Throughout this period, Lithuania remained to a large extent an agricultural economy. After the independence of the three Baltic States was proclaimed in 1918, their close economic ties with Russia were cut. During the inter-war period their industrial base deteriorated, particularly in Latvia. Industrialisation regained momentum during the Soviet period although, as in the past, at a somewhat slower pace in Lithuania. As in most socialist countries, industrialisation brought about an excessive emphasis on heavy industry at the expense of consumer goods production. As a result of Soviet planning the Baltics became over-industrialised by western standards, and under-supplied with services and housing. Industrialisation proceeded particularly rapidly in the 1960s and 1970s. By 1989,[4] the share of industry was comparable in the three Baltic countries (Table 3),[5] although Lithuania still differed in having a significantly larger share of agriculture and a smaller share of trade and housing.

Table 3. **Structure of gross domestic product in 1989**

Per cent

	Estonia	Latvia	Lithuania
Industry	36	37	35
Agriculture	20	19	27
Construction	8	8	10
Transport, communication	6	8	5
Trade, housing and other	30	28	23

Source: World Bank (1993*d*), pp. 182, 374, 422.

Enterprises were typically of large-scale. In 1990, the average number of workers in Estonian industrial enterprises was 790, in Latvia 760 and in Lithuania 840. The respective figure for Western Europe is around 160 and it is even much lower in the US and Japan (World Bank, 1993*a*, *b*, *c*). The bulk of industrial production consisted of quite energy intensive intermediate goods. Some of the large Baltic enterprises were single producers for the whole Soviet economy (see below).

These large enterprises were usually tightly linked to upstream or downstream partners in other Soviet republics. Heavy industry was mostly answerable to all-Union ministries based in Moscow.[6] As a result, all-Union enterprises with centralised decision-making accounted for 13 per cent of all industrial enterprises in Estonia, 35 per cent in Latvia, and as much as 40 per cent in Lithuania (Hansen and Sorsa, 1994; Sorsa, 1994*a*, *b*). By and large, only light industries remained under the control of regional ministries. Under Soviet planning, direct links with foreign (non-Soviet) enterprises were almost non-existent. At the end of the 1980s, only about 5 per cent of Baltic exports were directed outside the Soviet Union, and even in those cases the contracts with foreign partners were arranged by the Moscow authorities. Under these arrangements the direct ties between Baltic enterprises and the world economy were practically severed over a period of 50 years.

Hence, when the Baltic countries regained their independence in the early 1990s they shared broadly comparable economic conditions and structures of production. Their inheritance also made enterprise restructuring after independence extremely difficult. The large share of monopolistic enterprises created vested interests, which constrained restructuring (see Chapter V). This problem seems to have been more pronounced in Latvia and Lithuania, where the importance of large-scale enterprises was greater than in Estonia. Nevertheless, when compared with the other regions of the former Soviet Union, the Baltics, and especially Estonia, had relatively more employment in "private" firms[7] (Hanson, 1990).

... but some specific sectoral conditions

A number of sector-specific conditions may also be relevant to understanding the different paths of economic restructuring observed in the Baltic economies. In Estonia, the important economic sectors have for a long time been the extraction of shale oil and electricity production, phosphorite mining and related chemical production, and wood processing. Under Soviet rule, all these sectors were further developed. In particular, using shale oil,[8] Estonia started to produce electricity in excess of its own consumption to satisfy the needs of Russian Leningrad (Saint Petersburg). New sectors emerged, in particular machinery and metalworking, but their share in industrial production remained below the Soviet average. On the other hand, light industries developed significantly, notably textiles and food products (Table 4).

Table 4.   **Structure of industrial production in 1989**

Per cent[1]

	Estonia	Latvia	Lithuania
Fuel and energy	7	2	9
Metallurgy	–	2	–
Chemical industry	8	8	4
Machinery and metalworking	16	26	26
Forestry, pulp and paper	9	6	5
Construction materials	4	3	5
Textiles, clothing and footwear	22	18	21
Food processing	25	26	22

Note: The columns do not add up to 100 as some sectors are not shown.
1.   The numbers here may be taken as indicative only, due to the Soviet administrative pricing and peculiarities of the statistical system. Therefore, different sources give somewhat differing series. The broad lines, however, remain the same.
Source: World Bank (1993d), pp. 182, 374, 422.

Overall, Estonian industry was less dependent on the all-Union centralised decision-making that encompassed mainly heavy industry. This characteristic, and the comparatively higher share of light industry in Estonia, left the economy in a better position to adjust to the market than the other Baltic States. On the other hand, the shale oil production was and still is a handicap. Apart from the important environmental damages related to its extraction and use, shale oil production is located in a mono-industry region with a sizeable number of workers (around 10 000, mostly of Russian origin). These economic and social legacies point to one of the most difficult structural problems that Estonia still needs to overcome (see Chapter V).

During the inter-war period, Latvian industry consisted primarily of wood products, food processing, textiles and construction materials. In the Soviet period, emphasis was shifted towards the development of heavy industry, in particular machinery, metalwork and chemicals. By the end of the 1980s, engineering had become the most important Latvian industrial sector, producing mainly intermediate inputs for heavy machine building. Communication equipment and electronics were also developed. Latvia eventually became the most industrialised region in the Baltics, with some of the enterprises being the sole manufacturers in the Soviet Union for products such as passenger minibuses, milking equipment, electrical equipment for trains or telephone automatic switchboards. A specific feature was also the large proportion of military production. In 1985, it accounted for roughly 15 per cent of the labour force in Latvia, a much higher share than in Estonia and Lithuania (World Bank, 1993b), and employed mainly Russian workers. Latvia has remained one of the most important East-West transit hubs given the transport infrastructure (railways and ports) inherited from the Soviet period.

Lithuania was a distinctively agricultural economy before annexation to the Soviet Union. Industry and construction together only accounted for some 10 per cent of employment. Such a small industrial base was characterised by light industries such as food processing, textiles and wood products. During the Soviet period, a dual economy developed. On the one hand, agriculture remained relatively more important than in Estonia and Latvia. On the other hand, industrial development was typically even more concentrated than in the other Baltics. In contrast with Latvia, labour intensive production was also developed, contributing to the expansion of light industry, such as consumer durables, machine tools and computers. By the late 1980s, the electronics industry in Lithuania was quite modern compared with Estonia and Latvia, although much of its production was for military use. Lithuania also had a specific role in energy production with the only oil refinery and nuclear power plant in the Baltic region.

Management of the transition: different paths during 1990-98

The Baltics started their transformation towards a market economy the same time and, as noted above, shared many economic similarities from the outset. Looking retrospectively over the period 1990-98, a number of differences appeared in the way the transition process was managed in each country. In this respect, similarities and key differences in policies adopted by the three Baltic countries can be singled out. As the synopsis shows (see Table 5), the differences between the three countries are either more or less pronounced, depending on the policy areas under consideration. For example, in the mid-1990s there was a relative convergence of policy in the area of macroeconomic stabilisation.

Table 5. **A different management of the transition process, 1990-98**

An overview of the policy framework in Estonia, Latvia and Lithuania

	Estonia	Latvia	Lithuania
Macroeconomic stabilisation			
• Fiscal policy	Tight fiscal policy. 1994 VAT introduced (18 per cent). Flat rate for income tax (26 per cent).	Tight fiscal policy (except 1994-95). 1992 VAT introduced. Flat rate for income tax (25 per cent).	Moderate fiscal discipline. 1994 VAT introduced. 1998 Significant fiscal stimulus from distribution of privatisation revenues (Savings Restitution Plan).
• Monetary policy	1992 Positive real interest rates.	1992 Tight monetary policy; very high interest rates.	1991-92 Loose monetary policy. 1993 Tight monetary policy.
• Exchange rate policy	**Currency Board** since June 1992, with rate pegged to the DM (1 DM = 8 EEK).	Since February 1994, **fixed exchange rate** regime, stable *vis-à-vis* the SDR.	**Currency Board** since April 1994, with rate pegged to the US Dollar ($1 = 4 Litas).
Key structural reforms			
• Price liberalisation	Started in 1989 mostly completed by 1992. Energy and rent prices controlled/regulated. 1998 Regulated prices still account for about 26 per cent of CPI basket.	Started in 1991 mostly completed by 1992. Public transport, rents and heating controlled by municipalities. 1998 Share of administered prices in CPI is 22 per cent.	Started in 1991. Some restrictions remain on energy, transportation and housing prices. 1998 Significant share of administered prices in CPI.
• Trade liberalisation	1992-93 Full liberalisation of trade. 1994 (August) Full current account convertibility. 1995 Free trade with the EU. 1999 (November) Member of WTO.	1993 Tariffs ranging from 15 to 30 per cent. 1994 (June) Full current account convertibility. Overall very liberal trade regime. 1995 4-years EU adjustment period. 1996 Free trade EFTA. 1999 Member of WTO.	1993 Tariffs ranging 10-30 per cent. 1994 (May) Full current account convertibility. 1994 Export duties abolished. 1995 6-year EU adjustment period. 1996 Free trade EFTA. 1999 Final stage WTO membership.
• Foreign investment liberalisation	1991 FDI Law. 1993 Law amended, foreign investment, few restrictions. 1994 Tax benefits phased out. Few direct barriers remain, the most important restriction relates to availability of land.	1991 FDI Law. 1993 Law on foreign investment amended. 1995 Tax benefits phased out. Few direct barriers remain (notably, insurance market), the most important restriction relates to availability of land.	1990 FDI Law. 1992 Further liberalisation. Still some tax benefits. 1999 New Investment law: equal treatment for foreign investors. Few direct barriers remain, the most important restriction relates to availability of land.

Table 5. **A different management of the transition process, 1990-98** (cont.)

An overview of the policy framework in Estonia, Latvia and Lithuania

	Estonia	Latvia	Lithuania
• Banking sector	1992-93 **Banking crisis.** 1994-95 BIS C/A[1] enacted; IAS[2] introduced. 1994 Second banking crisis (Social Bank). 1995 Major five state-owned banks either liquidated or privatised. 1997 Last bank privatised. 1998 Supervision of consolidated banks' accounts enacted; further amendments in 1999 State temporarily holding one bank with 5 per cent of bank assets; dominant role of foreign strategic investors.	1992 IAS[2] introduced. 1993 Rapid increase number of banks. 1994 BIS C/A[1] enacted. 1995 **Banking crisis.** 1996 State: 32 per cent of assets of the 10 largest banks. 1999 Supervision of consolidated banks' accounts introduced. 1998 State owned banks account for 2 per cent of bank assets; foreign capital controls 68 per cent.	1995-96 **Banking crisis.** 1996 IAS[2] introduced. 1997 BIS C/A[1] enacted. 1997 Supervision of consolidated banks' accounts introduced. 1999 State: 28 per cent of capital and 44 per cent of assets; foreign investors control 38 per cent. Options for privatisation of the state-owned banks are being considered.
• Privatisation	1991-93 Small-scale privatisation. 1993 Privatisation Law adopted. Large-scale privatisation begins. 1998 Privatisation almost complete. Characteristics: Mainly direct sales; no insider advantages, important role of foreign capital.	1991-93 Small-scale privatisation. 1993 Privatisation Law adopted. 1994 Comprehensive privatisation of medium and large-scale enterprises. Characteristics: Initially voucher privatisation, with no insider advantages, since 1994 direct sales.	1991 Privatisation programme; vouchers to all citizens; Small privatisations: auctions. 1995 Cash privatisation begins. 1997-98 Inclusion of large strategic companies for privatisation. 1998 New State Property Fund. Characteristics: Mainly voucher privatisation, only recent introduction of direct sales; advantages to insiders.
• Land reform	1991 Tradability of land rights enacted: Vouchers used for privatisation. 1993 Land registry established. 1998 28 per cent land privatised. 1993 Foreigners can buy land by permission of county governors, but no restrictions on resale.	1993 Tradability of land enacted; Vouchers up to 50 per cent payment. Housing: slow voucher privatisation. 1997 Land registry established; legislation changes allowing for a liberalisation of the land market. 1998 40 per cent of property registered. 1994 Foreigners can buy land, under certain conditions, and can trade it.	1994 Land law enacted. Vouchers used for privatisation. 1998 Land registry established 1998, 55 per cent of land was privatised, for which restitution claims have been made. 1996 Foreigners can own land, but not trade it.

Table 5. **A different management of the transition process, 1990-98** *(cont.)*

An overview of the policy framework in Estonia, Latvia and Lithuania

	Estonia	Latvia	Lithuania
• Enterprise reform	1992 Bankruptcy law enacted. Relatively tough law applied actively. Structures of corporate governance have been shaped by the role of strategic investors and FDI; adopting "German model".	1996 Bankruptcy law applied actively; bankruptcy proceedings only partly effective. Corporate legal framework is rather complex. A new commercial code has been submitted to the Parliament.	1992 Bankruptcy law enacted; bankruptcy proceedings only partly effective. 1997 New bankruptcy law enacted. Insiders largely control the structures of corporate governance.
• Competition policy	1993 Competition Law, not very effective. 1998 New Competition Law following EU directives; the competition authority is subordinated to the Ministry of Finance.	1991 Competition Law, not very effective. 1998 New Competition Law following EU directives; changes are mainly institutional; the competition policy framework is being implemented.	1992 Competition Law, not very effective. 1999 New Competition Law following EU directives; changes are mainly institutional; the competition policy framework is being implemented.
• Pension reform	Pension law of 1998 in force from 2000. Work performed in 1999 and later will give a right to state pensions with both a contribution-defined component and a flat-rate component. A "second pillar" of private pension saving will be compulsory from 2001. Framework legislation for private pension saving is in place. Gradual increase of pension ages has begun.	New pension law adopted in 1995 introduced a notional defined contribution model for pay-as-you-go pensions. A "second pillar" of private pension saving will be compulsory from 2001. Framework legislation for private pension saving is in place. Gradual increase of pension ages has begun.	Plans exist for a reformed defined-benefit model for pay-as-you-go pensions, replacing 40 % of the final wage in typical cases. A "second pillar" of compulsory private pension saving has been proposed. Framework legislation for private pension saving is in place from 2000. Gradual increase of pension ages has begun.

1. BIS C/A = Bank of International Settlements capital adequacy ratio.
2. IAS = International Accounting Standards.
Source: EC (1998a, b, c), EBRD (1998, 1999), Nygind (1997, 1998), and OECD Secretariat.

A relative convergence of macroeconomic and liberalisation policies...

Monetary and exchange rate policies are an early achievement of macro-economic stabilisation and are characterised by a strong convergence across the Baltics (see Chapter II). This is particularly remarkable when compared with other former Soviet Republics. Price liberalisation in 1990-91 combined with a lack of control of monetary aggregates triggered a hyperinflationary process, with the consumer price index peaking at around 1 000 per cent in all three countries by end-1992. But, the Baltic authorities quickly understood the importance of intro-ducing monetary discipline and the need to build-up confidence through a cur-rency reform. Both Estonia and Latvia introduced tight monetary policies and new currencies (the Estonian kroon and the Latvian lat, hereafter EEK and LVL, respectively). This enabled them to bring year-on-year inflation down rapidly to about 35-36 per cent by end-1993. This required particularly high interest rates in Latvia. In Estonia, the introduction of a currency board in 1992 provided an additional element of credibility to the system. Latvia followed a similar approach by introducing a fixed exchange rate regime in 1994. In Lithuania, monetary policy was only tightened in mid-1993, together with the introduction of a new national currency (the litas, hereafter LTL). Consequently, the disinflation process gained momentum only in 1994, then was also reinforced by the introduction of a cur-rency board. By end-1998, all Baltic countries had converged towards single-digit inflation, with particularly low rates in Latvia and Lithuania.

Up to 1997, there was a certain convergence of fiscal policies, with pro-gress in either reducing budget deficits, or even generating surpluses as in the case of Estonia and Latvia (see Table 6). Lithuania is the only country that has accumulated consolidated budget deficits since 1993, though the establishment of the currency board in 1994 lead to a strengthening of fiscal discipline. This trend was reversed in 1998 when the government introduced a strong fiscal stimulus, partly compensating for the recessionary effect of the Russian crisis. The Russian crisis also had an impact in Estonia and Latvia, where the preliminary fiscal results for 1999 show growing pressure on expenditure and a shortfall of revenues (see Chapter III).

The three Baltic countries also adopted similar policies on price liberal-isation (see Chapter II). They followed roughly the same path as the more advanced transition countries of Central Europe. Between 1991 and 1993 price controls and regulations were removed on most food, industrial products and services. Nevertheless, in all three countries, regulated prices still account for a significant share of the consumer price index and affect an important part of the consumption basket, including items such as energy, heating, transportation and housing. In particular, Estonia is lagging behind in energy price liberalisation due to the difficulty in restructuring shale oil extraction and its continuing use in electricity production. In the area of competition policy, progress has been

Table 6. **Key macroeconomic indicators, 1991-99**

	1991	1992	1993	1994	1995	1996	1997	1998	1999e
Estonia									
Real GDP growth	-13.6	-14.2	-9.0	-2.0	4.3	3.9	10.6	4.0	0.0
Inflation (end-year)	304	954	36.0	42.0	29.0	14.6	12.5	4.4	4.0
Unemployment (registered basis)	..	..	..	5.1	5.0	5.5	4.6	2.0	5.5
Unemployment (ILO basis)	..	..	6.5	7.6	9.7	10.0	10.5	10.0	10.0
Fiscal balance[1] (% GDP)	5.2	-0.3	-0.7	1.3	-1.3	-1.5	2.0	-0.3	-4.0
Current account balance ($ billion)	..	0.0	0.0	-0.2	-0.2	-0.4	-0.6	-0.5	-0.5
Current account balance (% GDP)	..	1.5	1.3	-7.3	-4.4	-9.1	-12.0	-8.6	-8.0
Latvia									
Real GDP growth	-10.4	-34.9	-14.9	0.6	-0.8	3.3	8.6	3.6	0.5
Inflation (end-year)	262	959	35.0	26.3	23.1	13.1	7.0	2.8	3.0
Unemployment (registered basis)	0.6	3.9	8.7	6.5	6.6	7.2	7.0	9.2	10.0
Unemployment (ILO basis)	..	..	..	16.7	18.1	19.4	14.8	14.0	14.0
Fiscal balance[1] (% GDP)	..	-0.8	0.6	-4.4	-3.9	-1.8	0.3	-0.8	-4.0
Current account balance ($ billion)	..	0.2	0.4	0.2	-0.0	-0.3	-0.3	-0.7	-0.6
Current account balance (% GDP)	..	14.0	19.7	5.5	-0.4	-5.4	-6.1	-11.2	-9.0
Lithuania									
Real GDP growth	-5.7	-21.3	-16.2	-9.8	3.3	4.7	7.3	5.1	-1.0
Inflation (end-year)	383	1,163	189	45.1	35.7	13.1	8.4	2.4	3.0
Unemployment (registered basis)	0.3	1.3	4.4	3.8	6.1	7.1	5.9	6.4	8.0
Unemployment (ILO basis)	..	..	..	17.4	17.1	16.4	14.1	13.5	14.0
Fiscal balance[1] (% GDP)	2.7	0.5	-3.3	-4.9	-4.5	-4.5	-1.8	-5.8	-7.0
Current account balance ($ billion)	..	0.2	-0.1	-0.1	-0.6	-0.7	-1.0	-1.3	-1.1
Current account balance (% GDP)	..	10.6	-3.1	-2.1	-10.2	-9.1	-10.2	-12.1	-10.0

e: estimates.
1.   Consolidated general government fiscal balance: excluding privatisation revenues; for Lithuania it includes savings restitution payments.
Source: National authorities, EBRD (1998, 1999), IMF and OECD Secretariat estimates.

achieved by the recent adoption of new Laws in line with EU directives in all Baltic countries, but generally the effective enforcement and monitoring of competition policy is still in the early stages of implementation.

Foreign trade was liberalised rapidly and more extensively than prices. Baltic countries now have very liberal trade regimes embracing multilateral liberalisation though accession to the WTO. Latvia became a member in early 1999, Estonia became a member in November and Lithuania is an advanced stage of negotiation. To some extent the same applies to capital flows, with most of the remaining restrictions being related to the slow progress on land reform. The policy of liberalisation has been a powerful engine of economic restructuring although they have also dramatically revealed the weaknesses in the previous structure of supply (see below).

... but marked differences emerged in the management of structural reforms

Banking sector

Evidence from transition countries and emerging markets suggests that banking reform is central to establishing financial discipline. But privatisation and opening the market to new banks also requires a careful approach and adequate supervision. In retrospect, Estonia perhaps benefited from succumbing to the first Baltic banking crisis in 1992. This crisis, and subsequently those in the other Baltic countries, had a cleansing effect and led to consolidation in the banking sector, with more prudent behaviour emerging among the surviving banks (see Chapter IV). In this way, the stock of inherited bad debts was substantially reduced. From this base, the privatisation of the other state-owned banks could proceed rapidly in Estonia, notably with an especially strong participation of foreign capital. In 1999, Estonian banking is characterised by a core of two relatively sound banks, although recent cases of bank failure suggest that there is room for further improvement in banking supervision.

The development of the Latvian banking sector followed a different path. Resulting from low entry capital requirements, the banking sector developed rapidly in the early 1990s and state-owned banks progressively lost their dominant role. The number of banks peaked at 63 in 1993 (compared with a maximum of 43 in Estonia at end-1992, and 28 in Lithuania at end-1993[9]). Too many banks, the lack of adequate risk management and excessive currency exposure led to a serious crisis in the first half of 1995. The response of the central bank was to keep to its strict liquidity policy and none of the troubled banks was bailed out. The crisis, in which the largest deposit taker and other major banks went into liquidation, cleared out many of the bad debts from the system as well as eliminating a remarkable 40 per cent of deposits. Much tighter supervision and higher capital requirements were introduced following this crisis. Further privatisations took place, and now only the Land and Mortgage Bank (2 per cent of total banking assets) remains under full state ownership. But the fragmented banking sector of Latvia, a legacy of the early years of transition, is still evolving and further consolidation is expected to take place.

The governments in Lithuania were more prudent but also hesitant in their approach to bank privatisation and reform. In particular, they revealed a certain reluctance to accept foreign capital. As a result, substantial parts of banking sector privatisation remained only in the blueprints for structural reform and problem loans appear to be higher than in the other Baltics. This somewhat gradual approach towards bank reform didn't prevent a banking crisis in Lithuania, which occurred in 1996. An important difference here is that, contrary to what happened in Estonia and Latvia, the Lithuanian government committed to compensate depositors for losses incurred. This together with bank recapitalisation placed a large contingent liability on the public budget, which could amount to 3-4 per cent of GDP (World Bank, 1998). However, some progress in recent years should be acknowledged. The level of non-performing loans has fallen from 28 per cent of total loans in 1998 to 11 per cent by mid-1999. This decline is mainly the result of the privatisation of one bank and liquidation of another, with their bad loans being transferred to a rehabilitation bank (see also Chapter IV). Despite the more recent introduction of international prudential standards, on the verge of the Russian crisis Lithuanian banks appeared relatively more prudent and less exposed to the high-risk Russian assets than their counterparts in Estonia and Latvia. However, they are likely to suffer more indirect exposure given the relatively more intense economic relations between Lithuania and Russia.

Privatisation and enterprise reform

As in the banking sector, enterprise privatisation in Lithuania followed a specific path (see Chapter V). Up to 1997 its main characteristics were a reliance on a voucher scheme, the absence of privatisations to foreign investors and responsibility for privatisation was divided among many institutions, both central and local. Many companies were privatised under the voucher scheme, but property rights were mainly transferred to insiders and the state retained a significant stake in the enterprise sector. By end-1998, approximately 2800 companies still remained to be fully privatised, with the state having a majority stake in 239. Some 80 per cent of state entities had been privatised by September 1999, representing 70 per cent of total assets to be privatised; however, only 28 per cent of the Lithuanian companies are fully owned by private shareholders. With the establishment of a State Property Fund (SPF) in May 1998, privatisation in Lithuania changed track. In order to reform the weak and fragmented structures of corporate governance dominated by insiders, the SPF is now arranging for sale control "packages" of at least 51 per cent. This will facilitate the acquisition of majority stakes by strategic investors.

It is interesting to contrast Lithuanian and the Estonian approaches to privatisation. An important distinction is that since 1992 there has been no political support in Estonia to favour insiders. This may be partly attributable to the fact that many industrial firms had a majority of Russian employees and managers under the Soviet rule, but it also results from the liberal approach adopted by governments. There have also been few legal restrictions on foreign ownership. For large-scale privatisations, the emphasis in Estonia was on finding strong owners rather than fragmenting ownership though a voucher scheme. Overall, the approach has been to privatise and then restructure. By end-1995, most Estonian industrial companies had been privatised. The Estonian privatisation process has lost some momentum since 1995 as the more difficult and politically sensitive sectors of energy and infrastructure are tackled.

Two key factors appear to have contributed to a relatively speedy and effective process in Estonia. First, the bankruptcy legislation of 1992 was relatively tough and applied equally to state and private enterprises, giving the government no choice but to privatise state-owned entities or let them go bankrupt. With very few exceptions, companies were sold with all their liabilities, including tax arrears. Second, as discussed above, a private sound commercial banking system was quickly established. This both reinforced the effect of the bankruptcy procedures in establishing hard-budget constraints[10] and was a vital step in giving potential buyers of state assets access to finance (conditioned, of course, on a good business plan).

In Lithuania the government tried systematically to restructure state enterprises, rather than using liquidation. Despite that the new bankruptcy law enacted in October 1997 – in response to EU concerns – the state still appears to be playing an active role in bankruptcy proceedings, whether or not state-owned companies or debts to the state are involved. A particularly important decision is whether the enterprises concerned should be bankrupted, or should be "rehabilitated". This latter option is being considered in the case of large regional employers, and the resources may be drawn from the Privatisation Fund for this purpose. Examples from other transition countries suggest that this approach to enterprise restructuring can lead to misplaced incentives and a deterioration in financial discipline (*e.g.* OECD, 1999a).

Overall, the privatisation process in Latvia resembles that of Estonia, though it was implemented later and is still in the process of being completed. Since 1994, a case by case approach was used rather than mass privatisation, with the emphasis on seeking strategic partners and selling controlling interests in enterprises. There was a small-scale voucher scheme under which about 15 per cent of company shares were made available in public offerings. By end-1998, 95 per cent of all state owned companies were privatised but this represented only 50-60 per cent[11] of the initial capital to be privatised. The large utility companies are still under at least partial state ownership, including telecoms, with energy largely accounting for the rest (see Chapter V). A point to note is that the Privatisation Agency maintains monitoring rights over companies it has sold for three years following the sale (even if they are fully paid for). It has also some discretion to postpone loan payments from companies relative to the agreed schedule, and to cancel penalties in the case of companies running into financial problems. Until 1994 Latvian companies could also seek cheap loans from the State Privatisation Fund. This may have given room to some perverse incentives especially since the bankruptcy legislation was only partly effective in Latvia. In line with EU requirements, revisions are being considered in order to simplify the procedures under which companies are declared bankrupt.

In all three countries, land privatisation has been on a slow track. In Estonia, company privatisation excluded the land on which they were sited and, only about one-half the land available for privatisation has actually been sold. However, the process of land privatisation is expected to speed up following a reform enacted at end-1997 and as restitution cases are settled. Owners of build-ings have a pre-emption right, which they are exercising in most cases. In Latvia, privatisation of agricultural land began in 1993. But, as in Estonia, land privatisa-tion in Latvia only really gained momentum in 1998; before that, premises were sold but not the accompanying land. Enterprises can now choose either to buy their land or to enter into long-term leases with the state, and are being encouraged to take up the former option. Foreigners may buy and trade land, though they need the permission of local authorities to buy land where their home country does not have a bilateral investment protection treaty with Latvia.

Developments and problems in the real economy

Output decline and recovery

The Baltics suffered a deep fall in GDP during the 1990s, as did most transition countries. Different causes for the output declines have been discussed in the literature. For example, a disorganisation effect of the previous production and distribution networks (Blanchard and Kremer, 1997; Roland and Verdier, 1999) or the loss of CMEA markets. Nevertheless, the output patterns of a broad country group (see Figure 1) shows a striking difference between central Europe (Hungary, Poland, Czech Republic, Slovak Republic and Slovenia) and all the other transition countries (including the Baltics, Balkans and CIS). This can be partly explained by the lower level of pre-transition distortions and by a better management of the reform process in the former group of countries.[12] Before the transition central European countries had more contacts with western markets and some market-oriented reforms were already in place, leading to a more

Figure 1. **Output decline and recovery in transition countries**
1989 = 100

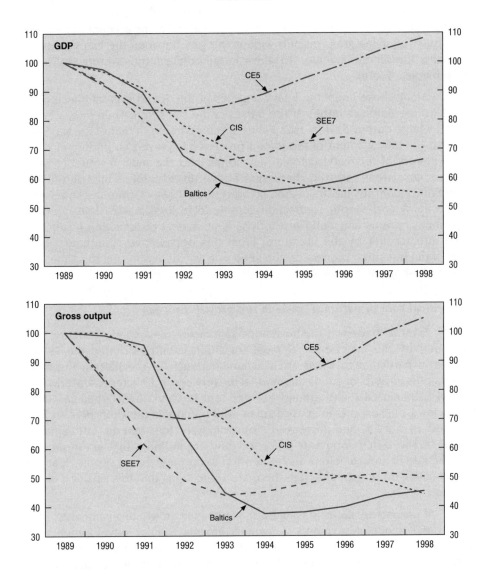

Legend: Baltics: Estonia, Latvia and Lithuania.
CE5: Czech Republic, Slovak Republic, Hungary, Poland and Slovenia.
SEE7: Albania, Bosnia, Bulgaria, Croatia, Romania, FYR Macedonia and Yugoslavia.
CIS: Commonwealth of Independent States.
Source: UN-ECE, *Economic Survey of Europe*, 1999, No. 1.

decentralised decision-making process. After the onset of transition, most central European countries also adopted reforms more quickly and more comprehensively, in a way that reinforced their favourable position. Overall, they had a less pronounced GDP decline and bottomed-out sooner. Taking account of intermediate inputs (*i.e.* using gross output) widens the gap between the two groups. This highlights the different degree to which intermediate inputs were wasted under the previous system.

Along these lines, the heavy legacies of the Soviet system affected similarly all three Baltic countries at the outset of the transition. Therefore, all experienced a large output decline (see Figure 2), comparable to that of Russia. Subsequently, the management of the reform process has played an important role for the dynamics of recovery. Estonia has, so far, had the most favourable profile, which is consistent with the discussion above. In addition, while output in all three Baltic countries has recovered steadily since 1994-95, time lost in reforming the economy and output contraction continued in Russia. The time needed to implement reforms and build institutions is an aspect of transition insufficiently taken into account by the literature. From this perspective, adequate management of the transition process can be seen as a way of minimising this time, which cannot be shortened *ad libitum*.

The critical role of external trade in the growth process

External trade was the most important factor in economic recovery. This is confirmed by the experience of most transition countries during the 1990s. It applies in particular to small open economies such as the Baltics: the sum of exports plus imports of goods and non-factor services in 1998 represented 170 per cent of Estonian GDP and around 110 per cent in Latvia and Lithuania. Starting from a low basis, exports increased seven-fold in Estonia between 1992 and 1998, doubled in Latvia, and increased approximately four-fold in Lithuania (see Figure 3). These developments preceded, and are in line with, the output recovery. The rate of growth of imports has tended to outpace that of exports leading to an increasing trade gap, although there are some signs that this position is being reversed.

If protracted, an increasing trade gap makes growth unsustainable. After a time, the balance-of-payments constrains growth. Similar developments have occurred in other transition countries and can be related mainly to structural factors.[13] The supply-side is one of the main structural weaknesses in a transition country. In an open environment, encouraged by policies of trade liberalisation, consumers have a natural preference for better product quality and variety. While consumer demands adjust quickly to new markets, supply needs time to restructure, and hence cannot meet changing consumer demand during the transition. The same applies to investment goods and the demand for intermediate inputs

Figure 2. **Output decline and recovery, Baltics and Russian Federation**
1989 = 100

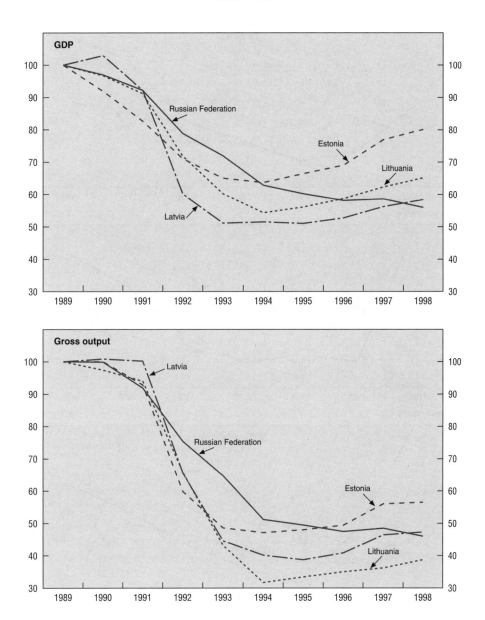

Source: UN-ECE, *Economic Survey of Europe*, 1999, No. 1.

Figure 3. **GDP recovery and trade trends**

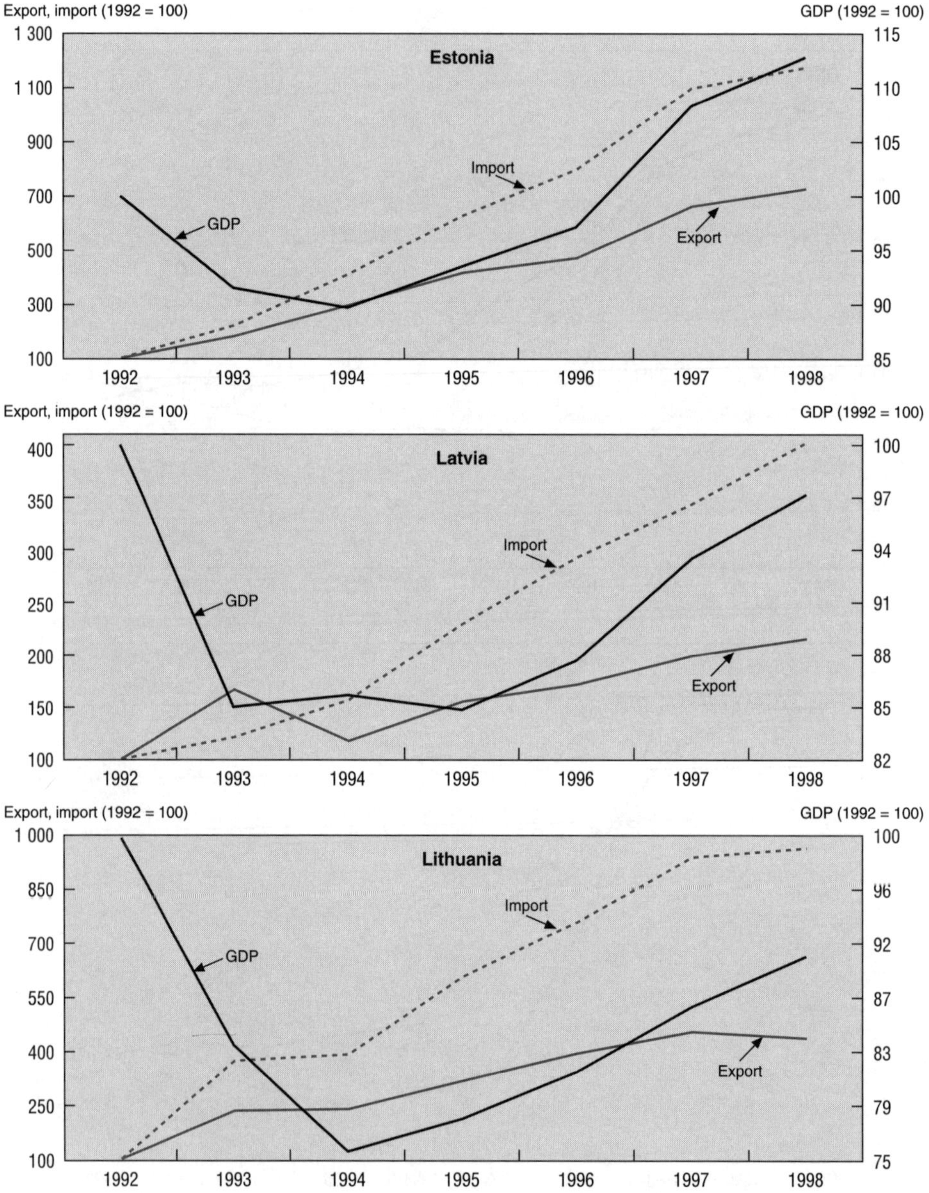
Export, import (1992 = 100)
GDP (1992 = 100)
Estonia
1 300
1 100
900
700
500
300
100
115
110
105
100
95
90
85
Import
GDP
Export
1992
1993
1994
1995
1996
1997
1998
Export, import (1992 = 100)
GDP (1992 = 100)
Latvia
400
350
300
250
200
150
100
100
97
94
91
88
85
82
Import
GDP
Export
1992
1993
1994
1995
1996
1997
1998
Export, import (1992 = 100)
GDP (1992 = 100)
Lithuania
1 000
850
700
550
400
250
100
100
96
92
87
83
79
75
Import
GDP
Export
1992
1993
1994
1995
1996
1997
1998

Source: UN-ECE, *Economic Survey of Europe*, 1999, No. 1.

by the enterprise sector. As a result, many goods are imported. Small open economies naturally import a wide range of goods, but the challenge during transition is that export growth tends not to generate a stream of revenues in line with domestic demand. Typically, exports have a limited product range and low quality; hence they also are characterised by low value-added and high price sensitivity (see Chapter VII). As residual producers, transition countries are also more than proportionally affected by external demand cycles. All these linkages make it difficult for a transition country, at least in the early years, to reconcile high rates of economic growth, needed for catching up, with a sustainable current account position.

As discussed in this Chapter, the management of transition is crucial in this context, because appropriate reforms in the enterprise and financial sector can save time in restructuring supply. Sound macroeconomic policies are critical. Lack of fiscal discipline and easy credit conditions fuel excess demand and only aggravate the structural problem.

The relative role of external trade and the other demand components provide further insights (see Figures 4a-c). However, before analysing the break-down of contributions to GDP growth, an important *caveat* applies. The coverage of national accounts differs significantly across the three Baltic States (see also Box 1). In particular, constant price statistics of GDP by expenditure were not available for Lithuania and were (roughly) estimated by the Secretariat.

The negative contribution of the trade balance to GDP growth in most years in all three countries illustrates the sustainability problem. Analysis of demand faced by domestic producers divided into foreign and domestic components (Panel B in Figures 4a-c)[14] shows that the peaks of GDP growth in 1997-98 for Estonia, 1996-98 for Latvia and 1996-97 in Lithuania were all driven by exports. Investment has had a limited role in the growth process. Only in Lithuania in 1998 domestic demand played a significant role, associated with the expansionary effect of the distribution of privatisation revenues to the population already discussed above. In general, given that fiscal policies are geared to curb fiscal deficits public expenditure has had a minor role in the growth process.

The sustainability of the current account deficit

The balance of trade gap is reflected in the current account. Current account deficits have reached record levels in the Baltics, even when compared with other transition countries. This raises the issue of the sustainability of the external deficits. Current account deficits emerged as soon as GDP bottomed-out in 1994-95. Since then, they have ranged from 4 to 12 per cent of GDP in Estonia, 4 to 11 per cent in Latvia and around 10-12 per cent in Lithuania. Whether such levels are sustainable depends on the dynamics of debt accumulation in relation to GDP growth. At a certain point in time, the ratio of net debt to GDP needs to

Figure 4a. **Contributions to GDP growth in Estonia**
As a percentage of GDP in previous year

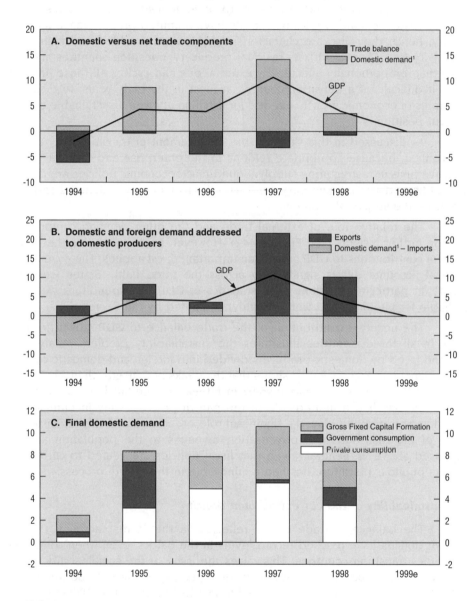

e: Estimate.
1. Including stock variation.
Source: Estonia Statistical Office and OECD.

Figure 4b.   **Contributions to GDP growth in Latvia**
As a percentage of GDP in previous year

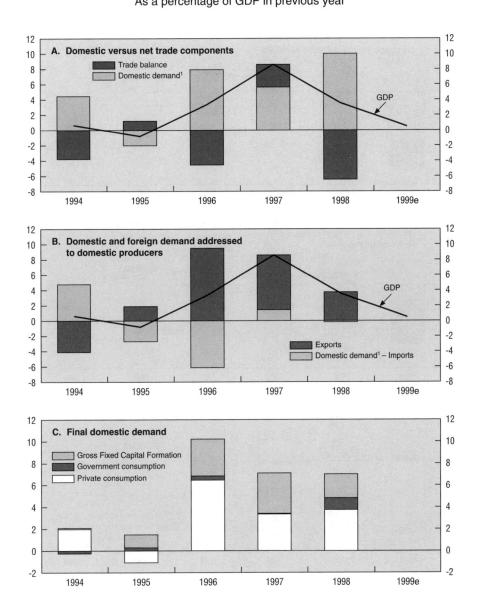

e: Estimate.
1.   Including stock variation.
Source: Estonia Statistical Office and OECD.

Figure 4c. **Contributions to GDP growth in Lithuania**[1]

As a percentage of GDP in previous year

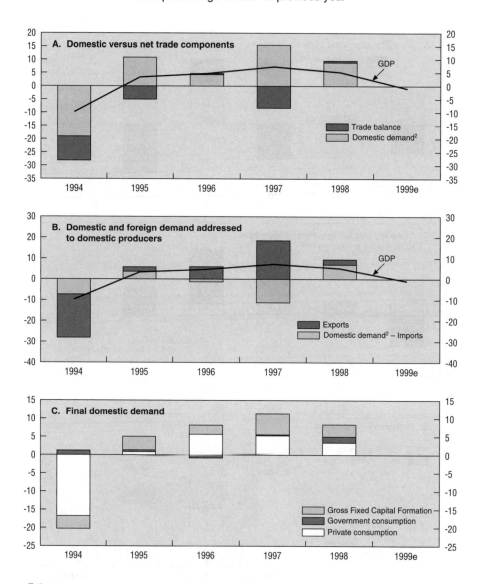

e: Estimate.
1.   The Statistical Office of Lithuania does not provide National Accounts by expenditure on a constant price basis.
     The data presented here estimated by the Secretariat (see text)
2.   Including stock variation.
Source: OECD.

Box 1.   National Account Systems in the Baltics: comparability
and progress

The Baltic countries have built up a National Accounts System, the quality of statistics has improved markedly. However, cross-country national accounts are not always reliably comparable since each country may treat the components differently. The statistical offices of the Baltic countries started to introduce the system of national accounts according to SNA93 in 1994. At that time national accounts data were estimated back to 1992; Lithuania subsequently made estimates for 1990-91. According to EU standards, the Baltics have recently been focusing on the implementation of the ESA 95.

All three countries publish annual and quarterly GDP at current and constant prices compiled by the production approach, basically using enterprise financial surveys. Estonia and Latvia also publish the annual and quarterly GDP compiled by the expenditure approach at current and constant prices with the respective breakdown by major categories of expenditure. Lithuania provides GDP by expenditure only at current prices, but is developing the corresponding annual and quarterly GDP estimates in constant prices. For the purposes of this study, disaggregated expenditure in constant prices underlying Figure 4c have been estimated by the Secretariat.*

In the case of Lithuania experience shows that estimates of GDP using the production approach may be underestimated when compared to levels using expenditure. The size of the statistical discrepancy has varied between 1-7 per cent of GDP. Latvia and Lithuania incorporate the statistical discrepancy between production and expenditure approaches under "change in inventories" while Estonia shows it separately under the expenditure approach. All three countries publish annual GDP using the income approach at current prices *only*. Estonia and Lithuania publish this on a quarterly basis as well.

There are other problems in comparing the Baltic National Accounts Statistics:

– The different frequency of stock valuation.
– Inconsistency between stocks of fixed assets and gross fixed capital formation, and lack of investment data for the agricultural sector. Consumption of fixed capital is likely to be understated as a result of using historical cost accounting methods for valuing the capital stock. Replacement costs should be used, and the depreciation rates used to calculate the consumption of fixed capital must be carefully chosen.
– Poor estimates for the imports and exports of services
– Lack of harmonisation in procedures for estimating agricultural production. This concerns the use of basic agricultural prices and the kind of activity unit (taking into account the large number of agricultural plots of households).
– Concerning constant price estimates, the main problems concern the deflation of services, allowance for productivity change and deflation of agricultural production. A specific problem for Lithuania which emerged at a recent OECD workshop devoted to national accounts, concerns the estimates of agricultural production at constant prices, which are flawed by the use of fixed prices for 12 products.
– Finally, the lack of a uniform approach in balancing the accounts.

_____

* In estimating expenditure in GDP at constant prices, the following deflators have been used: for final consumption, the CPI; for gross capital formation, the capital investment deflator; for imports, the import prices of the other Baltic countries adjusted for changes in the exchange rates; for exports, a weighted average of the PPI in agriculture and non-agricultural sectors.

stabilise at a certain level which international lenders rate as appropriate or sustainable. Using the approach outlined in OECD (1999a), the path of current account deficits and net debt relative to GDP has been mapped in Figure 5a.[15]

From this simplified measure, the trend current account deficits appear to be unsustainable in Estonia and Lithuania. The cumulated current account balance from the early 1990s (an estimate for net debt) reaches a rather high 40 per cent of GDP in both countries. The situation in Latvia appears to be less worrying, as the current account surplus of the years 1992-94 (equal to 20 per cent of GDP in 1993) can be used to finance the subsequent deficits, while the net debt ratio remains, in 1999, still below 20 per cent of GDP.

The picture changes if other elements are taken into account. The financing of the current account deficit is an essential component. In other words, what matters is not so much the level of the deficit but the way it is financed. Typically, if the deficit is mainly financed through short-term capital, the risk of sudden and large outflows is high. Conversely, a situation in which the deficit is mainly financed through long-term capital, a fortiori by foreign direct investment seems less fragile. In the case of the Baltics, a different picture emerges if the deficit is evaluated net of foreign direct investment (Figure 5b). Under this alternative assumption the current account deficit situation in Estonia is practically reversed. The deficit disappears in Latvia, but still holds for Lithuania, although to a lesser extent. Irrespective of whether the stock of FDI is viewed as part of the external debt, these calculations illustrate the important role that foreign investment can play. FDI not only interacts positively with enterprise restructuring (Chapter V), but it also helps to finance the pathological external gap which characterises transition and adjustment to market.

Developments in the wake of international and Russian financial crises

Together with macroeconomic policies, there was a relative convergence in the economic situation across the three Baltic countries up to 1998, the latter also stimulated by the goal of accession to the EU. While the inflation rate and fiscal positions improved remarkably, the current account continued to worsen from 1995. Estonia managed to finance the current account deficit through capital inflows, but these inflows have become increasingly weighted towards portfolio investment, much of which is short-term. This helped fuel a short-lived stock market boom. Between June and August 1997 stock prices doubled and turnover quadrupled, before collapsing equally rapidly in the final quarter of the year.

The monetary authorities in each country responded promptly to booming capital inflows. In Lithuania the central bank withdrew additional liquidity from the market at the time of the boom, and the Estonian authorities counteracted the overheating of the economy by increasing reserve requirements, plus a number of other measures. This averted major problems in the last

Figure 5*a*. **Sustainability of the current account**[1]

Per cent in GDP

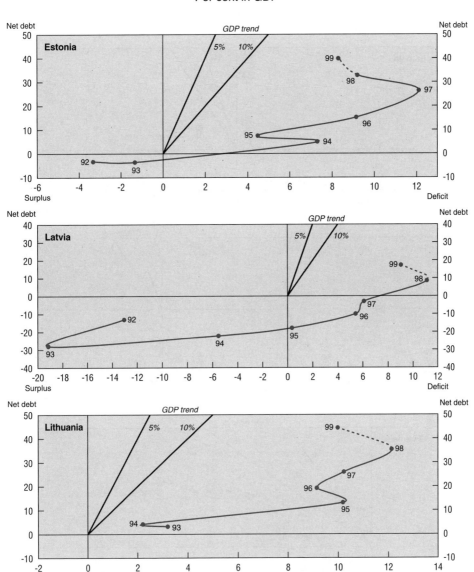

1. All variables are expressed in per cent of GDP. The lines represent the combinations of nominal GDP growth and current account deficit that stabilise the share of net debt in GDP. Hence, points to the right of the line give rise to an increasing debt to GDP ratio, which increases the external vulnerability over the long-run.
Source: National sources and OECD.

Figure 5b.   **Sustainability of the current account net of FDI flows[1]**

Per cent in GDP

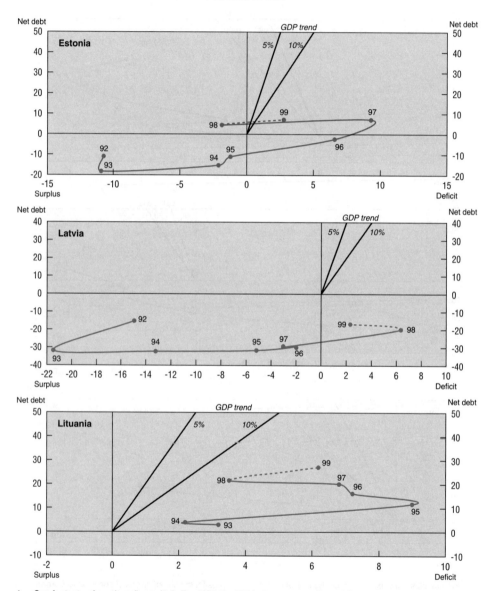

1. See footnote of previous figure (5a). For 1999 the FDI balance was estimated from the average of FDI to GDP ratios over the period 1995-1998.
Source: National sources and OECD.

quarter of 1997 when demand for foreign currency and forward currency operations suddenly increased. A rise in interest rates also raised the cost of engaging in forward transactions, helping to stem speculative pressures. Overall, the mini-crisis of late 1997 abated relatively quickly and, apart from a fall in the stock exchange, the economy as a whole did not suffer.

The robust growth during 1996 and 1997 also obscured the remaining problems in the path of transformation to a market economy. The Russian crisis acted as a catalyst to re-surface these problems. Depending on political choice, this may perhaps prompt more determined action to address them. The effects of the Russian crisis on the economy were both direct and indirect. In 1998, the current account deficit of Latvia and Lithuania jumped from 6 and 10 per cent of GDP respectively, to 11 and 12 per cent. In Estonia the current account deficit decreased from 12 to 8 1/2 per cent of GDP, mainly due to a sharper adjustment in the commodity balances and a decline in import growth. Import values in the first quarter of 1999 declined considerably in all Baltic countries.[16]

The Russian crisis provoked a slowdown of growth. GDP growth in Estonia decreased to 4 per cent from a peak of 10.6 in 1997. In Latvia, growth slowed down to 3.6 from 8.6 per cent, while Lithuania seemed the least affected with 5.1 per cent growth in 1998 compared with 7.3 in 1997. In the first half of 1999, GDP decreased by 3.9 per cent in Estonia, by 2 per cent in Latvia and by 4.8 per cent in Lithuania. Given these and Russia's post-crisis developments, the estimates for 1999 show a significant fall in growth rates (see Table 6). Only in 2000 may the situation be improved in the light of stronger economic performance amongst EU trade partners.

The crisis immediately prompted a fall in exports, and industrial production in the Baltics has been declining steadily compared with early 1998, especially in Estonia and Latvia. By September 1999, the year-on-year growth rates are still negative, but there were some signs that industrial output was recovering from the shock (Figure 6). This picture is somewhat of a contrast to the situation in retail sales (Figure 7). After an initial drop, a certain recovery has taken place in Estonia. Growth has continued in Latvia, although at variable rates during the second half of 1998 and has tended to slowdown up to mid-1999. Likewise, in Lithuania there is a steadily declining trend suggesting that the effects of the crisis took longer to materialise. Another puzzling but perhaps related development in Lithuania is the apparent continuous growth in credits to the economy (Figure 8) during 1998-99. Lending in Lithuania does not seem to have been much affected by the Russian crisis, while in Estonia and Latvia there is a clear downward trend reflecting both the disinflation trends and the credit contraction by the banking sector.

To sum-up, the way each Baltic economy reacted to the Russian crisis is revealing of different adjustment mechanisms. In Estonia there was an increase in the number of bankruptcies and enterprise liquidation. This in turn was reflected

Figure 6.   **Recent trends in industrial production**

Year-on-year growth in per cent

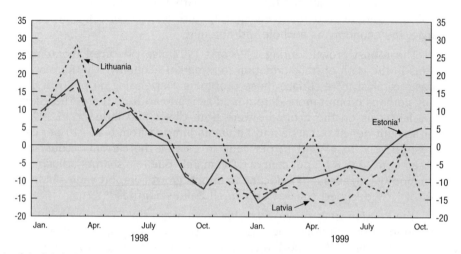

1.   Sales in industry.
Source: National Statistical Offices.

Figure 7.   **Recent trends in retail sales**

Year-on-year growth in per cent, real terms

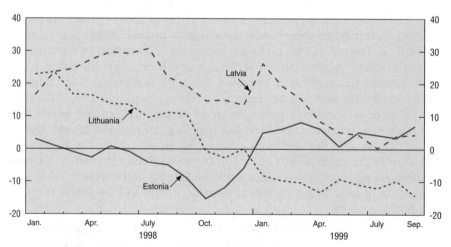

Source: National Statistical Offices.

Figure 8. **Recent trends in credit growth**
Year-on-year growth in per cent

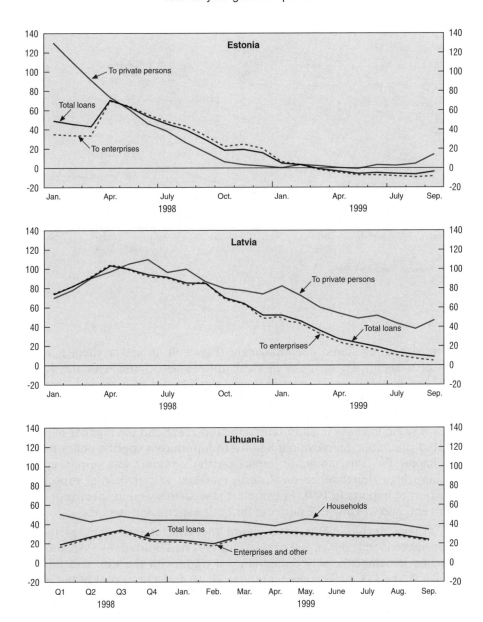

Source: National Banks.

Figure 9. **Recent trends in registered unemployment**
Per cent

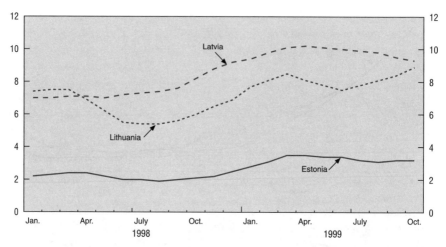

Source: National Statistical Offices.

in an increased registered unemployment (Figure 9). In Latvia, there is no evidence of a significant increase in bankruptcies associated with the Russian crisis,[17] but unemployment increased very significantly from around 7 per cent mid-1998 to above 10 per cent in early 1999 suggesting a relatively high degree of flexibility in the labour market. In Lithuania, growth persisted during 1998, though there was some increase in short term unemployment and the number of lay-offs prompted the Public Employment Service to introduce a specific policy package (see Chapter VI). This moderate impact on the economy was surprising given Lithuania's high dependence on Russian markets: 17 per cent of exports and 20 per cent of imports in 1998. In Estonia, these shares were respectively 13 and 11 per cent, and in Latvia 12 per cent for both exports and imports.

These developments have shown the structural weaknesses that the spectacular economic dynamism of 1996 and 1997 had blurred. By 1998, the Baltic economies remained heavily dependent on trade with the CIS, and Russia in particular.[18] The CIS markets accounted for 21, 19 and 35 per cent of the exports respectively for Estonia, Latvia and Lithuania. While, by itself, this dependence could be explained by the former ties, geography and transport infrastructure, and could turn out to be a source of competitive advantage for the Baltics, the outlook is more problematic from the perspective of effective restructuring. It

Figure 10. **Recent trends in bilateral exchange rates**

Rate per local currency, January 1997 = 100

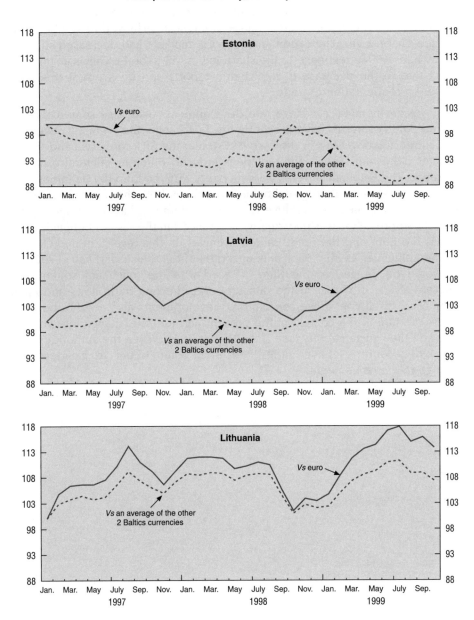

Source: National Banks and OECD.

raises doubts about the quality of exported products: as the recent crisis has shown, most of the products exported to the CIS are not exportable to more developed countries. This brings about the issue of the effective degree of transformation and competitiveness on the world scale achieved by the Baltics to date (see Chapter VII). The export shares to CIS markets had decreased substantially by mid-1999 in response to the sharp fall in CIS imports. This is a statistical artefact due to the decrease in total Baltic exports and does not at this stage represent a reorientation of trade.

Recent nominal exchange rate developments also raise some concerns. All three Baltic countries have presently fixed exchange rate regimes, pegged to major currencies (the Euro in the case of Estonia, the SDR for Latvia and the US dollar for Lithuania). These different pegs induced different bilateral exchange rate trends. The Estonian currency kept its parity with the Euro (by definition) and depreciated *vis-à-vis* its Baltic neighbours. In contrast, both the Latvian lat and the Lithuanian litas appreciated relative to the Euro. Being exclusively pegged to the dollar, the appreciation was particularly pronounced in the case of Lithuania, both vis-à-vis the Euro and the other Baltic currencies. In this regard, in mid-October 1999 the Lithuanian Central Bank announced that from the second half of 2001 the litas would be pegged to the Euro.[19] Faced with the tough adjustment to a significant shock, in particular the difficulty of redirecting trade flows and maintaining fiscal discipline, these concomitant developments also need to be given proper attention in the context of the present and future exchange rate arrangements and their sustainability (see also Chapter II). However, the authorities in all three Baltic countries have underlined their commitment to existing fixed exchange rate arrangements.

II. Monetary developments and policy

Background: institutional parallels and similar policy choices

The Baltic economies provide a number of valuable insights into the process of macroeconomic stabilisation and adjustment. While there have been some differences among these countries regarding the approaches to and timing of stabilisation, all three economies have been far more successful than others in the former rouble area in lowering inflation and building the credibility of their respective currencies. In retrospect, it can be seen that the Baltics abandoned the rouble early enough to avoid the worst of the currency turmoil that emerged early in the 1990s and has persisted for most of this decade in Russia and elsewhere in the former Soviet Union. More was required than this, however. The monetary authorities in each country put in place policy frameworks that have to date been robust to the various pressures arising during the stabilisation period, including real appreciation of their currencies, banking crises, and the recent tensions in international financial markets. Particularly noteworthy, in view of current debates about the relative merits of alternative exchange rate regimes, is the fact that two countries – Estonia and Lithuania – introduced currency boards while Latvia has adopted much the same approach under a more conventional fixed exchange rate regime.

While much progress has been made, the stabilisation process is not over. Inflation in the region has only recently come down to levels comparable with those of trading partners in Western Europe, and significant upward pressures on price levels are still present. As discussed in other chapters, the Baltic economies have not been immune to the Russian crisis and the general increase in international financial uncertainty (see Chapter I). The real economies have been severely affected and developments inevitably raise questions about the strength and resilience of the monetary framework in each country. Widening interest differentials have periodically signalled deteriorating international confidence in the ability of the authorities to maintain the exchange rate at the existing level (see below). Measures showing relatively low levels of monetisation and high shares of foreign currency deposits in each country are indicative of the progress still to be made in increasing the credibility and depth of domestic financial systems. Of particular importance for the conduct of macroeconomic policy is the continued viability of the current exchange rate regimes.

Central Banks were founded in each of the Baltic Republics shortly after World War I, and re-established in 1990 by decree of the respective Supreme Councils. The process of separating central banking operations from commercial activities began as a result of the latter decisions. However, the Banks in their current form came into being only after the Republics became independent in 1991: the key statutes establishing the governance, objectives and functions of the Banks date from 1992 (Latvia), 1993 (Estonia) and 1994 (Lithuania). In the case of Latvia, the Central Bank's principal objective is to conduct monetary policy so as to maintain price stability. With Estonia and Lithuania, the Central Banks' objectives are defined in terms of stability of the currency. This requirement is given more precise meaning under additional (and overriding) legislation that establishes currency boards in these two countries (discussed in more detail below).

The Banks in all three countries appear to have a high level of independence, in the sense of lack of political interference, in their governance and conduct of policy. Under their establishing legislation, each of the Banks is independent of government agencies, is not bound by government decisions, and reports to Parliament. The latter body or the President is responsible for appointing the Chairman of the Bank Board. In terms of monetary policy operations, the currency board arrangements in Estonia and Lithuania clearly limit significantly the scope for discretionary policy adjustments, even by the Banks themselves. The Bank Law in Latvia authorises the Central Bank to determine the official exchange rate of the national currency and, implicitly, the exchange rate regime. There are nevertheless some interesting nuances of difference between the Central Bank statutes. The Bank of Lithuania is required to support the government's economic policy, provided that this action does not conflict with the Bank's principal objective of currency stability. Until recently, if the Minister of Finance of Latvia disagreed with a decision of the Bank Council, the office had the right to request that execution of the decision be delayed for ten days. This provision was not used, however, and was removed when the Bank of Latvia Law was amended in early-1999. The same amendment also abolished the possibility for the Bank to lend directly to the government, matching similar restrictions in place in Estonia and Lithuania.

First steps towards monetary stabilisation

The initial stages of monetary stabilisation in the Baltic States have been well documented elsewhere (*cf.* Saavalainen, 1994, IMF *Economic Reviews* (1993, 1994), and Lainela *et al.*, 1994), and will be reviewed only briefly here. The crucial step in this process was the introduction of national currencies and, in particular, the shifting of exchange rate linkages from the rouble to hard currencies. The success of these moves can be seen most clearly by considering the economic context within which they occurred.

Inflation increased dramatically in all three countries in 1991 and 1992, moving from annual rates of 260-380 per cent at the end of 1991 to a peak of 960-1500 per cent in late 1992. *Monthly* inflation rates in the region peaked at 60-90 per cent in December 1991 and January 1992 (Figure 11). The principal reason for this trend was the liberalisation of domestic prices, involving increases in regulated prices, removal of many price controls in conjunction with large reductions in explicit and implicit subsidies, and monetary overhang. Liberalisation began when these countries were granted increased economic independence at the end of the 1980s, and proceeded rapidly in the 1990-1992 period. In Estonia, for example, the proportion of goods with free prices rose from 10 per cent in December 1989 to 40 per cent in April 1991 and 90 per cent in January 1992 (World Bank, 1993a).[20] Much the same pattern applied Latvia and Lithuania, albeit with some small differences in timing. Overall, the liberalisation process for items in consumer and producer price baskets was largely completed in 1992, although controls were still in place on prices of energy, certain public services, and rents.

Figure 11. **Monthly inflation, 1991-94**

Per cent

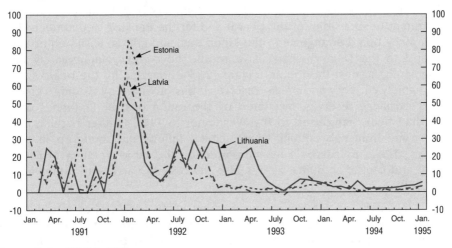

Source: National Statistical Offices.

External effects on prices were also important. Russia, providing the largest share of imports to the region, was also in the process of liberalising prices during this period – although at a slower pace than in the Baltics.[21] In particular, the increase in prices of energy exports from Russia to world levels contributed to a dramatic decline in the Baltic economies' terms of trade: these fell by 30-40 per cent in 1992, equivalent to 10-15 per cent of GDP.[22] Prices of imports from the West were driven up by the collapse in the rouble – which depreciated from around 20 to over 100 to the USD in the course of 1991 and with an accelerating decline from mid-1992 – prior to the Baltics' exit from the rouble zone.

Introduction of the new currencies and exchange rate regimes

The surge in inflation in the Baltic region, combined with the increasing instability in the rouble, created urgent pressures for currency reform. Adding to these pressures were a severe shortage of cash roubles in the first half of 1992, the loss of foreign exchange reserves as residents placed funds abroad and increased use of foreign currencies in domestic transactions.

Estonia introduced its new currency in June 1992, with the kroon immediately becoming the sole legal tender. The use of foreign exchange deposits was initially severely restricted, although this provision was later relaxed. In the space of a few days, individuals' holdings of cash roubles were converted at a rate of 10 roubles per kroon for up to 1 500 roubles, and 50 roubles per kroon above this level. The use of different conversion rates reflected the authorities' concerns about the potential for high rouble inflows, possibly of dubious origin, prior to the exchange. The standard rate of 10 to 1 also applied to bank deposits and cash held by enterprises. At the same time, a currency board was established by introducing separate sections in the Bank of Estonia's balance sheet for the Issue Department (responsible for the board) and for the Banking Department. Under the currency board arrangement, the kroon was, and still is, anchored at a fixed rate of 8 to the Deutschemark; as a result, the currency immediately began strengthening against the rouble (Figure 12). Full backing for the board's liabilities – namely currency and banks' reserves – was provided by Estonia's gold and foreign exchange reserves, facilitated by the return of over 11 tonnes of gold which had been transferred to the West prior to 1940. Further backing for the kroon came from subsequent strong capital inflows and build-up in foreign reserves. These processes were supported by the rapid opening of Estonia's current and capital accounts, as was also the case in Latvia and Lithuania (see Chapter I).

In Latvia, an interim currency (the Latvian rouble) was introduced in May 1992, largely as a means of overcoming shortages of Russian roubles. The two currencies exchanged one-for-one. The Latvian rouble became the only legal tender in July, a move that allowed the currency to fluctuate independently from

Figure 12. **Roubles per unit of local currency**
June 1992 = 1

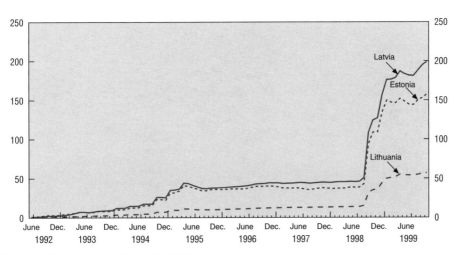

Source: National Statistical Offices, IMF, OECD.

– and appreciate strongly against – the Russian rouble (Figure 12). Nevertheless, many transactions continued to be made (quite legally) in foreign currencies, including Russian roubles, for some time after this date.[23] As of March 1993, the new currency – the lats – was introduced, exchanging at a rate of 1:200 against the interim rouble which was being undermined by a large number of counterfeit notes. The lats was initially allowed to float, with intervention by the Bank of Latvia to limit the currency's appreciation. This appreciation was strong – around 40 per cent in nominal effective terms relative to a dollar-Deutschemark basket – throughout 1993, under the influence of tight monetary conditions and strong capital inflows (Figure 13). In February 1994, the Bank introduced an informal peg against the SDR (at a rate of 0.8 lats to the SDR, implying just under 0.6 lats to the dollar). This informal regime has been maintained since.

Lithuania also introduced an interim currency, referred to as the talonas (*i.e.* coupon), in May 1992, circulating at par with the rouble. The talonas became the sole legal tender in October, hence allowing the link with the rouble to be broken. With monetary conditions loose at first, the currency depreciated strongly against hard currencies during 1992 and the first quarter of 1993, hence appreciating only weakly relative to the rouble (Figure 12). As in Latvia, a large proportion of transactions – estimated at 30-50 per cent – continued to be conducted in foreign currencies over this period. Monetary policy was tightened in the second

Figure 13.   **Nominal effective exchange rates**[1]
January 1994 = 1

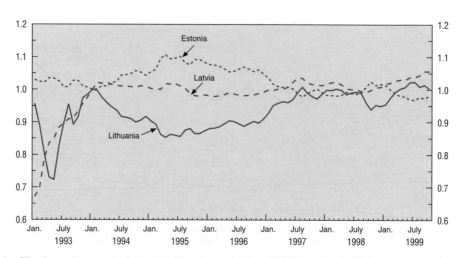

1.   Effective exchange rate (weighted with currency basket: 60% DM and 40% US$), growth in the index denotes appreciation of the money and *vice versa*.
Source: National Statistical Offices, IMF, OECD.

quarter of 1993, and the currency strengthened against the hard currency zone (Figure 13). The talonas was replaced by the new national currency, the litas, in June 1993, and this stabilised at just under 4 to the dollar in the second half of the year. The exchange rate was formally pegged at 4 to the dollar through a currency board that came into effect in April 1994. Providing initial backing for the board's liabilities were gold returned from abroad (around 6 tonnes) and reserves purchased from the IMF.

Securing stabilisation and building monetary credibility

With price liberalisation largely over and much more stable currencies in place, inflation in the Baltic region fell rapidly during 1993. Monthly inflation in Estonia and Latvia fell durably into the single-digit range in the final months of 1992, and the same happened by mid-1993 in Lithuania (Figure 11). The pace of reduction then slowed, partly because of the removal of remaining elements of subsidisation (especially on rents, public transportation and utilities), but mainly reflecting the convergence of tradeable goods' prices with world levels (Saavalainen 1994). In this regard, the currency appreciation in Latvia prior to the introduction of a fixed exchange rate absorbed some of this convergence shock and contributed to Latvia's lower inflation in 1994-1996 compared with its Baltic neighbours. By end-1996, the annual inflation rates of 13-15 per cent in the region were comparable with those of other transition economies in central Europe (Figure 14). By end-1998, annual inflation dropped sharply to under 3 per cent in Latvia and Lithuania and 4.4 per cent in Estonia.

Figure 14. **Annual CPI inflation**
Per cent

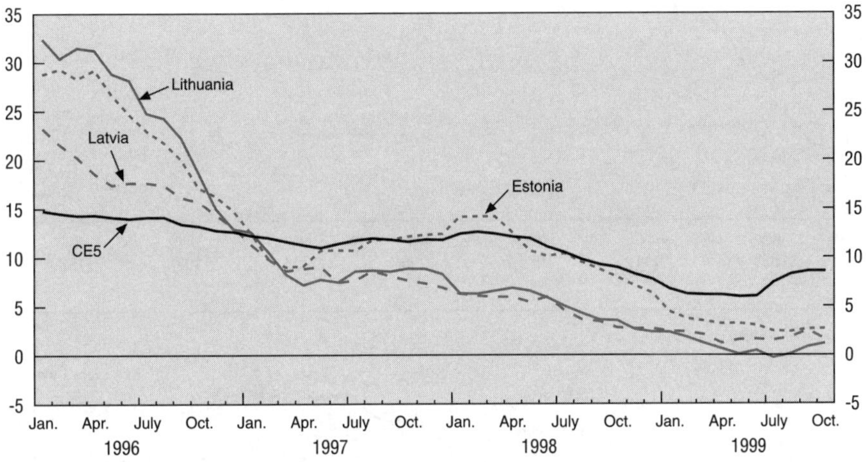

Legend: CE5: Czech Republic, Slovak Republic, Hungary, Poland, and Slovenia.
Source: National Statistical Offices.

These inflation trends, combined with nominal exchange rate stability, imply a strong increase in the price-based real exchange rate indices relative to the Baltics' trading partners in the West (Figure 15). For example, between 1994 and end-1998, the real exchange rate on a CPI basis roughly doubled in Estonia and Lithuania, and increased by 70 per cent in Latvia (reflecting the latter's generally better inflation performance in this period). A similar pattern, although with somewhat lower rates of increase, is evident on a PPI basis. To a large extent, these trends need to be viewed as an equilibration mechanism drawing attention to the large initial under-valuation in the currencies, the price convergence process noted above, and the fact that productivity growth has also been strong. On a unit labour cost basis, for example, the real exchange rates of

Figure 15. **Real effective exchange rates**[1]
January 1994 = 1

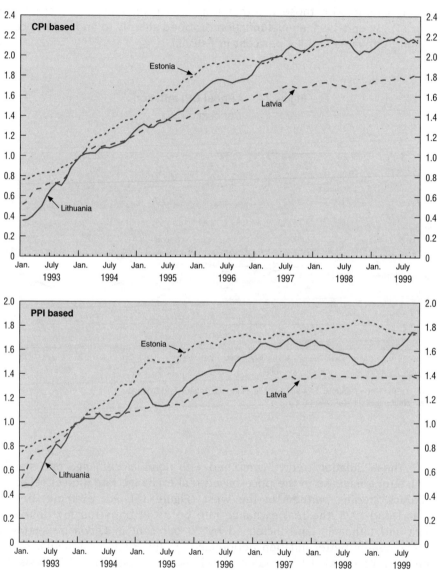

1. Effective exchange rate (weighted with currency basket: 60% DM and 40% US$), growth in the index denotes appreciation of the money and *vice versa*.
Source: National Statistical Offices, IMF, OECD.

the Baltic countries have been much more stable. It is also notable that prices in the non-tradable sector have been growing more strongly than those in the tradable sector, reflecting the latter's better productivity performance and the greater competitive pressures in this area. Hence, the rise in price-based real exchange rates overstates the loss of external competitiveness in the Baltic economies. Nevertheless, over the longer-term, an ongoing rise in the Baltics' real exchange rates could impose difficulties on their trading performance, especially in the aftermath of the rouble devaluation in August 1998. Consequently, the rather sharp decline in inflation in 1998 is clearly a positive development.

In line with currency board requirements in Estonia and Lithuania, official reserves have been maintained above the money base, with a comfortable margin between the two totals; indeed, reserves have been close to and at times exceeded M1 in Lithuania (Figure 16). Even in Latvia, with a more standard fixed exchange rate regime, reserves have consistently exceeded the money base. This margin did however move close to zero in the second half of 1998 when the central bank intervened to support the lats which was coming under selling pressure, largely due to concerns about the exposure to domestic banks to the Russian financial crisis.

As regards money and credit developments more generally, the overall level of monetisation of the Baltic economies was low compared with other transition economies, although it is on an upward trend. For example, in 1997 broad money as a share of GDP was around 20-25 per cent, compared with 30-40 per cent in Poland and Hungary and close to 70 per cent in the Czech Republic and Slovakia (Figure 17). In part, this comparison may simply reflect the lower levels of income per head in the Baltics: on this basis, the three countries do not appear substantially out of line regarding monetary depth (Figure 18). Furthermore, this measure of monetisation does not reflect the full extent of financial development. For example, it does not directly capture the increasingly important role played by leasing companies (see Chapter IV), and direct foreign borrowing by enterprises.

The process of monetisation has been slowed by the various banking crises that have hit the Baltic countries during the transition period. These have had an important and, to some extent, enduring influence on the level and volatility of money growth and other aspects of monetary development (Figure 19). For example, the crises in Latvia and Lithuania during 1995 and 1996 led to a sharp contraction of money and credit, with deposits as a share of GDP being roughly cut in half over this period. Reflecting this fall in deposits and increased reliance on cash, currency in circulation jumped to over 40 per cent of broad money in Latvia and Lithuania in 1995-1996 and is still high at around 35 per cent, while this share has declined to under 20 per cent in Estonia. By mid-1999, there was still a high share of foreign currency deposits in total

Figure 16.　**Official reserves and money aggregates**

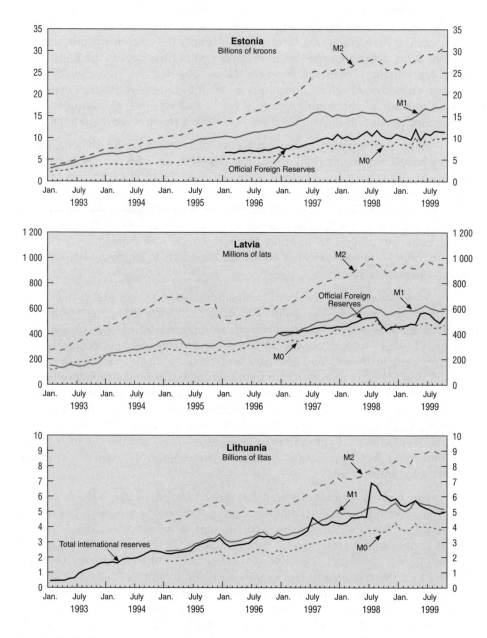

Source:　National Banks.

Figure 17. **Broad money as share of GDP**

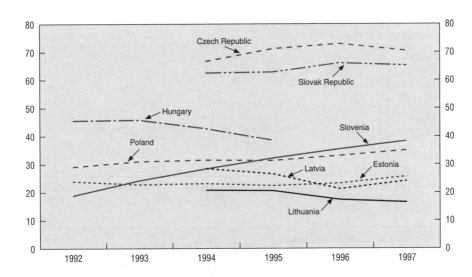

Source: World development indicators, World Bank 1999.

Figure 18. **Monetisation ratio relative to GDP per capita, 1997**

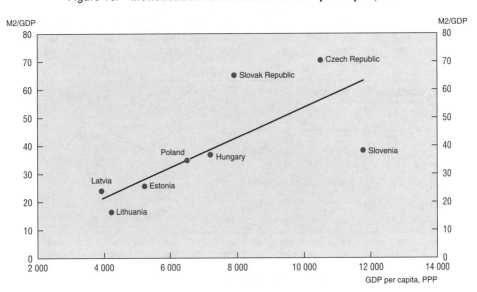

Source: World development indicators, World Bank 1999.

Figure 19.   **Developments in deposit and currency holdings**

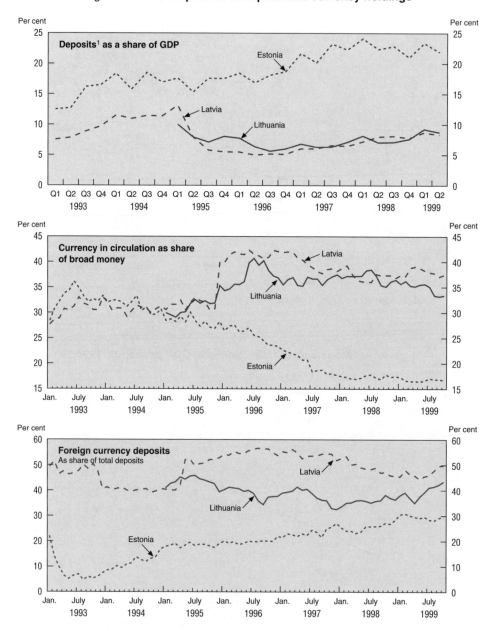

1.   Deposits consist of demand deposits and time deposits.
Source: National Banks.

deposits – around 45 per cent in Latvia, 43 per cent in Lithuania and 30 per cent in Estonia. This share, which rose in the mid-1990s in Latvia and Lithuania during their banking crises and has increased in Estonia since late-1997, suggests there is still a sense of caution about the strength and robustness of the local currencies. Historical factors may also be important in this regard, however, including restrictions that Estonia placed on holdings of foreign exchange deposits in the early years of stabilisation and, in the same period, the more widespread use of foreign currencies in Latvia and Lithuania (Lainela et al., 1994).

Money and credit grew rapidly in Latvia and Lithuania in 1997 and the first half of 1998, off the lower base for these aggregates after the banking crises; in Estonia, the upward trend continued, with marked acceleration up to mid-1997 (Figure 20). For example, broad money in the three countries grew by 34-41 per cent in 1997, well above nominal growth rates ranging from 14 per cent in Latvia to 24 per cent in Estonia. With inflation declining in the region, these trends imply strengthening real demand for the domestic currencies over this period. On the credit side, domestic credit increased by just under 40 per cent in Latvia and Lithuania in the year to end-1997, and an astonishing 88 per cent in Estonia. This growth was driven by the region's improving economic performance, high capital inflows and declining international risk margins applied to borrowers (prior to the Asian crisis). Consistent with growing economic confidence, there was also a general tendency towards lengthening the maturity structure of loans. Some differences are nevertheless apparent between the composition of credit growth. In Lithuania, an increase in net claims on central government (which became less negative in the period) accounted for one third of credit growth while, in Latvia and Estonia, lending to the private sector grew by 80-90 per cent. The private sector credit growth in Estonia included a rapid increase in lending to non-bank financial institutions (such as leasing companies), which peaked at annual growth of 240 per cent in mid-1997. Strong credit growth helped fuel a short-lived stock market boom: between June and August, 1997, stock prices doubled and turnover quadrupled, before collapsing equally rapidly in the final quarter of the year.

Concerned with this rate of credit growth, together with a deteriorating current account position, the Estonian authorities introduced several measures in 1997 to reduce risks of overheating in the economy. Fiscal policy was tightened, with the targeted budget surplus transferred to a Stabilisation Reserve Fund (see Chapter III). Beginning mid-year, the Bank of Estonia tightened policy settings in several areas: these included an expansion of reserve requirements to cover banks' net liabilities towards non-resident credit institutions; several increases in minimum liquidity requirements; and an increase in the capital adequacy ratio from 8 to 10 per cent, with a further reserve of 5 per cent of risk-weighted assets also established (Bank of Estonia, 1998). Latvia and Lithuania were under less pressure in this period to tighten monetary policy settings, given their lower current account deficits (especially in Latvia) and lower inflation than Estonia. The

Figure 20. **Recent growth rates in money aggregates**

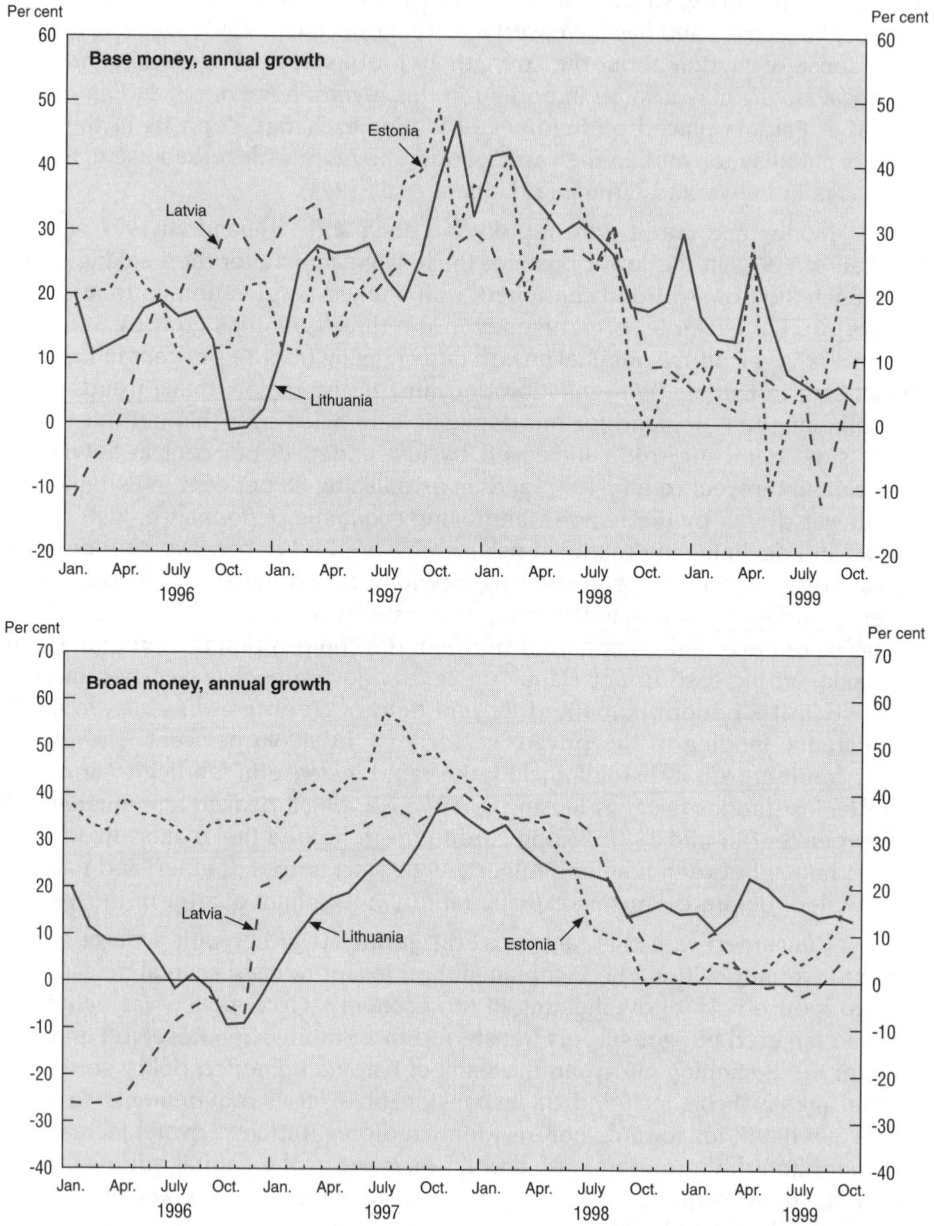

Per cent

Base money, annual growth

Estonia

Latvia

Lithuania

Jan. Apr. July Oct. Jan. Apr. July Oct. Jan. Apr. July Oct. Jan. Apr. July Oct.
1996   1997   1998   1999

Per cent

Broad money, annual growth

Latvia

Lithuania

Estonia

Jan. Apr. July Oct. Jan. Apr. July Oct. Jan. Apr. July Oct. Jan. Apr. July Oct.
1996   1997   1998   1999

Source: National Banks.

Bank of Lithuania did however withdraw liquidity from the market in the final quarter of 1997 to limit the scope for speculation against the currency at the time of increased turmoil in the international financial system. Given the policy measures taken in Estonia, combined with broader macroeconomic developments in the region (particularly the decline in inflation and in GDP growth), there was a general slowdown in the rate of money and credit growth during 1998. Broad money growth to end-1998 ranged from 0 per cent in Estonia to 14 per cent in Lithuania, while domestic credit grew by 17-31 per cent (Tables A34-A36 in the Statistical Annex).

Interest rate data provide a variety of perspectives on financial market developments and progress with macroeconomic stabilisation (Figure 21). At least up to mid-1997, nominal interest rates declined and converged among the three countries, sharply so in the earlier years of transition, indicating the important reductions in inflation and improvements in economic prospects over this period. Similarly, the generally declining spread between domestic and foreign currency deposit rates in each country suggests growing confidence in the stability of the local currencies. Conversely, this spread rose in the second half of 1997, especially in Estonia and Lithuania, in response to the increase in international financial market tensions in this period and specific concerns about the robustness of the exchange rate regimes in each country. This episode is discussed in further detail below. The difference between foreign currency deposit rates and interest rates in the benchmark country (typically the US and Germany) can indicate changing perceptions regarding the strength and stability of the banking systems in each country (as banking sector problems would affect their holdings of both domestic and foreign currency deposits). In this regard, the overall trend is again towards growing stability and convergence between local and international interest rates. However, the influence of banking sector crises in Latvia and Lithuania clearly stands out, as does (to a lesser extent) the banking sector problems experienced in Estonia in the first half of 1998 (see Chapter IV).

The interbank market is small in these countries and becoming increasingly integrated with international capital markets. Nevertheless, short-term interbank rates reflect directly the pressures that may arise on the currency and foreign exchange reserves, given the limited scope under currency boards for liquidity smoothing by the central banks. Even in Latvia, the authorities are prepared to accept a greater degree of interest rate volatility than under a standard fixed exchange rate regime in consequence of emulating the currency board arrangement. Overall, interbank rates have trended downwards for most of the transition period, although staying at relatively high levels in Latvia and Lithuania in 1995 and the first half of 1996 during the period of banking sector concern (Figure 22). The increased uncertainty in international financial markets beginning in the second half of 1997 then had a clear upward influence on short-term rates, with a particularly strong reaction evident in Estonia.

Figure 21. **Interest rate developments**

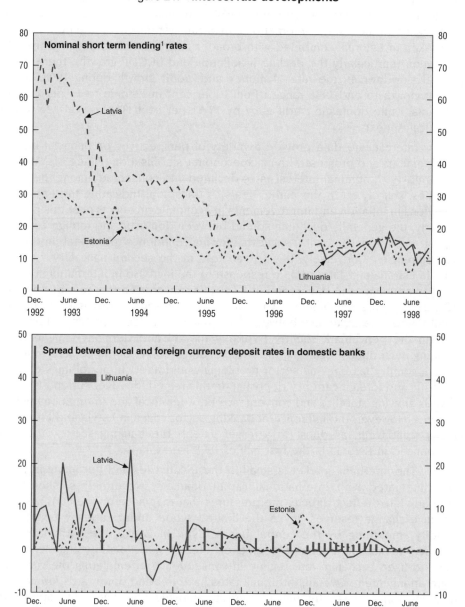

1. Up to 3 months.
Source: National Banks.

Figure 22.   **Interbank market average interest rates**

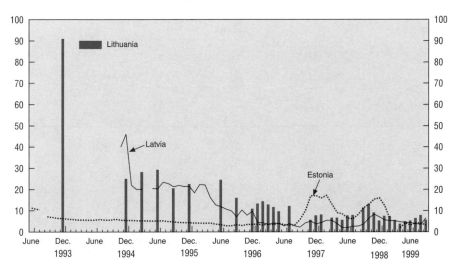

Source: National Banks.

It is instructive to look more closely at this episode in Estonia, as it provided a clear test of the robustness of the currency board framework.[24] As noted above, high capital inflows and declining interest rates fuelled a rapid increase in money and credit in the first half of 1997. This situation turned around dramatically in the second half of the year when the Asian financial crisis led a more general re-assessment of emerging market economies. Capital inflows slowed, with interest rates rising and maturities shortening. For example, the financial account of the balance of payments declined from a surplus of close to 25 per cent of GDP early in the fourth quarter of 1997, to a low of 5 per cent of GDP in the first quarter of 1998. With the measures introduced by the Bank of Estonia earlier in the year also taking effect, liquidity tightened, the stock market bubble burst, and interest rates began rising as of August. In September and October, concerns about the currency led to a sharp increase in forward sales of the kroon matched by forward purchases of the Deutschmark,[25] and increased holdings of foreign currency deposits in domestic banks. However, the capacity for speculation against the currency was severely constrained by the currency board arrangement, which automatically prevented the central bank from providing more liquidity to the market (as noted above, the same constraint applying in Lithuania was reinforced by the central bank withdrawing additional liquidity from the market). The resulting rise in interest rates added to the costs of engaging in forward transactions, and speculative pressures abated. Interbank rates remained

Figure 23. **Real interest rates on local currency deposits**
Using forward CPI, per cent

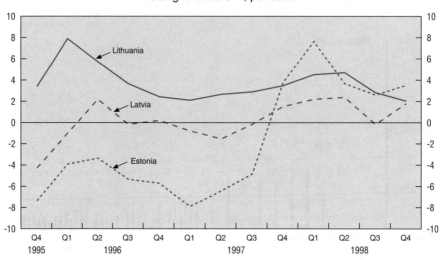

Source: National Banks and OECD.

high but stabilised in the final part of the year, and market pressures eased in the Spring – before re-appearing at the time of the Russian financial crisis in August 1998.

Real interest rates – even using forward-looking inflation results[26] – have been low and even negative (especially in Estonia) for much of the transition period, becoming consistently positive in all three countries only since late-1997 (Figure 23). While such low real rates may at first be surprising, they reflect the steady convergence of nominal interest rates with western levels, in systems with fixed exchange rates and open capital accounts, combined with inflation rates which until recently have been relatively high. Nevertheless, the maintenance of positive real rates through lower inflation is an important development, particularly given the need to increase the level of monetisation and overall financial market activity in the region.

Sustainability of the monetary framework

All three Baltic states have expressed the strong desire to join the EU and Euro area as soon as this is feasible. However, given that it will still be some time before these aspirations are realised, the question arises whether the current full or *de facto* currency boards should in the meantime be maintained or replaced by some alternative exchange rate regime.

Currency board systems have been subject to increased interest and scrutiny recently. It is generally acknowledged that these arrangements have been beneficial. They have enhanced credibility and delivered a higher quality, more trusted, domestic currency in some emerging markets. In general, it can be said that the relatively simple, mechanistic aspect of a currency board arrangement is at the same time its main area of strength and of weakness (for a full discussion of these issues, see IMF, 1997). For example, under currency boards the central banks are severely constrained in their ability to fulfil a lender of last resort function (although, as noted below, this capacity is not totally absent). As a result, the concern arises that central banks may be unable to provide sufficient assistance to otherwise sound commercial banks exposed to a severe liquidity squeeze and even failure from factors beyond their immediate control, especially from contagion effects. On the other hand, the very fact that the scope for central bank intervention is known to be limited may reduce moral hazard risks that can occur when owners (and also clients) in this sector expect that publicly funded bailouts of banks would be available if needed. More generally, the currency board constraints put additional, but desirable, pressure on the supervisory authorities and on the banks themselves to ensure that the prudential framework and financial positions are sound. Similar arguments can be applied in the case of public sector finances (see Chapter III).

A broader concern with currency board arrangements is that they may impair the development of the overall monetary and financial system. By design, these arrangements imply limitations on central banks' ability to develop and use the full range of monetary instruments. It has been suggested that the resulting central bank inexperience in these areas could slow their readiness to take part in the euro zone, given the responsibilities assigned to individual member banks under the common currency arrangement (Pautola *et al.*, 1998). And financial market development may be slowed by this limited scope for central bank inter-action with the market, especially regarding the instruments of day-to-day liquidity management. If liquidity is instead determined largely by net capital flows, interest rate volatility is then likely to be higher than under more standard fixed (or floating) exchange rates, possibly with adverse consequences for the real economy.

These concerns should not be overstated, however, at least as far as the Baltic States are concerned. A general point is that overall increases in monetary stability and credibility that currency board systems can offer – and that have apparently been achieved in the Baltics – may well compensate for the limitations these arrangements place on the financial sector. In particular, the currency board constraints have required the authorities to take a firm approach towards banking sector restructuring (see Chapter IV), helping to clear the system of non-viable banks and promoting the development of a more robust banking sector. Furthermore, the scope for monetary policy interventions and liquidity management need not be totally lacking under currency boards. For example, the margin between official foreign reserves and the monetary base (see Figure 16) provides a buffer within which policy interventions can and do take place – especially for purposes of liquidity smoothing, but even extending to lender of last resort-type activities. Adjustments in reserve requirements have also been used as a means of controlling liquidity growth – for example, to slow the rapid credit expansion in Estonia in 1997 (see above). Overall, as indicated in Table 7, the Baltic area central banks have a substantial range of monetary instruments available to them. Although some may be used to only a limited extent, the central banks and financial market do appear to have the opportunity to develop their experience with a reasonably standard range of policy tools.

With fixed exchange rate regimes more generally, countries cede a potential means of adjustment to economic shocks – an issue that may be of particular importance to small open economies such as the Baltics. Related to this, countries with fixed rates may need to withstand the pressures of strong real appreciation in their exchange rates. As noted above, however, the real exchange rate appreciation in the Baltics has come on top of substantial undervaluation, and may to some extent be an equilibrating phenomenon reflecting price convergence and differential productivity growth between tradeables and non-tradeables (the Belassa-Samuelson effect). It is probably also the case that the high current account deficits in the Baltic region do not reflect a weakening in these countries' competitive positions, but rather are driven by the strong growth in investment and other components of domestic demand (see Chapter I). Nevertheless, it is important for the Baltic States to hold on to the important gains made with disinflation in recent years, both to ease real exchange rate pressures that do exist and to support overall macroeconomic stabilisation.

While keeping to the underlying principles of currency boards (whether full or de facto), the Baltic States are nevertheless introducing or considering various changes in their monetary arrangements. These developments are generally technical in nature, usually involving adjustments in policy instruments designed to improve liquidity management and smooth short-term fluctuations.[27] The impact of – and desire for – closer economic and monetary relations with western Europe are also apparent. Linkage with the Euro is now in place in Estonia (through the Deutschemark peg), and closer ties are also being considered in Latvia and Lithuania.

In this regard, the most significant changes are planned for Lithuania: the authorities intend to change from the peg from the dollar to the euro in the second half of 2001. However, monetary emissions would continue to be

Table 7. **Monetary policy strategies, instruments and procedures**

	Estonia	Latvia	Lithuania
Strategy: Intermediate target[1]	XR	XR	XR
F/X Bid-asked spread at the Central Bank, %	–	2.0	1.0
Reserve requirements	Yes	Yes	Yes
Ratio	10	8	10
Maintenance period	1 month	1 month	1 month
Remuneration	See below[2]	No	No
Open Market Operations (OMO)			
Operating objectives[3]	SCI	NDA	SST
OMO types:[4]			
Outright in domestic securities[5]	–	Intermediate	See below[6]
Reversed transactions in domestic securities[5]	High	High	Intermediate
Foreign exchange swaps	No	Yes	No
Main operations:[7]	CD	RP	RP, TD
Maturity	4 weeks	1 week, 1 month, 3 months	1 week, 2 week
Frequency	1 per month	1 per day	1 per month
OMO procedures:[4]			
Volume tender (auction)	–	–	–
Interest rate (price) auction	High	High	High
Standing facilities at:			
Lending facilities at:			
Below market rate	No	No	No
Market rate	No	No	No
Marginal rate[8]	RP	OLa, L	OLa
Deposit facilities	Yes[2]	Yes	No
Special liquidity loans			
Below market rate	N/A	No	No
Market rate	N/A	No	No
Marginal rate	N/A	Yes	Yes

1. XR – exchange rate target.
2. Since 1 July 1999 all bank reserves held at the Bank of Estonia are remunerated at the ECB deposit rate.
3. SCI – smoothing of fluctuations of currency issue; NDA – net domestic assets of the Central bank; SST – smoothing of significant cyclic fluctuations of interbank market interest rates.
4. Importance in OMO: low, intermediate, high.
5. These are certificates of deposit by the Central bank in the case of Estonia, T-bills in the case of Latvia and Lithuania.
6. The Bank of Lithuania used outright purchases on secondary T-bills market in December 1995-January 1996. However, these operations were strictly limited and made up to 2 per cent of monetary base.
7. CD – Auctions of certificates of deposits; OT – Outright OMO; RP – Repo auctions; TD – Time deposit auctions.
8. RP – Repo transactions; Ola – automatic lombard lending for overnight (collateralised overdraft of banks' correspondent accounts with the Central bank); L – lombard lending on initiative of the bank – borrower for 1 to 30 days.

Source: National Banks.

constrained by foreign reserve holdings, hence keeping the monetary framework within the scope of the current Law on the Credibility of the litas. These changes, bringing the monetary arrangements in Lithuania closer in practice to those in Latvia, represent a more modest version of reforms announced in 1997. Under the Bank of Lithuania's original Monetary Programme for 1997-99, there would have been a *de jure* exit from the currency board beginning in 1998, and introduction of a more standard fixed exchange rate pegged to the Euro (see Bank of Lithuania Annual Report, 1997). These reforms were subsequently put on hold in view of the increased tensions and uncertainty in international financial markets.

All in all, the current exchange rate regimes have served the Baltics well. In providing currency stability and significant progress with disinflation, these regimes have undoubtedly made a major contribution towards overall economic and financial sector development. The constraints imposed by the currency board principles have had an anchoring effect on fiscal policy, helping to keep public debt at low levels, and have contributed to a generally rapid and robust restructuring of the banking sector. It is interesting to note in this context that the Governor of the Bank of Latvia is reported to have suggested (at least as a theoretical proposition) that the Euro could be adopted as the national currency in the Baltic region even before these countries are admitted to the EU.[28] Also noteworthy is the point that there seems to be broad-based public and political acceptance of monetary policy arrangements in each country. Moreover, substantive changes in the current regimes, even if conceptually sound and carefully implemented could potentially increase these countries' exposure to elements of uncertainty that they have so far largely avoided. This may be too high a price to pay for the possible advantages of such a move.

The exchange rate has been used as an anchor of stability and a promise of certain value in order to attract foreign investment. But, it is also a price that reflects the relative position of economies in terms of productivity, quality of production and, more generally, trade and capital flows. Where this price is fixed, the burden of adjustment in response to external shocks, or shifts in relative positions, falls on domestic relative prices and the real economy. The balance between the exchange rate as an anchor of stability and a means of adjustment is the product of many factors. Notably, small open economies may place greater emphasis on the exchange rate as an adjustment mechanism, as through time they are more likely to face a variety of external pressures or shocks. An example of the latter, has been the effect of the rouble devaluation on the Baltic economies. But, this may be outweighed where a country needs either to establish institutions or improve their credibility, as is initially likely to be the case in transition economies. This suggests that the option of a currency board or a fixed exchange rate is unlikely to be a permanent policy choice.[29] Rather, it is linked to the economic environment at a specific point in time and the nature of expected economic developments (*e.g.* as the prospects for EU integration in the case of the Baltics).

When the governments or monetary authorities judge that the advantages of a currency board may be exhausted, the question then becomes how to achieve an orderly exit. There is no experience on which to draw, as, in the recent past, there has been no exit from a currency board. Credibility of the policy framework need not be damaged where the macroeconomic conditions and market sentiment are such that the previous exchange rate arrangement was not sustainable. However, the chances of achieving an orderly adjustment are improved when other areas of potential macroeconomic concern – notably the fiscal positions, current account deficits and inflation – are held within reasonable bounds. This is the policy dilemma that the Baltic economies may have to confront in the foreseeable future.

III. Comparison of developments in fiscal policy

Fiscal policy at the centre of macroeconomic policy making

As discussed in the previous chapter, the decision to adopt currency or quasi-currency boards implied a very limited role for the active use of monetary instruments. This has placed fiscal policy at the centre of macroeconomic policy making in the region. To support fixed exchange rates all three Baltic economies adopted a tight fiscal stance, which led to a substantial reduction of their budget deficits, though this has not been at the cost of neglecting essential government activity. Notably, the Baltics countries have maintained, and indeed increased, revenue collection. However, these benign developments have been severely tested by the Russian economic crisis that began in August 1998. As growth has slowed, the process of fiscal reform has had to contend with a less favourable environment. This raised a new set of issues.

Divergent responses to the Russian shock have revealed differences in the sustainability of the apparent fiscal convergence. As discussed in Chapter II, global financial turbulence in 1997-1998 has also renewed concerns about the sustainability of current account deficits in all the Baltic countries. Given the limited range of monetary instruments, keeping current account deficits within sustainable limits requires a particular discipline in setting fiscal policy. Moreover, control of expenditure has become more demanding as the initial targets of macroeconomic stabilisation have given way to a system of more decentralised decision-making, involving local budgets and off-budget funds. Early rapid progress in fiscal transformation lost momentum as needed reforms have become politically more sensitive and administratively more difficult to implement. To address these issues, the Baltic economies face the challenge of strengthening budget management, increasing the effectiveness of public spending and re-examining how expenditure is prioritised. Less immediately, fiscal policy will also have to deal with the appropriate level at which social safety nets are set, and how to manage the burden of future pension liabilities.

The same starting point...

The fiscal systems in the Baltic countries shared similar features at the beginning of transition.[30] Public spending was high, reaching 45-50 per cent of GDP. The fiscal system relied on definitions of the tax base peculiar to central planning; fiscal institutions such as tax administration, excise duties and treasuries either did not exist or were underdeveloped.

As well as sharing institutional similarities, the Baltic economies embarked on their programme of fiscal reforms against the difficult background of macroeconomic stabilisation. Along with other transition economies they experienced a sharp drop in output and high inflation partly due to monetary overhang following the general adjustment of relative prices that took place once prices had been liberalised. Living standards generally fell, particularly so for some segments of the population, leading to popular demands for more public spending to protect vulnerable groups such as pensioners. Governments faced this pressure to increase expenditure at the same time as economic recession eroded the tax base, a situation that was magnified by the failure of inherited tax structures to be effective under the prevailing, new, conditions.

Though the Baltic economies shared these structural weaknesses in their fiscal account, they also shared two advantages. Firstly, in 1989 the three Baltic States inherited none of the Soviet debt outstanding at the time of their independence, either domestic or foreign. Secondly, all the Baltic States, and in particular Latvia, had also been significant net contributors to the Soviet Union's budget.[31] After regaining independence these transfers ceased, significantly improving their fiscal position.

... and, after a time, apparent fiscal convergence

Strong fiscal adjustment took place in all three Baltic countries, although not at the same time. Estonia led the way in 1992, followed approximately two years later by Latvia and Lithuania (see Figure 24 and Box 2). This would not have been possible without broad political consensus that tax reform and improved control of expenditure was necessary to achieve a successful transition to a market economy. An important feature of fiscal outcomes in Estonia, Latvia and Lithuania has been stability in revenue following an initial hiatus.[32] All three countries avoided the rapid revenue decline observed in many transition economies, although, as discussed below, maybe not for the same reasons. The experience of Russia is a case in point (see Figure 25). It is notable that the Baltic countries attained high levels of fiscal revenue mobilisation even within the Soviet system during the decade prior to the start of transition. Resilient patriotic sentiment that was important in the campaign for independence may also have contributed to relatively good rates of tax collection. In a national accounting sense, the stability of revenues is remarkable, in so far as they evolved rapidly

Figure 24. **General government balance, 1993-98**
Per cent GDP

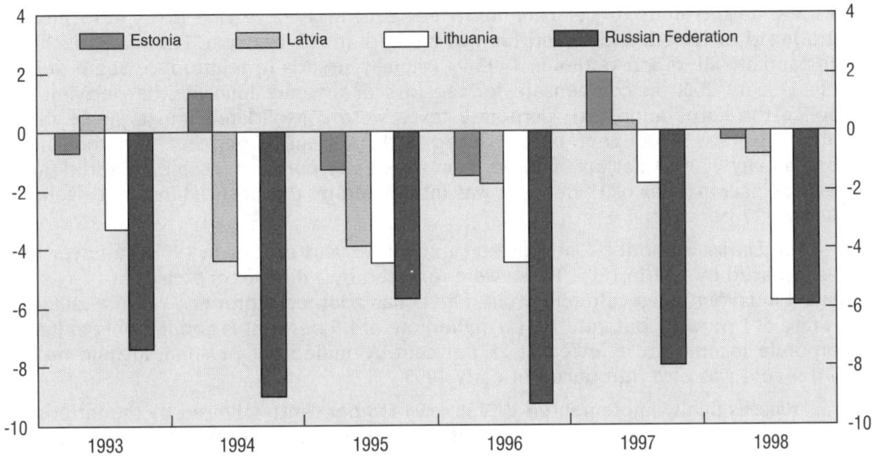

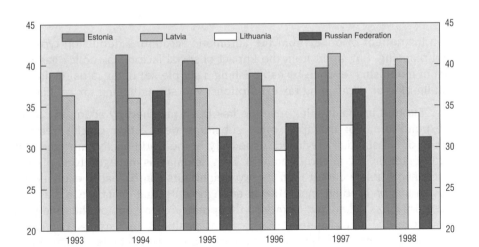

Source: IMF and OECD.

Figure 25. **General government revenues, 1993-98**
Per cent GDP

Source: IMF and OECD.

Box 2. Overview of tax reform

Estonia started in 1991 to establish a simple and efficient tax system. The rate of VAT was raised from 10 per cent to 18 per cent in 1992. Excise taxes were newly introduced or raised, and a land tax was created at $1/2$-2 per cent. Estonia abolished substantially all import duties in 1992-93 (though intends to reintroduce some tariffs from January 2000 to compensate for the loss of revenue following its decision to abolish the corporation tax). Corporate taxes were consolidated into a single rate, initially fixed at 35 per cent, later reduced to the current 26 per cent, and abolished from January 2000. A flat tax of 26 per cent applies to personal income. In addition, a medical insurance tax of 13 per cent was introduced on top of social insurance contributions (20 per cent).

The *Latvian* authorities introduced turnover tax and excises in 1992. Turnover tax was replaced by VAT in 1995. These were replaced by a new set of excises in 1996, still biased in favour of agricultural output. Latvia has adopted a property tax at a uniform tax rate of 1 percent, but until 2001 a higher rate of 1.5 per cent is applied only to land. Corporate income tax is levied at 25 per cent. A unified flat personal income tax at 25 per cent was also introduced in early 1995.

Lithuania finally implemented VAT in 1994 (18 per cent), followed by the introduction of *ad valorem* excise taxes varying between 10 and 50 per cent, mainly on alcohol, tobacco and fuel. Land, rental of land and property are taxed at, respectively, 1.5 per cent, 1.5-6 per cent and 1 per cent. The system for personal and corporate income taxes remains relatively complex, despite several attempts to simplify it. Corporate income tax is currently 29 per cent, though the government intends to lower this to 24 per cent in 2000. The standard rate of personal income tax in Lithuania is 33 per cent.

---

into an instrument of policy from the automatic accounting deduction typical of central planning. But, apart from the impact of social factors, tax policy has been crucial in mobilising revenue by establishing a simple set of tax rates (mainly flat rates), limiting or eliminating tax exemptions, and strengthening tax collection.

Success in maintaining revenue has been matched by action in controlling expenditure. For example, price subsidies were either quickly removed (Estonia) or substantially reduced, especially in the traditionally important agricultural sector (in Latvia and Lithuania). That Estonia has managed to implement a tighter fiscal policy earlier than its two neighbours can be partly explained by the adoption of binding institutional arrangements that mandate a balanced budget. This has taken out some of the political heat out of the budgetary process. General improvement of the fiscal positions in Estonia, Latvia and Lithuania was supported by the implementation of predictable budget procedures and a clear legislative framework that accorded with the constitution. In support of the formation and execution of fiscal policy, all countries have made good progress towards establishing fiscal institutions, such as a treasury system, state revenue service and a customs service. A record of modest fiscal deficits has allowed governments in the region to avoid the excessive accumulation of public debt. Another similarity is that fiscal adjustment has brought about budgets dominated by current spending while capital spending has been restrained, particularly in Latvia and Lithuania.

Reform of the tax system

Uniform tax rates have proved effective

As in other transition countries the emerging private sector had little incentive to report profits and pay taxes. Therefore, the Baltic countries gave particular consideration to the advantages of a simple tax system. Reforms have simplified administration, eliminated exemptions and largely set flat rates of tax. The share of indirect taxes in the Baltic States has steadily increased reflecting governments' policy to shift the tax burden from production to consumption, but also to comply with EU tax directives. Indirect taxes have also proved more efficient in terms of tax collection rates and lower administration costs.

Replacing the complex turnover taxes, value added tax (VAT) is levied in all three Baltic States at a uniform rate of 18 per cent. The most important excises (*e.g.* fuel, tobacco and alcohol) are expected to rise in the future to harmonise with EU legislation. The share of trade taxes (mostly consisting of customs duties) is low and on a decreasing trend in all the Baltic States, reflecting their choice of liberal multilateral trade regimes, although countervailing pressures may arise from EU membership requirements. Estonia will anyway raise some tariffs, within WTO limits, to make up for revenue lost as a result of its decision to abolish corporation tax.

Amongst direct taxes, the share of personal income tax has increased in all Baltic countries in relation to corporate tax as the pattern of tax collection has moved closer to that found in market economies: a remarkable difference compared with Russia. A comparison with the OECD (see Figure 26) suggests that the share of personal income taxes could further increase at the expense of the share currently taken up by payroll taxes.

The share of corporate income tax revenue has fallen in all three countries since the onset of transition. This reflects the fall in output, with declining enterprise profitability, and also a degree of tax evasion (see below). The share of corporate taxes is expected to continue its decline given the increasing mobility of the corporate tax base. While, in spite of periodic discussion, Latvia and Lithuania have not taken further action in light of the need to preserve aggregate revenues, as stated above Estonia passed legislation to abolish corporation tax

Figure 26. **Composition of revenues, 1998**
Per cent GDP

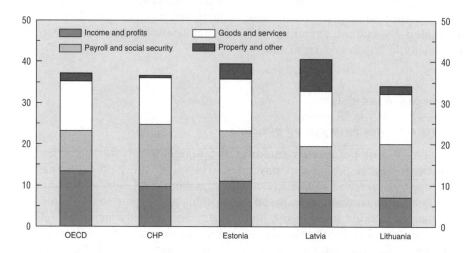

Legend: CHP: Average of Czech Republic, Hungary and Poland.
Source: IMF, OECD.

from 1 January 2000. Lithuanian corporate taxes are lower, and less transparent, than are those in either Latvia or Estonia and favour the agricultural sector. Local government also has significant discretion to grant tax exemptions; a power that has in practice further reduced revenue.

Interest income is not taxed in Latvia, but non-residents are subject to a 10 per cent withholding tax. In Lithuania corporations pay tax on interest income, and non-residents are subject to a 15 per cent withholding tax. Dividends are treated as tax-paid[33] in Estonia and Latvia, though non-residents suffer a 10 per cent withholding tax in Latvia. In Lithuania, dividends are taxed as income, with some exceptions for foreign enterprises where this is covered by an international agreement.

To a different extent all the Baltic States use their corporate tax systems as an instrument of industrial and/or regional policy. Both Latvia and Lithuania try to support agriculture and small business, for instance using corporate tax credits or reduced tax rates. Lithuania and Estonia have attempted to encourage investment using corporation tax allowances. While Estonia has finally decided to abolish corporation tax. Latvia has opted for accelerated depreciation allowances. Latvia and Lithuania have both tried to attract foreign investment by offering tax incentives,[34] although there is no strong evidence that these play a significant role in the decision about where to invest. Other than in Free Economic Zones, these practices have been discontinued.[35]

Property taxes have been adopted in all transition economies. These typically yield high rates of collection, and the Baltic countries are no exception: revenues from property taxes already account for about one percent of GDP in Latvia and Lithuania and half percent of GDP in Estonia. Property tax is also attractive because of its redistributive effect. But this effect relies on a well functioning market for land. Lower income groups in transition countries, who acquired land via restitution, could be the worst hit. Collection from tax on property should increase as land privatisation accelerates.

Collection of personal income taxes has been more mixed. Estonia has been the most successful in collecting personal income taxes, providing evidence of the effectiveness of a flat tax system. With the highest tax rates, Lithuania has the lowest rates of collection. While it is difficult to single out any particular factor explaining Estonia's relative performance, distinctive features in Estonia are that it has the broadest tax base, including, for instance, a higher proportion of the self-employed, and has eliminated most tax-allowable deductions. Different policies towards tax allowances may go some way to explaining lower rates of collection in Latvia. All three countries allow individuals to deduct a minimum amount in arriving at taxable income; in Latvia these deductions are also conditional on the number of dependants. These contrasting experiences suggest there is considerable scope for increasing proceeds from personal income tax in Latvia and Lithuania by broadening the tax base and synchronising personal and corporate income taxes. In this regard, a unified Income Tax Law is in preparation in Latvia. Moreover, the experience of the Baltic States suggests that high tax rates have encouraged informal economic activity and discouraged formal employment.

Payroll taxes are used to fund high levels of social expenditure, a significant part of which relates to fiscally unsustainable "pay-as-you-go" pension systems (see section below on underlying pressures). Payroll taxes have also suffered widespread avoidance, leveraging up the tax rate on the shrinking base, as there was only a weak link between contributions and benefits received. The underground economy contributes to this problem. A portion of the payroll tax in Estonia and Lithuania is transferred to the health insurance fund; in Latvia an analogous transfer is made out of income tax receipts. Payroll tax rates in the Baltics are by and large comparable to those in western European countries (see Figure 27).

In light of the relatively high level of taxation already in place, the revenue effort will need sustained progress in the quality of tax administration. Tax administration has already been strengthened by moving towards a more functional system (of assessment, collection and enforcement), though also by

Figure 27. **Payroll taxes and social security contributions, 1999**
Per cent

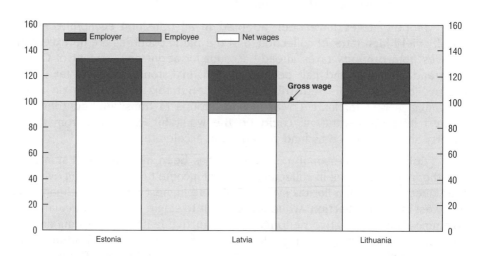

Source: National Authorities.

extending self-assessment, simplifying tax returns, introducing selective auditing and investigation, and bringing in taxpayer identification numbers and computerisation. But more can be done.

Tax arrears and the informal sector remain significant

Despite their good record in maintaining tax revenues, the countries in the Baltic region can take further action to restrict tax evasion and reduce tax arrears. Latvia faces the most significant challenge: tax arrears are some 6 per cent of GDP, mostly related to the energy sector. Although the volume of tax arrears stabilised in 1996-97 and decreased through the first half of 1998, it increased again after the rouble crisis in August 1998. This was partly due to the policy of allowing farmers to postpone payments of their taxes. According to the Latvian Ministry of Finance the downward trend in the volume of arrears has again taken hold during 1999. In contrast, Estonia established a firmer stance towards this problem despite concerns to protect debtors and some opposition from the courts. Total tax arrears amount to about 1.6 per cent of GDP in 1998 but increased to 3 per cent by September 1999. The government has put in place a mechanism for debtors to settle overdue tax liabilities; also in some cases accumulated tax liabilities have been forgiven as part of privatisation. In Lithuania, low tax arrears are largely due to the government having written-off outstanding tax arrears on several occasions. In January 1999, the amounted to some 4 per cent of GDP.

Tax evasion is in part a product of weak institutional co-operation, particularly between tax collection agencies. Countries also need to develop legislation that balances the need to protect banking confidentiality against the benefit to the tax authorities of gaining access to banks' transaction details. Legislation also needs to be developed to allow the authorities effectively to pursue cases of tax evasion through the courts; presently the law makes it difficult to pursue even flagrant cases of tax evasion. Border controls will also have to cope with the incentive to tax evasion in parallel with increasing customs duties and excises in the Baltic countries, aiming to integrate with the EU. The differential in tax rates between the Baltic region and its eastern neighbours is likely to increase. However, governments in this area face a difficult task. A too heavy-handed approach in dealing with tax evasion could damage dynamism of small business and the informal sector. These tend to emerge together, as barriers to enterprise creation of make it difficult for a small entrepreneur to become established. However, this is a vital element in the transition process.

Free Economic Zones: a risk of revenue reduction

Free or Special Economic Zones (FEZ/SEZ) are another area where there is a perceived trade-off between current tax collection and higher future revenue expected from economic growth. FEZ are specified geographical areas where tax incentives to producers are offered in order to attract industrial development. These incentives include tax rebates for investors and usually also VAT and/or duty exemptions for goods transiting the FEZ. Free ports, such as Ventspils and Riga in Latvia, benefit only from VAT and duty exemptions. While the temptation to tackle structural problems by setting-up FEZs in not unique to the Baltics, this issue deserves special attention as there is potential for harmful competition between countries in the region. Where different FEZs engage in a "beauty contest" to attract potential investment there may be significant negative externalities. This effect could become particularly pronounced where alternative sites are located in different countries but serving the same market. This danger should not be under-estimated by the Baltic countries given, in particular, the regional perspective through which many outside investors approach the Baltic area. Presently, there are FEZs in all three Baltic countries (see Chapter V).

The short-run risk to the government's fiscal position in terms of revenues foregone needs to be weighed against the potential for future revenue growth expected from higher levels of economic activity. There are to date no studies in the region of whether the potential benefits of these zones, in terms of job creation or skills development, have indeed materialised. FEZ may also have

---

Box 3.   Case study: the informal sector in Latvia

It is notoriously difficult to estimate the size of the informal economy. Latvia has made various estimates, based on: energy-consumption, cash in circulation and discrepancies in reporting of international trade flows (see Steinbuka and Kodolina, 1998).

In 1995 the Latvian Statistical authorities launched a study on the informal economy in co-operation with EUROSTAT. The informal sector was estimated at 14 per cent of GDP. But this study was based on the labour market survey and only captured unregistered and "parallel" activities. According to the Latvian Ministry of Finance, which based its estimate on tax evasion and (uncovered) illegal activity, the informal sector amounted to 35 per cent of GDP in 1994. This rose to 37 per cent of GDP in 1995 following the banking crisis that took place in that year. The informal sector started to decrease as the economy grew and tax administration was strengthened. It is now reckoned to be about 30 per cent of GDP.

Latvia has experienced a general shift towards formal activity as transition has progressed. According to various sources, uncollected payroll taxes have declined from 31 per cent to 28 per cent between 1994 and 1997. A similar trend has been observed for personal income tax. The creation of effective customs control has contributed to a sharp decline in smuggling: lost excise taxes have decreased from 50 per cent in 1994 to 17 per cent in 1996. VAT collection also indicates a shift to formal activity. But, overall, all tax collection is expected to deteriorate following the Russian economic crisis, not least because of an increase in less formal employment arrangements. For example, in order to avoid redundancies, employees may be prepared to forgo social security benefits in order to reduce the costs of employment to the employer.

---

structural implications. An important prior question is whether the forgone revenue might have been used more efficiently. For example, by investing in infrastructure, but above all there is the question of whether FEZ incentives actually influence investment decisions. With its comparatively high level of FDI, Estonia experience suggests that there are other ways to induce FDI. Evidence from Russia (Brock, 1998) suggests that market size and the perceived level of criminality and lawlessness are rather more important determinants of foreign investment flows.

Management of expenditure

Changing patterns of public expenditure

Public expenditure in the Baltic States as share of GDP[36] is higher than in countries at similar income levels, and almost as high as in lower income members of the EU. What stands out is how stable the shares of expenditure by different categories has been over time (see Figure 28).

However there are differences between the Baltic States in the comparative level of expenditure in different areas. In relative terms, Estonia has directed more public expenditure at education. Social security and welfare is the highest item of expenditure in all the three countries; but spending in this area is also significantly higher in Latvia than in either Estonia or Lithuania. Nearly all of this expenditure is financed through the central budget, local expenditure accounting for only some one per cent of the total in Latvia and Lithuania, and about half that in Estonia. There are also pronounced differences between the countries in expenditure on housing. Latvia spends more than four times as much as Estonia (1.7 versus 0.4 per cent of GDP). This expenditure is also financed in different ways: entirely from the central budget in Estonia, exclusively from local budgets in Lithuania and a mixed solution in Latvia (though biased towards local spending).

There are also significant differences between types of expenditure in the Baltic countries (see Table 8). In particular capital spending is lower in Latvia and Lithuania than in Estonia; though in Latvia this expenditure has more than doubled since 1995 whilst it contracted in Lithuania over the same time period. Commitments to public investment made during this period of catching-up in Latvia could have implications in the present period of fiscal restraint induced by the Russian crisis, as there is a cost to suspending investment projects once they are under way. The counterpart to low capital spending is relatively high current spending. Its most important component is wages and salaries which, as a share of GDP, tended to fall in the years after 1995, but has more recently increased in all three countries.

Social security expenditure has been the highest in Latvia. All three countries increased the share of GDP devoted to these expenditures during 1999. Rising pensions, and pensioners, are behind the high level of social and welfare expenditure. The 1998 the net replacement rate (pensions/after-tax wages) in Latvia was 52 per cent versus 40 per cent in Estonia and Lithuania (see Table 18). Although these simple estimates probably overstate the true position, they accurately reflect a difference between the countries. Indeed, pre-retirement income typically exceeds average income, wages tend anyway to be under-reported and newly granted pensions tend to be below the average. Thus the average net replacement ratio is likely to be biased upwards, but this bias should be equivalent in all three countries. As a result, pension expenditures in Latvia as a percentage of GDP are the highest among all the former Soviet republics. Aiming to respond to these long-term pressures on expenditure, all the three Baltic states have embarked since 1995 on a comprehensive pension reform aiming to

Figure 28. **Shares in government expenditure, 1993-98**
Per cent

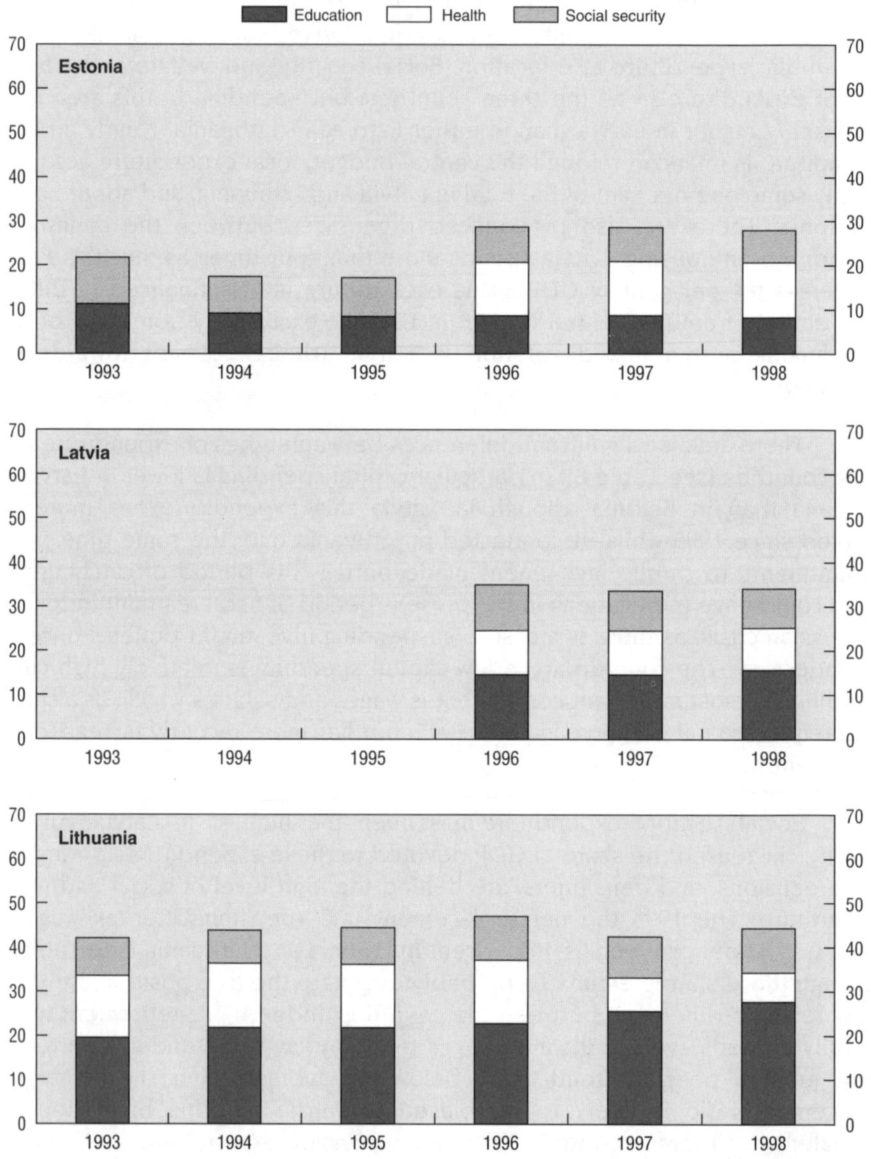

■ Education   □ Health   ▨ Social security

Table 8. **Government expenditure by type, 1995-99**

Per cent GDP

	1995	1996	1997	1998	1999p
Estonia					
Total expenditure	**41.4**	**40.4**	**37.7**	**39.7**	**41.7**
Current expenditure	36.7	35.5	33.9	35.4	37.8
Wages and salaries	*10.4*	*9.4*	*8.3*	*9.3*	*10.5*
Goods and services	*14.3*	*14.3*	*14.6*	*15.1*	*14.9*
Subsidies	*0.5*	*0.4*	*0.3*	*0.4*	*0.5*
Transfers to households	*11.0*	*11.1*	*10.4*	*10.3*	*11.5*
of which: Pensions	*7.1*	*7.6*	*7.2*	*7.1*	*8.2*
Other	*0.5*	*0.3*	*0.4*	*0.3*	*0.3*
Capital expenditure	4.7	4.9	3.9	4.2	4.0
Latvia					
Total expenditure	**40.5**	**39.0**	**40.7**	**41.3**	**43.6**
Current expenditure	40.0	36.9	38.3	37.4	39.5
Wages and salaries	*8.9*	*9.4*	*9.1*	*9.4*	*9.9*
Goods and services	*9.1*	*9.5*	*9.7*	*8.1*	*7.9*
Subsidies	*0.0*	*0.8*	*5.2*	*4.5*	*5.3*
Transfers to households	*17.4*	*15.8*	*13.3*	*14.2*	*15.7*
of which: Pensions	*9.6*	*10.2*	*10.4*	*10.6*	*11.8*
Other	*4.6*	*1.4*	*1.0*	*1.1*	*0.8*
Capital expenditure	*0.9*	*2.1*	*2.4*	*3.9*	*4.1*
Lithuania					
Total expenditure	**34.9**	**32.1**	**34.1**	**38.5**	**39.0**
Current expenditure	29.9	29.4	30.6	34.1	35.0
Wages and salaries	*9.2*	*9.6*	*8.7*	*10.0*	*10.6*
Goods and services	*9.2*	*7.7*	*9.7*	*11.7*	*10.2*
Subsidies	*1.1*	*1.3*	*0.9*	*0.7*	*0.7*
Transfers to households	*9.9*	*10.0*	*10.5*	*10.5*	*12.0*
of which: Pensions	*6.2*	*6.1*	*6.4*	*7.0*	*7.6*
Other	*0.4*	*0.9*	*0.8*	*1.2*	*1.5*
Capital expenditure	3.8	2.7	2.7	2.7	*1.7*
Savings restitution	0.0	0.0	0.0	1.0	*2.2*

p: projection.
Source: National authorities and IMF.

modify existing "pay as you go" systems and gradually to introduce a multi-pillar system (see Box 8, below).

This comparison between the Baltic countries' public expenditure has been carried out on a consolidated basis. However, one should bear in mind that there is a lack of transparency in the public spending in the region. Consolidated figures are sometimes not available for central and local government expenditure;

Table 9. **Scope of the national budget**

Categories of expenditure included in the national budget

	Estonia	Latvia	Lithuania
Central government	Yes	Yes	Yes
Local government	No	No	Yes
Social insurance	Yes	Yes	No
Medical insurance	Yes	Yes	No

Source: National authorities.

the coverage of national budgets differs, and a varying scale of expenditure is passed through off-budget funds. In Latvia 46 per cent of government expenditure in incurred by "special funds".[37] The differences between the three countries concerning the coverage of the national budget are summarised in Table 9.

The Baltic countries have also adopted different approaches to the degree of expenditure that is incurred by local governments. These differences amount to between one-fifth and one-quarter of total expenditure (see Table 10). While a certain degree of decentralisation may be desirable, it may make it harder to achieve fiscal consolidation when this becomes needed. Indeed, greater fiscal discipline in Estonia seems to be associated with a generally larger share of central government financing.

Public debt in all Baltic countries stands at reasonably low levels as a result of the fiscal convergence discussed above and thanks to privatisation revenues as a source of budget financing. This may change in the aftermath of the Russian crisis (see below). Although the EU does not require the accession candidates to adhere to the Maastricht criteria for entry to the European Monetary Union, to date all the Baltic countries comfortably satisfy the public debt criteria, none having debt of more than 30 per cent of GDP (see Figure 29).

Table 10. **Shares in selected government expenditure by tier, 1996**

Per cent

	Education		Health		Social security		Housing	
	Central	Local	Central	Local	Central	Local	Central	Local
Estonia	49	51	96	4	96	4	100	0
Latvia	71	29	52	49	93	7	14	86
Lithuania	35	65	51	49	91	9	0	100

Source: National Statistical Offices.

Figure 29. **Gross stocks of public debt, 1998**
Per cent GDP

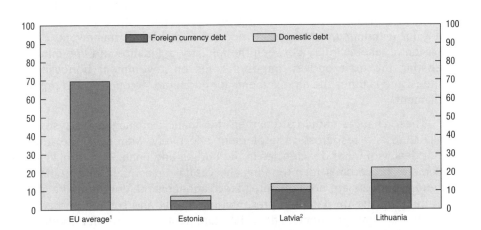

1. For the EU, refers to total general government consolidated gross debt.
2. For Latvia, domestic debt comprises lat-denominated T-Bills and bonds, bank recapitalisation bonds, some of which are held by non-residents.
Source: International Financial Statistics, 1999 and Eurostat for the European Union.

The budget process needs improvement

Preparing the budget should be an opportunity for governments to estab-lish economic priorities and to communicate public policy choices. National fiscal authorities undertake a careful review of existing programs and consider the introduction of new programmes for managing government activities in line with the identified priorities. The approved national budget should be a clear state-ment of the government's intentions and targets. Notably, local governments, as well as central government, should be bound into an overall fiscal strategy. It is not yet the case that local government and municipalities adhere to a common policy framework, though authorities in the Baltics have recently begun to appre-ciate the need for an approach based on a consolidated budget.

In all three countries the ministries of finance have been moving ahead with certain initiatives in order to modernise their systems of budgeting and financial control, and to meet the requirements of future membership of the European Union. In particular, the European Commission demands high stan-dards of financial management and control in the use of pre-accession funds. In *Estonia*, a modern treasury system, covering both cash management and debt management procedures, was introduced in 1996 and is in the process of being fully computerised. A new version of the Law on the State Budget was passed in June 1999. It includes a comprehensive concept of what constitutes public money and the scope of the budget (reducing the number of extra-budgetary funds); provides for a (minimum three-year) medium-term budget framework; clarifies the division of responsibility between the Ministry of Finance and line ministries in preparing the draft budget; imposes limits on government borrowing and guarantees; and clarifies the arrangements for budgetary accounting and reporting to parliament.

These changes should strengthen the financial management system but will take time and resources to implement effectively. Moreover, the new law does not deal with other deficiencies in the budget and financial control systems. For example, procedures for preparing the capital investment and operational expenditure budgets are not fully integrated, arrangements for internal audit are not set out, and the preparation, presentation, format and content and external audit of the annual government financial statements need further clarification. The public audit office is currently undergoing a process of modernisation and development to strengthen the effectiveness of public sector external audit and is preparing new audit legislation.

In Latvia, progress has been made, for example, in approving a Law on Budget and Financial Management (April 1994) and establishing a treasury system (1993). Priorities in the Ministry of Finance are to control the spending and proliferation of autonomous agencies, whose spending is not included in the budget and hence is not subject to the same degree of control.[38] Other priorities are to introduce stronger internal audit and financial control systems in line ministries; to develop procedures for ex-post evaluation of the efficiency of public expenditure; and to integrate the budget planning and policy process into a realistic medium-term framework. Consideration should be given to integrating procedures for preparing the capital investment budget, which are at present divided between the Ministry of Finance and the Ministry of Economy. As in Estonia, the public audit office is currently undergoing a process of modernisation and development to strengthen the effectiveness of public sector external audit and is preparing new audit legislation.

Lithuania has made progress towards establishing a modern treasury. However, work on computerisation and integration of the treasury procedures with budget preparation and debt management operations needs to be completed. A draft Law on the Budget has been prepared which would strengthen the budget system in a number of ways. For example, it would create a three-year medium-term planning framework for the budget; facilitate the introduction of a new performance budgeting structure and clarify the role and responsibilities of the "appropriation managers", i.e. the senior officials in the line ministries responsible for preparing and implementing the budget. However, these changes are still under review by the government and parliament and will require intensive and sustained efforts to implement. Procedures regarding annual reporting, clearance of financial accounts, and internal audit and financial controls also need to be strengthened.

The Russian crisis: a source of divergence

The benign picture of fiscal convergence in the three Baltic States that emerged during 1993-97 has begun to disintegrate in the wake of the rouble crisis that took place in August 1998. Within six months the rouble had depreciated by more than 70 per cent against each of the three Baltic currencies (and a similar amount against the US dollar). Russia's output fell by about 5 per cent in 1998, after a modest pick-up in 1997. As already discussed in Chapter I, this has had a dramatic effect on economic performance in the region and revealed more profound differences in the state of progress on structural reforms. The sharp reduction in Russian growth not only made itself felt directly through the impact on the balance of payments. There was a general reassessment of the potential of the Russian market that dented confidence and raised risk *premia*. Growth slowed. Governments in the region found themselves starting 1999 with budgets based on overly optimistic assumptions about GDP growth and hence tax revenues. In fact, fiscal performance had already deteriorated significantly in the last two quarters of 1998 (see Figure 30).

The responses in the region to this external shock have differed. In Estonia, expenditure was not reduced to match lower revenues and the deficit during the second half of 1998 rose to 2.8 per cent of GDP, though the deficit for the year as a whole was a modest 0.3 per cent of GDP. A supplementary budget was passed by parliament in June 1999 to cut expenditure and restrict the 1999 deficit to 4.0 per cent of GDP.[39] Half of the privatisation revenues have been used to finance the fiscal deficit, but the other half has been accumulated in a fund located outside the country (see Box 4). Estonia also suffered a contraction of indirect tax revenues during the first quarter of 1999 that may be related to the economic turbulence in Russia. VAT receipts suffered from a fall in private consumption, and from a sharp deterioration in imports, which decreased by 16 per cent in the first quarter.

Impending parliamentary elections in both Estonia and Latvia made agreement on revised budget projections in response to the expected economic slowdown difficult. As a consequence budgets were approved with only minor changes relating to the composition, rather than the level, of revenue and expenditure. The consolidated deficit widened sharply in the first half of 1999 in both countries.

Figure 30.   **General government balance by quarter**

Per cent GDP

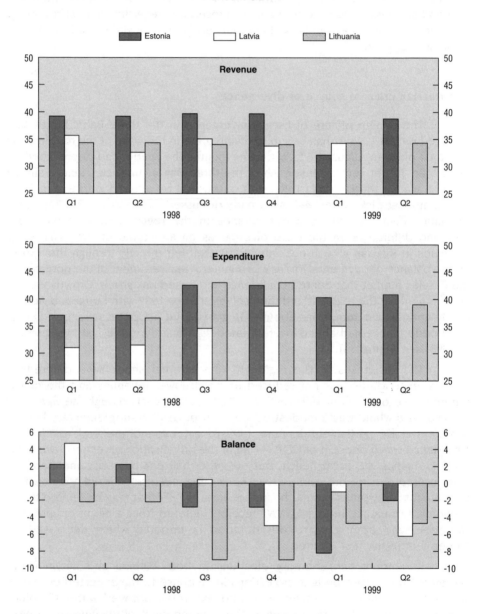

NB: Revenue and expenditure for Latvia in 1999-Q2 are not available.
Source: Ministries of Finance and IMF.

Box 4.   The Estonian Stabilisation Reserve Fund (SRF)

The SRF was set up in late 1997 as an instrument for saving budget surpluses and privatisation proceeds abroad. It may not be used to invest in domestic securities. It is to be used as a contingency reserve, and to finance long-term reform and investment. During late 1997 and early 1998 Estonia was experiencing a period of considerable growth in domestic credit, and the SRF was used to withdraw liquidity from banks by transferring public savings abroad and, in the first quarter of 1999, to sterilise proceeds following some large privatisations. By March 1999 the balance on the SRF amounted to 3.5 per cent of projected GDP for the year. It is envisaged that this will be used to finance infrastructure investments and a systemic reform of pension provision. From January 2000, all privatisation receipts will mandatorily be transferred to the SRF, although this will have a limited impact given that the privatisation process in Estonia is nearly complete.

Latvian fiscal performance had in fact deteriorated after the first quarter of 1998, though the fiscal account remained in surplus until the fourth quarter. This deterioration appears to have been due to higher spending rather than a marked fall in revenue. The outcome for the year was a fiscal deficit of 0.8 per cent of GDP, notwithstanding the pronounced downward trend in fiscal performance. Since then, preliminary figures for the first half of 1999 show that the deficit has increased, to 1 per cent in the first quarter and 6 per cent in the second quarter. The government in Latvia passed a supplementary budget in August 1999 to contain the deficit to about 4 per cent of GDP in 1999. The authorities in both Estonia and Latvia have signalled that larger cuts would be desirable but that this may not be politically feasible.

Modest revenue gains in Lithuania have been more than offset by higher spending, mainly as a result of the Savings Restitution Plan (SRP) which returned cash payments to citizens following some large scale privatisations. The government has also increased direct support to enterprises, notably in the agricultural sector, affected by the economic crisis in Russia. The fiscal deficit has been hauled back from the 9 per cent of GDP it reached during the third and fourth quarters of 1998, but the deficit remains significantly higher than at the same period during the preceding year. This fiscal stimulus largely compensated for the real effects of the Russian crisis and explains the apparent paradox that Lithuania, the country most exposed to Russia, seemed the least affected by the loss of export markets. As a consequence, there has been a significant weakening in the current account balance, which reached 14 per cent of GDP in the last quarter of 1998. This pattern replicates the experience of other transition economies (see OECD, 1999a). In November 1999, the Lithuanian government announced its intention to freeze further payments under the SRP for at least two years.

The fiscal and current account deterioration in the three Baltic countries must be seen in the light of their commitments to fixed exchange regimes. The main line of defence against a negative external shock is to tighten fiscal policy, without which there is a danger that the countries will expose themselves to increased external vulnerability. After a delay, governments now seem to be taking fiscal action. But the anatomy of the fiscal deterioration is different between the region's three countries. In Estonia it was driven by a fall in (indirect) revenue in the first quarter of 1999; the government has nonetheless moved quickly to reduce expenditure and the deficit in the second quarter of 1999 was less than 2 per cent of GDP. In both Latvia and Lithuania the fiscal deterioration has also been driven by higher expenditure. In Lithuania, in particular, this was due to the one-off transfer to households under the SRP.

Policy challenges ahead

The short run fiscal challenges are based on maintaining the macroeconomic stability that has underpinned recent growth in the region. In the medium term the countries of the region face three main challenges. They have to continue reforms designed to qualify them for accession to the European Union; they need to develop mechanisms for making and enforcing (at all levels of government) policy choices in prioritising public expenditure; and, lastly, they need to address the universal problem they share in funding their pension systems where 26 per cent of their population is drawing a pension.[40]

The prospect of EU accession places significant obligations on the applicant countries, many of which will have fiscal consequences, though these cannot be reasonably quantified. Although the accession countries are not obliged to adhere to the parameters of the EMU "stability pact", in practice it is natural that many commentators will measure them against that yardstick.[41] This provides an added incentive, on top of the self-imposed constraint implicit in maintaining fixed exchange rate regimes, for the Baltic countries to maintain tight fiscal policies. Little further harmonisation is needed in direct taxation, though more needs to be done with respect to indirect taxes. This would include harmonising VAT exemptions and excise duties and, in Estonia's case raising customs tariffs from zero to current EU rates. In approximating their standards and practice to EU norms the countries will benefit from EU technical assistance drawn from funds such as PHARE (enterprise, employment and regional development), ISPA (transport and environment) and SAPARD (development of agriculture, food, fisheries and rural areas). The scale of the support available to applicant countries has not yet been decided, but national strategies will need to identify resources for co-financing projects eligible under these initiatives.

Improvements to budget management and transparency will support better public policy choice. Consolidated budgets should cover all sources of revenue, all domestically and foreign funded expenditure, and all forms of domestic and foreign financing. Improved transparency should also help governments to test the control mechanisms they put in place to cover local governments' finances and the operation of currently off-budget funds. It will also support the better allocation of public resources towards projects and activities designed to promote macroeconomic stability and sustainable economic growth. Ongoing reform of direct tax includes broadening the tax base and reducing high rates of tax, particularly payroll taxes. There is a danger that governments will allow the pressure to reduce expenditure to bear disproportionately on capital expenditure whereas medium run sustainability requires reform of (persistent) current government expenditure.

The Baltics face a specific pressure on expenditure due to their rapidly ageing populations. A substantial amount can still be done to reform the existing social security systems and improve their effectiveness, but existing pension systems are not fiscally sustainable over the long-run. Although all three countries have initiated reform of their pension systems (see Box 8 in Chapter VI), it will still be necessary to maintain tight control on spending in order to ensure sustainable fiscal positions.

IV. Banking and financial sector reform

Financial markets in Estonia, Latvia and Lithuania have undergone substantial development throughout the last decade. The main institutions are now in place, working reasonably well after a series of crises helped promote rationalisation in the financial sector and encouraged a trend of openness towards the international capital market (Psalida, 1998). The choice of monetary policy has been central to the development of the financial sector. As described in Chapter II, all the Baltic countries used the exchange rate as an anchor for monetary stability. Tight monetary policy favoured the emergence of the financial market discipline by reducing liquidity available to the banking system, forcing banks to manage the available liquidity more effectively and to build up their own liquidity buffers.

Free movement of capital has been integral to development of the financial system, allowing greater diversification of risk in liquidity management, and reducing the dependence of banks on domestic inter-bank and securities markets that lacked sufficient quantity and volume of high quality financial instruments. Deliberate lack of discretion in monetary policy has left little room for bailing out the financial sector.[42] This has promoted prudent behaviour by financial sector institutions, and hence has contributed to growing confidence in the sector both at home and overseas. The common goal of accession to the European Union (and the perspective of EMU membership) has been a strong contributory factor in leading all the Baltic countries to pursue a stable monetary and financial framework, and to open up their financial markets.

The financial markets in Estonia, Latvia and Lithuania have generally adopted the "universal banking" model. The absence of mandatory separation between banking and securities businesses has allowed banks to dominate the financial sector. Banks have acquired a dominant role in financial intermediation, taking a leading position in other segments of the market either directly or via non-bank subsidiaries. This development was accelerated in an environment, characterised by economic uncertainty and an incomplete legal infrastructure, that favoured strong personal relationships. The delays and uncertainty in undertaking pension reform[43] created unfavourable conditions for the development of an insurance sector, particularly life insurance, further constraining the emergence of alternative financial intermediaries.

Initial explosion in the number of banks...

The first phase of financial markets reforms in the Baltic States, as in other transition economies, started with the demolition of mono-bank system and progressed to establishing a two-tier banking system. These reforms coincided with macroeconomic stabilisation, and were to a large extent complete during the first half of the 1990s. New banks were set up and existing Soviet banks[44] were broken-up and transformed into independent banks as joint stock companies. At this point, the Baltic countries also re-established their central banks and started to regulate commercial banking activities, though with initially rather limited powers as regional offices of the Soviet Gosbank remained in operation. Dual central banking came to an end only in 1992 when then the Gosbank branches were wound up and national currencies reintroduced.

At the beginning of the 1990's the Baltic States were still part of the Soviet economic and monetary space. As a consequence, they endured the liberalisation and decentralisation of the Soviet economy and with it a regulatory framework that was accompanied by lax monetary and fiscal policies. This contributed to overly fast growth in both the volume of credit and the number of banks. Given extremely low barriers to entry[45] and lack of supervisory control the number of banks increased dramatically in the beginning of 1990's. By the end of 1991 24 new commercial banks had been established in Estonia, and were responsible for about one-third of outstanding loans; by the end of 1992 there were more than 40 banks operating in Estonia. The number of banks increased even more rapidly in Latvia where some 50 new banks were granted licenses in 1991-1992, and the total number of banks peaked at more then 60. Similar developments took place in Lithuania, though growth in the number of new banks was less pronounced: between 1991 and 1994, 21 new banks were established, bringing the total number to 27. The financial operating environment changed drastically once the Baltic countries introduced their own currencies.

... but, weak supervision invited banking crises

In the early years of transition, the Baltic countries' banking industry was overwhelmingly focused on the domestic market. The level of financial intermediation was low, for example in Estonia domestic credit amounted only to 13 per cent of GDP in 1993. In Latvia 18 per cent. The share of loans in banks' balance sheets was also low. The only link with international markets was for liquidity management. Exiting the rouble zone had revealed the extent of underlying weaknesses in each of the countries' banking sectors, but the timing of subsequent banking crises essentially reflected the speed with which they had adopted monetary reform (see Table 11).

Table 11. **Some financial sector indicators, 1995-99**

	1995	1996	1997	1998	1999 Q2
Estonia					
Domestic credit (per cent GDP)	16	21	29	31	32
Total banking sector assets (per cent GDP)	36	42	60	56	63
External liabilities (per cent total liabilities)	12	21	39	39	36
Foreign exchange loans (per cent total loans)	12	33	57	76	73
Ratio of average capital adequacy	n.a.	12	13	17	17
Number of banks	18	13	11	6	6
Stock Market Capitalisation (per cent GDP)	8	26	38	20	42
Leasing portfolio (per cent GDP)	2.0	3.5	8.0	8.7	8.7
Gross insurance premiums (per cent GDP)	1.2	1.4	1.6	1.7	1.7
Latvia					
Domestic credit (per cent GDP)	14	12	15	17	17
Total banking sector assets (per cent GDP)	31	39	54	46	48
External liabilities (per cent total liabilities)	41	51	56	59	55
Foreign exchange loans (per cent total loans)	56	64	68	66	n.a.
Ratio of average capital adequacy	20	23	21	17	n.a.
Number of banks	42	35	31	27	25
Stock Market Capitalisation (per cent GDP)	n.a.	3	6	6	12
Leasing portfolio (per cent GDP)	n.a.	n.a.	n.a.	n.a.	n.a.
Gross insurance premiums (per cent GDP)	n.a.	n.a.	n.a.	n.a.	n.a.
Lithuania					
Domestic credit (per cent GDP)	15	11	11	12	15
Total banking sector assets (per cent GDP)	28	23	24	25	28
External liabilities (per cent total liabilities)	7	13	15	19	18
Foreign exchange loans (per cent total loans)	32	33	42	56	59
Ratio of average capital adequacy	n.a.	11	11	24	23
Number of banks	12	12	11	10	10
Stock Market Capitalisation (per cent GDP)	4	11	18	14	15
Leasing portfolio (per cent GDP)	n.a.	n.a.	n.a.	n.a.	n.a.
Gross insurance premiums (per cent GDP)	n.a.	n.a.	n.a.	n.a.	n.a.

Source: National Banks.

Estonia was the first to experience a wave of banking failures, in 1992-93, which was not emulated by Latvia and Lithuania until mid-1995. The ingredients of banking failure were ongoing mismanagement resulting in poor quality loan books[46] – basic credit and internal controls and the essential elements of risk management were often missing – combined with a drastic change in the macro-economic environment as the countries undertook currency reform. Declining output and the trade shock that accompanied the collapse of the Soviet economy helped expose the true worth of banks' assets, leading to a number of high-profile banking failures. These naturally led to a loss of confidence in the sector, though low levels of financial deepening meant this had only a limited effect on the real economy.[47] Symptoms of banking vulnerability in Latvia and Lithuania were increasing dollarisation, withdrawal of deposits and capital outflows. The loss of confidence was least pronounced in Estonia, which avoided similar flight to foreign currency or cash.

Banks in Estonia and Latvia have been less troubled than other transition economies by exposure to troubled state-owned enterprises. In the first instance, persistently higher rates of inflation eroded the real value of inherited debt allocated by central planning to state owned enterprises. But banks' freedom to set interest rate and credit policy was used to pursue profitable business as new entrants have dramatically reduced the market share held by existing banks. Relatively quick privatisation of state-owned banks reinforced this tendency to break up existing, potentially detrimental, relationships between banks and management in state enterprises. However, poor banking regulation led to the emergence of a new structural weakness in the sector. Although banks were not directly instructed, or under political pressure, to lend to state-owned enterprises, a significant part of the sector in Lithuania remains in government ownership. Pursuit of market share also resulted in some reckless lending, unchecked by national supervisory agencies. And in another example of weak supervision, banks were able to lend to their, often anonymous, shareholders, at the very least raising the possibility that lending took place on other than commercial grounds.

Although Estonia took a commendably tough approach to banking failures in 1992-93, improvements in supervision were not sufficient to prevent a further crisis in 1994. In 1992 all the insolvent banks had been liquidated,[48] owners lost their investments and depositors in all troubled banks bore a significant share in the burden of restructuring. Accounting standards were tightened. Prudential regulations and loan loss provisioning were strengthened. Formerly state owned banks continued to lose market share, but at the same time the government declined to issue any further banking licenses for about a year, until the end of 1993. But in 1994 the Social Bank collapsed, largely as a result of excessive lending to shareholders and connected parties. The bank had been privatised, but senior management had remained in place; there was no system to review the suitability of major shareholders,[49] and the failure had serious implications for the inter-bank market in which Savings Bank was the largest borrower.[50] This time the response to the crisis was less decisive. The situation was eventually resolved through successive measures (sale of branches, changes in management and ultimately the withdrawal of license) only in the spring of 1995.

Unlike the first crisis, depositors' claims were safeguarded in full and the cost of restructuring was borne by authorities. It was followed by a revision of the regulatory framework in a new banking law that included increased capital requirements, presentation of financial statements based on international accounting standards, audit of annual accounts to be carried out only by international auditing firms, and provision for increased competition. As a consequence there was substantial consolidation in the banking market towards the end of 1995. Administrative regulation forced four mergers as the number of banks fell from 21 to 15. Monetary measures and prudential regulation have subsequently focused on discouraging the rapid expansion of domestic credit and increasing the share of liquid assets in banks' portfolios.

Progress prior to 1995 in Latvia and Lithuania was limited. Regulatory requirements were gradually tightened; for instance, Lithuanian banks were required to access borrowers' credit worthiness and make specific loan-loss provisions, and the National Bank of Lithuania introduced an early warning system. But there was not yet a requirement for banks to be audited according to international standards, or for audit to be carried by international auditing firms, although according to the National Bank all banks were audited by international firms. More widespread tightening and enforcement of the supervisory framework could to a certain extent have substituted for evolving domestic supervision. Latvia was the first of the Baltic countries to require international audit for the largest banks' accounts as of end 1993, and Lithuania followed suit as of end-1994. As in Estonia, banks did not suffer from a particularly poor inherited stock of assets but exploited lax supervision to expand more quickly than was prudent, and in ways that bordered illegality.

By 1995 the situation was ripe for a crisis in Latvia and Lithuania. At this time the Bank of Latvia introduced a requirement that all commercial banks had to be audited by international auditing firms, and a number of large and medium sized banks had great difficulty in complying with new regulations. In 1995 some 15 banking licenses were withdrawn, including that of the then largest bank, Bank Baltija, which held about 30 per cent of the market.[51] The banking crisis led to consolidation in the banking sector; the number of institutions decreased, as did concentration, though the number of banks remained still high compared with its neighbours.[52] Similarly, by the end of 1995 it became clear that six Lithuanian banks were insolvent. Fifteen out of the 27 banks operating at the time were closed by end-1996. Bankruptcy procedures were initiated in both countries and the regulatory framework was strengthened with banks all having to report their results according to international standards.[53]

Latvia introduced a higher capital requirement on banks that were eligible to accept household deposits,[54] and the Bank of Latvia also intensified its surveillance activity, with a particular emphasis on on-site inspections. Lithuania chose to recapitalise the largest two banks and issued bank-restructuring bonds to meet the cost and has created a special asset management company to take over the non-performing loans of troubled banks. As a result the state has remained a significant player in the financial markets, with the danger that decisions on credit allocation may be influenced by political considerations. Tighter prudential regulations encouraged banks towards conventional banking activities of deposit taking and lending, explicitly limiting the scope for currency speculations and short-term high risk lending operations.

Banking crises have had a purgative effect. By 1998 bad debts had been reduced to manageable levels (Table 12). But the emergence of healthier banking systems in the Baltic countries has depended on the degree to which the crisis was used as a catalyst to hasten the destruction of non-market based networks and linkages which had endured from the days of the command economy. Continuing state ownership and failure to deal with lack of transparency have hindered this process. Better banking supervision was needed to ensure that the new structure survived and that banks complied with the rules of a competitive market where bankruptcy is a real threat. However, regulation also needs to mature to the point where it can effectively deal with systemic risks without compromising the incentives on individual financial sector institutions to behave prudently. The Baltic countries have concentrated their efforts in reducing moral hazard in the financial sector by rigorously enforcing bankruptcy rules for banks. As discussed below, this was tested during the Baltic banking crises. However, reducing moral hazard is not a perfect substitute for sound banking supervision, as it does not address the systemic risks involved with a generalised banking failure. Given the developments in the Baltic banking sector, the countries could benefit from looking at the experience of others in developing banking and financial supervision (see Box 5).

Faster international integration and financial deepening followed financial crisis

Following the first phase of restructuring, Baltic financial markets started to become increasingly international and regionally integrated. Strong export performance and increased investor confidence in the Baltic region were the foundation for economic recovery. High investment demand and a relatively low domestic saving rate led to a widening current account deficit that was, however, more than covered by capital inflows. Over time the financing pattern of the current account deficit shifted from FDI (especially in Estonia) to portfolio investments and debt creating inflows. The financial sector has become the chief intermediary of these flows.[55] Declining interest rates and an easing liquidity constraint contributed to financial deepening and development of non-bank financial intermediation, though the pace of financial market development has been somewhat uneven in Baltic countries.

The Estonian banking sector has been the most active in pursuing regional expansion. An Estonian bank has established an institutional presence in Lithuania through leasing subsidiaries and the acquisition in 1996 of a commercial

Table 12. **Loan classification and provisions, 1995-99**

Percentage of total loans

		Estonia	Latvia	Lithuania
Standard (I)	1995	–	66	69
	1996	–	72	55
	1997	–	87	60
	1998	–	88	68
	June '99	–	89	68
Watch (II)	1995	–	15	14
	1996	–	7	13
	1997	–	4	12
	1998	–	5	20
	June '99	–	4	21
Total I-II	**1995**	**100**	**81**	**83**
	1996	**93**	**79**	**68**
	1997	**93**	**91**	**72**
	1998	**95**	**93**	**88**
	June '99	**90**	**93**	**90**
Substandard (III)	1995		7	4
	1996	3	5	8
	1997	3	3	5
	1998	2	3	4
	June '99	6	3	3
Doubtful (IV)	1995		10	6
	1996	1	6	8
	1997	1	2	4
	1998	1	2	2
	June '99	1	2	3
Bad (V)	1995		10	7
	1996	3	9	16
	1997	4	5	19
	1998	2	2	6
	June '99	4	2	4
Total III-V	**1995**	**0**	**27**	**17**
	1996	**7**	**20**	**32**
	1997	**7**	**10**	**28**
	1998	**5**	**7**	**12**
	June '99	**10**	**7**	**10**
Provisions	1995	3	20	16
	1996	2	16	22
	1997	2	7	19
	1998	4	4	6
	June '99	3	5	5

Source: National Banks.

Box 5. Organisation of a financial supervisory authority*

OECD countries have only recently started to create unified structures for integrated financial sector supervision. Single supervisory authorities, covering banking, securities and insurance, have been established in some six OECD members including the UK and three Scandinavian countries. Their experience could be helpful to the Baltics as they seek to develop their regulatory capabilities.

The regulator can be established as a government agency, an independent statutory authority or an agency founded under a central bank. The choice in practice reflects the general legislative and political contexts of each particular country and seems to be less important than the issue of how to ensure that the regulatory authority is held accountable, but remains independent and has sufficient powers to carry out its duties effectively. The objectives, roles and responsibilities of the authority are usually clearly defined by law in order to separate the body from direct government control. The authority is then typically held to account by board members appointed by the government, by the requirement to report its activities, and by the obligation to conduct regular meetings with the relevant ministry (usually the Ministry of Finance). There seems to be emerging consensus that financial supervision should be separated from the central bank which is responsible for conducting monetary policy. This is to avoid conflicts of interest which may lead a central bank to loosen monetary policy to protect the financial position of banks; or loss of public confidence in the central bank where there is a case of perceived supervisory failure.

Although it can act independently from the government an integrated financial supervisor is required to follow government policy and/or to report to the government. In many cases, the budget of supervisory authority is subject to the approval of the government, even if this budget is industry-funded. Financial supervision is fundamentally a part of the administrative power of the government. Government rightly has to hold the supervisory authority to account, but this should be at arms' length. For example, by submission of an annual report and/or responding to *ad hoc* inquiries from members of parliament. In Finland, the Financial Supervision Authority co-operates with the central bank rather than the government, which may be justified by the fact that, in this country, the central bank is a constitutional institution independent from the government.

Some continue to argue in favour of central bank supervision of the financial sector on the grounds that monetary and financial stability are inter-related, and that the central bank cannot adequately guarantee the former without the latter. This reinforced by the central bank's role as a lender of the last resort. Mixed solutions are possible, though rare. Finland has an independent financial supervisory authority that is accountable to the central bank rather than the government: the supervisory board of the bank appoints the board of the authority.

---

* From *Financial Market Trends*, OECD, No. 68 (November 1997), No. 71 (November 1998) and other editions.

bank in Latvia. Since that time they have also been active in international markets in raising equity and in widening their choice of funding facilities. A strengthened capital base enabled banks to expand their lending activities and to meet high growth in credit demand. The share of credit in banks' total assets increased steadily and has reached a higher level than in either of the other Baltic countries.[56] Banks also established leasing subsidiaries and became increasingly active in securities market.[57]

Although international integration was slower in Latvia and Lithuania, they also experienced financial deepening as the financial sector recovered its profitability following the banking crisis.

In Latvia, banks' assets doubled between 1995 and 1998 and the aggregate loan portfolio increased threefold during the same period on the back of declining lending rates and increasing competition in the domestic market.[58] The sector also became increasingly internationalised: majority foreign owned banks accounted for more than 70 per cent of the total assets of the banking system by end 1997, and about two-thirds of assets and liabilities were foreign currency denominated. But it should be noted that the high degree of foreign involvement both in terms of equity participation and funding was to a large extent based on non-institutional investors, in particular before 1998. However, the degree of foreign participation resulted in part from tax incentives which encouraged Latvians to make domestic investments through offshore companies, and use of the Latvian banking sector by many Russian and CIS companies as a perceived safe financial channel for their core activities. Likewise many of Latvian banks had developed wide information and business networks in Russia and were exploiting the interest rate differential between the domestic and Russian markets. This was encouraged by declining margins in the domestic market, but also by standard regulatory incentives.[59] There remains a question mark over the quality of the outstanding loan portfolio, which can only be answered after the next downturn in Latvia's economic cycle.

The development of non-bank financial intermediaries and increasing integration of different segments of the financial market were also evident in Latvia. Banks became increasingly involved in the leasing industry[60] and performed strongly in the local stock market.

The Lithuanian banking sector also benefited from the banking crisis. The volume of bank's assets continued to grow and banks returned to profitability in 1998. Banks' capitalisation improved and average capital adequacy calculated according to EU and BIS standards rose to almost 24 per cent by the end of 1998 from 10.8 per cent in 1997, but the maturity structure of deposits remains short term. Unlike Estonia and Latvia the sector remains influenced by two state-owned banks with a market share of about 44 per cent (see Tables A32 and A36 in the Statistical Annex). Though this share is falling and both banks are now expected to be privatisated. Banking assets grew by around 28 per cent, and domestic credit by some 37 per cent, in 1997, though foreign currency lending considerably outpaced domestic currency loan growth over 1997-98, and exceeded half of all lending in 1998. Despite these developments the level of credit to the private sector remained low, about 12 per cent of GDP, and lagged well behind of that in Estonia and Latvia though it has started to grow quite quickly: during the first-half of 1999, loans grew by 15 per cent. Ownership of private banks has become more international but, again unlike its Baltic neighbours, this initially took the form predominantly of portfolio investments rather than strategic partnership.[61] By mid-1999 two foreign banks had established branch offices, and five banks had majority foreign ownership. In order to diversify the funding structure Lithuanian banks started to borrow from international capital markets more aggressively in the second half of 1997, benefiting from positive investor sentiment and declining margins for emerging market borrowers.[62] The level of external borrowing remained however relatively modest amounting to 6 per cent of total liabilities as of end 1997 though banks became net external borrowers in 1998.

There were modest developments in non-bank financial intermediation. Leasing companies, generally banks' subsidiaries, recorded strong growth and stock market capitalisation increased to 18 per cent of GDP in 1997. Foreign investors controlled about one fifth of brokers operating in the stock exchange, but turnover and liquidity in the market remained low.

Testing the new financial structures: the Asian and Russian crises

The effects of the Asian crisis were especially felt in Estonia...

Developments exposed the industry to new risks and, in particular, increased its dependence on investor sentiment prevailing on global markets. Challenges associated with unrestricted capital movements were clearly revealed at the onset of financial markets turmoil in South East Asia in October 1997 when the consistency of economic policy was tested in many emerging markets. Among the Baltic countries Estonia was the most affected by financial contagion, experiencing considerable pressure on its exchange rate,[63] and recorded a significant adjustment in asset price, which led eventually to a number of banking sector mergers. In contrast, Latvian and Lithuanian financial markets were more indirectly affected by the crisis.

The immediate impact in Estonia was on short term interest rates in the money market: three-month rates doubled, reaching 15-16 per cent. Longer maturities remained largely unaffected due to somewhat segmented money and credit markets, and so the main impact was felt by financial institutions and individuals who faced significantly higher interest rates (under the currency board) and smaller loan volumes; the industrial sector was the least affected. Interest rates had subsided by April 1998. There was little pressure on the Latvian lat, reflecting Latvia's better current account position, and credit growth remained strong. As a result, interest rates in Latvia also remained significantly lower than in Estonia.[64] Turbulence in the Tallinn stock market did however have a knock-on effect in Riga (Figure 31). Overall, the three Baltic stock markets appear to be quite closely synchronised and have been significantly influenced by developments in Russia.

There was also a differential impact on financial sector institutions. Whilst the Estonian banking industry stagnated, Latvian and Lithuanian banks continued to grow in the first half of 1998 showing the limited impact of contagion in those

Figure 31. **Russian and Baltic States stock market indices**

Dollar value, normalised data

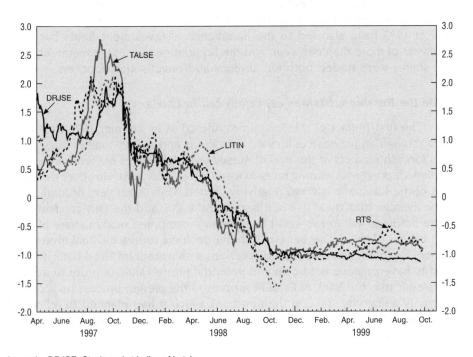

Legend: DRJSE: Stock market indice of Latvia.
          LITIN: Stock market indice of Lithuania.
          RTS: Stock market indice of Russia.
          TALSE: Stock market indice of Estonia.
Source: National Stock Exchanges.

countries. In Latvia total banks assets and credit grew by 11 per cent and almost 35 per cent respectively during the first half of 1998. The same trend was evident in Lithuania, though at a lower pace. During the first half of 1998 total assets and credit to private sector grew by 9.7 per cent and 7 per cent correspondingly. This also fed through to banking profitability.[65] After the two years of negative earnings Lithuanian banks' return on equity became positive in the first quarter of 1998. Likewise banking profitability improved in Latvian, although this was partly due to strong revenues from high-yielding Russian securities. Despite poor results, a strong capital base allowed the Estonian banking system to absorb poor earnings and a certain deterioration in asset quality without calling into question the ability of the system to withstand further shocks. The Estonian authorities also moved quickly to put in place measures to discourage excessive foreign borrowing and increased liquidity requirements on banks in light of the short term structure of maturities.

Securities markets fell sharply in the wake of the Asian shock. The Tallinn exchange lost nearly three-quarters of its value from its peak in August 1997. Since then the stock market has largely lost its importance as a financial intermediary, and was little affected by the rouble crisis (see below). In Estonia the events of 1997 have also led to the emergence of investment funds based on instruments of more than one year, and the liquidation of those investment funds whose shares were traded both for currency and privatisation vouchers.

... while the Russian crisis was especially felt in Latvia

The first impact of the Russian rouble crisis in summer 1998 was felt in Estonia through an increase in forward quotations and money market rates. Turnover in forward markets at the end of August was eight times higher than normal; inter-bank deposit and lending rates to rose to 16-17 per cent. However the direct impact of the Russian crisis was relatively limited. Only 2 per cent of total assets were on average directly at risk in Russia and the CIS, and the only concentration of these holdings was in two small banks with a combined market share of 7 per cent.[66] In one of these the Bank of Estonia decided to initiate bankruptcy proceedings. The other was in merger discussions with a medium sized bank and was judged to have positive net worth and potential future value. In order to ward off any systemic risk, the Bank of Estonia supported the merger process by acquiring temporarily a majority stake in the new bank which it had planned to relinquish by the end of 1999. Estonian banks have also benefited from increasing levels of domestic deposits.

Russian exposure in Latvian banking sector was more than 10 per cent of total assets in August 1998. Latvian banks had built up sizeable positions in Russian sovereign and corporate debt instruments as domestic yields had shrunk. Falling yields reflected an improvement in the Latvian fiscal position and increased competition for domestic lending. In contrast, in the first half of 1998 Russian securities yielded more than 30 per cent per annum: some six times more than was available to investors in Latvian T-bills.[67] Excess capacity generated by an over-banked market created additional incentives to engage in high-risk activities, not mitigated (as discussed in Chapter II) by watchful supervision. Hence, devaluation of rouble and Russia's default on government bonds (GKO's) considerably strained the liquidity of the Latvian banking sector. As inter-bank credit limits were reduced and banks' willingness to lend was minimal, there were runs on some banks whose exposure to Russia became known. The Bank of Latvia had to inject additional liquidity to the market. The Bank of Latvia's credit to banks increased from LVL 7.6 million at the end of 1997 to LVL 52 million by the end of 1998, with the majority of this lending taking place during the fourth quarter.[68] Some banks were unduly exposed to the Russian market. Three smaller banks were closed, and a moratorium was announcement on the fifth largest bank: Riga Komercbanka. Latvian banks posted consolidated losses of LVL 53 million for 1998 and average capital adequacy dropped to around 17 per cent, some 3.5 percentage points lower than in 1997.[69]

The Lithuanian financial sector seems to have been little affected by the Russian crisis directly. Banks held only 1.4 per cent of their total assets in Russia at the start of the crisis. This had fallen to 1.1 per cent by a year later. This situation reflects that from 1997-98 all assets related to Russia and the CIS carried a 100 per cent risk-weighting in calculating capital-adequacy ratios. But as in the other countries there has been an indirect impact. Enterprises have found it difficult to replace their Russian trade, turnover has stagnated and this has complicated loan servicing.

Further bank consolidation and financial deepening is needed

The Estonian experience could provide an insight into what developments can be expected in Baltic banking and financial sectors. The turbulent external economic environment and toughening competition in Estonia and its neighbouring countries brought about consolidation in the banking sector during 1998. The monetary environment combined with external shocks revealed hidden management weaknesses, problems with corporate governance and excessive risk-taking that resulted in number of exits from the market as well as in mergers and acquisitions. A highlight of the period was the purchase of significant stakes in banks and insurance companies by Swedish banks and other Nordic investors. This particularly affected Estonia: new capital injections came from two Swedish banks, Swedbank and S-E-Banken (SEB), which acquired a 49.98 per cent stake in Hansapank and a 30 per cent stake in Ühispank, respectively. As of end-1998, non-residents owned a 60.7 per cent stake in Estonian banks, up from 14.7 per cent in 1994 and 44.2 per cent in 1997. However this concentration, replicated to a lesser extent in Latvia and Lithuania, brings with it the danger of banking sector consolidation undermining medium run financial health by eliminating competition. There is a similar risk where the government, as currently in Lithuania, continues to own a significant share of the sector. In November 1999 the State owned about 39 per cent of the Lithuanian banking sector. The equivalent figures in Estonia and Latvia were five per cent and two per cent. Plans by the Lithuanian authorities to privatise two major banks (the Savings and Agricultural banks) will not by itself address the dangers of concentration.

Ultimately, about 85 per cent of the Estonian banking, 90 per cent of the leasing and 30 per cent of the insurance market became concentrated into two major financial groups – Hansapank and Eesti Ühispank (Table 13). This has considerably strengthened the Estonian banking system and created preconditions for its further progress. There has also been a shift from investment banking

Table 13. **Top regional banks, ranked by assets end-1998**

	EEK million	US$ million
Estonia		
Hansapank	21 285	1 595
Eesti Uhispank	13 530	1 014
Optiva pank	3 174	238
Eesti Krediidipank	508	38
Tallinn Aripanga AS	261	20
Top five banks' assets (per cent total bank assets)	95	

	LVL million	US$ million
Latvia		
Latvia Unibanka	307	541
Parex Bank	301	531
Hansabanka	145	255
Rigas Komercbanka	115	203
Rietumu Banka	110	193
Top five banks' assets (per cent total bank assets)	91	

	LTL million	US$ million
Lithuania		
Lietuvos Taupomasis Bankas AB	3 212	803
Vilniaus Bankas AB	2 757	689
Bankas Hermis	1 551	388
AB Lietuvos Zemis Ukio Bankas	1 466	367
Bankas Snoras	501	125
Top five banks' assets (per cent total bank assets)	55	

Source: National authorities and Central European Economic Review.

to conventional banking, reflecting a more cautious approach in corporate govern-ance of banks.[70] The overall decline of the stock market and the need to protect portfolios from further losses were behind the decline in securities portfolio by EEK 2.2 billion (25 per cent), which constituted 15.5 per cent of total assets by year-end compared to 21 per cent a year previously. During last months of 1998, banks increased their investments into high-quality EEK-denominated instru-ments, issued by foreign financial institutions as an alternative to keeping the money with the central bank or non-resident credit institutions. In 1999, however, the banks have started to place funds abroad as a response to decreased domes-tic interest rates and continuously conservative credit policies. More stringent credit policies have also contributed to falling loan growth rates and the legacy of the Russian crisis can be seen in more overdue loans: the proportion of overdue loans has increased from 5 per cent to 10 per cent of total loan portfolio by mid-1999 (Table 12 above).

In the first quarter of 1999, Estonian banks became profitable after three consecutive quarters of negative results. The main underlying reason for the change is declining total costs. Strong capitalisation, improved maturity structure of term liabilities and increased efficiency as a result of the consolidation process, are a good basis for positive results provided there is no further stagnation in the domestic real economy, or external shocks. There has been a constant growth in loans with maturities from two to ten years, mainly at the expense of loans with maturities up to three months.

V. Enterprise reform and economic restructuring

A comparison of the privatisation process in the Baltics

In recent years, all the Baltic countries have achieved substantial progress in terms of privatisation, with Estonia being clearly the most advanced country, followed by Latvia. Compared with its neighbours Lithuania is still lagging somewhat behind. As discussed below, the success of privatisation in Estonia was based in strong political support from the beginning and seems to be attributable mainly to two factors. Firstly, the bankruptcy legislation was quite tough and effectively implemented (see Chapter IV). This accelerated the privatisation process since companies had to choose between either privatisation or liquidation. Secondly, the prospects of liquidation proved a strong incentive to find a strategic partner, matched by willingness to welcome foreign capital. The privatisation process in Latvia resembles that of Estonia, albeit at a slower pace. A case by case approach was also used – rather than mass privatisation – with emphasis on seeking strategic partners and selling controlling interests in enterprises. The privatisation process in Lithuania has differed from that in the other two countries. Notably, greater use was made of voucher schemes and, until 1997, there were practically no privatisations to foreign investors. There was also a greater effort to restructure state enterprises before privatisation rather than making more direct use of bankruptcy procedures; with the establishment of the State Property Fund in May 1998, privatisation now appears to be on a somewhat clearer and faster track.

The early steps favoured insiders

The process of privatisation began before independence in all three Baltic countries (see Table 14a). The first private enterprises were established during a period of liberalisation that followed Gorbatchev's policy of *perestroika*. They included small individual enterprises, co-operatives, and joint ventures. The nature of the political changes taking place during this period make it difficult to define strictly the boundary between early spontaneous privatisation and

Table 14a. **An overview of the privatisation process, 1989-98**

	Estonia	Latvia	Lithuania
Early stages of privatisation	– Small SOEs[1] and new co-operatives, mostly owned by management. – Before independence (12), employee-owned. – After independence (200), management owned.	– New co-operatives mostly owned by management. – Before independence leasing to employees.	– New co-operatives mostly owned by management. – 1990-91: Before independence leasing (60) employee-owned. – Employee-shares, 2-3% of assets.
Small enterprises	– Legislation (December 1990): insider advantages, 80% of 450 employee-owned. – Advantages were limited May 1992, and cut away June 1993. – Most privatised by end of 1992.	– November 1991 legislation partly by local municipalities. – Below 10 employees. – Auction bidders > 16 years of residency. – Trade, catering, service. – 1994: 85% privatised mainly by management, some to employees.	– LIPSP vouchers (see text) and cash quotas can be used in auctions. – Conditions: employment cannot be reduced more than 30% and same activity 3 years. – Sold 57% (1992), 70% (1992), 76% (1993), 100% (1995). – No advantages for employees.
Large enterprises	– 1989: peoples enterprises (7). – 1991: SOE[1] experiments (7). – Mostly employee owned. – 1992: EPA Treuhandmodel. – Advantage: outsiders, foreign tenders based on price and investment, and job-guarantees. – 1994: peak of privatisation, mostly privatised 1995 and nearly all by end of 1998. – Autumn 1994: Public offering of minority shares for vouchers, and by end-1997: 39 holdings for 2.3 billion kroons (most vouchers for housing). – End 1998: 483 enterprises for 4.7 billion EEK (400 million US$). 4.6 billion EEK investment Guarantees; 56 000 job guarantees; few utilities remaining.	– 1991: 6 SOEs[1] sold to insiders. – 1992-94: decentralised privatisation by sector ministries, ca. 50 firms privatised, 78 corporatised. 234 leased, mainly to insiders. – May 1994: centralised at LPA. – August 1994: Voucher market. – January 1996: 2.9 billion LVL vouchers distributed to 2.4 million people (97% of the population). – 1997: Peak of privatisation, and nearly all by end 1998. – 1995-98: 82 public offerings 1 billion LVL vouchers (most vouchers for housing). – End-1998: 1 009 tender privatisations for 190 million LVL (350 million US$). 244 million LVL debt taken over, 127 million LVL investment guarantee, 47 735 job guarantees, few remaining utilities and large enterprises.	– September 1991: LIPSP privatisation. – Sale of shares through Vouchers and cash quotas. – December 1991: Investment Funds – Increase in the share purchasing of employees at preferential terms i.e. 1991: 10%, 1992: 30%, 1993: 50%. – Sold 38% (1992), 62% (1993), 75% (1994), 99% (1995) of LIPSP's 2 928 enterprises, tenders of min. shares utilities, 48 SOEs were sold in "hard currency". – 1992: Peak of privatisation. most medium and large firms privatised by end of 1994 remaining shares had a very long and slow process. – 1996: Lit. Privatisation Agency formed. privatisation for cash funding ministries and municipalities slowed down the process. – 1998: Centralisation of process in State Property Fund (SPF), faster remaining privatisations including some of larger firms. – End 1998: remaining utilities and large enterprises, and remaining residual shares following LIPSP.

1. SOE: State-owned entrerprises
Source: Mygind (1999) and OECD.

subsequent more regulated developments. For instance, Estonia dabbled in early "small privatisation" from 1987, and in 1989 an economic reform programme included a proposal for "people's enterprises". The political situation in Latvia was different to that in Estonia and so privatisation was slower in starting, while Lithuania began transferring shares in some enterprises to their employees in October 1990. By the time of independence in 1991 all the Baltics had already introduced elements of their own economic legislation.

Privatisation had its root in Soviet legislation on co-operatives and leasing. In Estonia, co-operatives employed more than 10 per cent of the workforce, and new co-operatives were emerging particularly quickly in construction, trade and information technology.[71] This gave insiders the opportunity to take over enterprises, but also supported start-ups. The new co-operatives often used Soviet leasing legislation to appropriate assets from state owned enterprises.[72] The first Latvian law on co-operatives was approved in August 1991 (and implemented in October), though the legislation on privatisation was rather unclear in the early stages. The new co-operatives were not as widespread in Lithuania as in the other Baltic Countries, though in 1990 they still made up around 4 500 enterprises with some 5 per cent of the total workforce.[73]

The 1987 Soviet law on state enterprises had also given the general meeting of employees some rights concerning future production plans and the right to elect the enterprise's director. Latvia was the first Soviet republic to implement employees' right to elect the director of their enterprise.[74] But this early move may have had unintended consequences: in six privatisations completed in 1991, ownership was transferred to insiders. Government fairly soon realised that the use of Soviet legislation was dissipating state assets at rather less than fair value. As a result they introduced legislation to stem the flow. All Latvian co-operatives had to restructure and re-register before March 1992, and the activities open to co-operatives were restricted, forcing the dissolution of many. Latvians could continue to lease state companies, but the legal status of this remained unclear until February 1993 when new legislation made it possible for concerned groups of employees to make a new leasing contract.[75] Estonia ruled out the leasing option in 1993, and majority ownership of most leased enterprises passed to the former leaseholder. Prior to this, in July 1991, Soviet legislation had been relaxed to allow leasing by the management and outsiders as well as employees. About 200 enterprises were registered under the new rules, and it seems that the state bureaucracy favoured management take-overs.[76]

Early legislation favoured employees in all three countries. In Estonia "small state enterprises" (often established and controlled by a large state-owned enterprises) acquired a high degree of operational autonomy and proved popular.[77] There was a tendency to spin these off into a private firm controlled by the management of the original holding enterprise. Many of the successful Estonian entrepreneurs first established their businesses as "small state enterprises".[78] Leasing legislation also had built-in preferences for employees.[79] In Latvia a 1990 law allowed companies to issue shares worth up to 10 per cent of the authorised capital to employees at a discount, or free of charge. These shares carried full voting rights, but value had to be paid in full on the employee's departure from the company.[80] But, as in Estonia, most of the advantages initially enjoyed by insiders were removed in 1992. Some sixty, previously leased, Lithuanian firms transferred shares to their employees in October 1990. This was intended to compensate in part for delayed wage payments. Enterprises with capital exceeding a threshold could also sell up to 10 per cent of their capital to their employees, part of which could be paid by vouchers. Somewhat more than half of all state enterprises took advantage of this programme up to July 1991, when another programme was approved.[81] Take-overs by foreign companies were permitted under leasing legislation, but not widespread. Estonians were the most active in the former Soviet Union in creating joint ventures. The first joint ventures had already been established in Estonia in 1987. There were 11 joint ventures in 1988 and 320 by the end of 1992.[82]

The use of vouchers and "small" privatisation strengthened the position of insiders

The three Baltic countries all issued vouchers to be used in the privatisation of state assets. Their motives for using vouchers were a combination of the need to act quickly[83] and the notion that this method of privatisation was in some sense 'fairer' than the alternatives. In Lithuania's case voucher privatisation was also an element in the campaign for independence: the Law on the Initial Privatisation of State-owned Property (LIPSP) was passed in February 1991. The scheme was designed to achieve greater economic self-management, and included privatisation of enterprises formally owned and controlled by the central authorities in Moscow.

Lithuania, inspired by the Czech voucher privatisation, was the first Baltic country to implement its voucher scheme: vouchers were distributed in April 1991, the first enterprises were sold in September 1991. Latvia passed a law on vouchers in November 1992 after a long political debate, but did not distribute vouchers until September 1993 and the scheme was not really operational until the summer of 1994. Latvia adopted the most restrictive approach to issuing vouchers. Distribution was based on residency, favouring those resident prior to World War II; later immigrants received fewer vouchers, and people connected with the Soviet Army or KGB none at all.[84] As a result 87 per cent of vouchers were issued to Latvian citizens.[85] Lithuania made its distribution based on age,[86] but assignments were made only to residents in order to prevent substantial inward flows of roubles (and hence an ebbing of domestic control) from the rest of the former Soviet Union. Estonia issued two separate vouchers,[87] subsequently used in parallel in the privatisation of both property and enterprises. Capital vouchers were distributed to all residents during 1992-96 in proportion to the number of years worked. Compensation vouchers were distributed after 1994 to owners (or their descendants) of property nationalised in the early Soviet period if they either did not want the property, or if it was not possible to return it to them.[88]

Having issued the vouchers, the countries took different views on their use and tradability which, in the end, had a considerable impact on the ownership structure. Estonia made vouchers freely tradeable in 1994, since when the market price has remained lower than face value, although rising modestly in later years. This led to a considerable concentration of vouchers, and hence ownership structure. Latvia also authorised direct trading of vouchers in 1994, but subject to a special transaction tax of 2 per cent and a fee payable to the bank administering the "special privatisation account".[89] As in Estonia the market price of vouchers has remained much below the face value,[90] exacerbated by the absence of legislation approving the use of vouchers in the privatisation of property until 1995, and enduring uncertainty over enterprise privatisation. Lithuania took a different approach. Before 1993, vouchers could not be traded directly but could be used to acquire a shareholding in an investment fund, which could be traded.[91]

As in other transition countries, investment funds were introduced, although with somewhat different developments. The role of investment funds is a further factor differentiating the Baltic countries' experience of voucher privatisation. Lithuanian investment funds were approved in December 1991 after some funds had spontaneously been established during the autumn. They became very popular and were most active during 1992-93.[92] Shares in investment fund shares could be sold for cash, and in March 1994 about one-third of privatised capital was owned by Investment Funds.[93] Legislation in July 1995 strengthened regulations on auditing and reserves, and required investment funds to apply for a license either as a mutual fund or as a holding company.[94] Many investment funds were dissolved after regulation was strengthened, but by the end of 1998 there were still 22 "investment companies" in existence. Estonia's experience with investment funds was essentially terminated in March 1995 when the biggest investment fund crashed resulting in losses exceeding those incurred during the Estonian banking crisis in 1992-93.[95] By June 1996 there were only six privatisation investment funds, and their holding of vouchers amounted to only 1 per cent of the total.[96] By October 1999, five of them had been wound up and the remaining one functions as an ordinary closed-end corporate investment fund.

While people in Estonia used vouchers mainly in the privatisation of housing, the authorities also intervened with policy aimed at attracting foreign investors. The authorities also removed some EEK 2.3 billion worth of vouchers from circulation between 1994 and 1997 by offering minority holdings in some 39 large and medium sized companies, previously privatised to a "core owner", via public offerings in which only vouchers could be used.[97] In addition, from spring 1994 the compulsory initial payment in purchasing an enterprise was increased from 20 per cent to 50 per cent of the price, but up to 50 per cent of the purchase price could be paid in vouchers. Foreigners bought vouchers and used them in privatisation. According to the Estonian Privatisation Agency, by 1995, on average 33 per cent of the price paid by foreigners was met by vouchers, and vouchers had been used in three out of the five enterprises taken over by foreign capital. Most privatisations exploited the option to meet half the down-payment using vouchers. The average figure for vouchers used in privatisation is considerably lower because some of the largest privatisations, especially to foreigners were for cash.

Lithuanian vouchers could be used to acquire all state assets: at auctions of small enterprises, in share subscriptions to large enterprises and in the privatisation of housing and land. Assets were sold for a combination of cash and vouchers, with a ceiling on the proportion that could be paid in cash, though this ceiling was typically relaxed where existing tenants were bidding to buy their apartment, or where enterprises had failed to sell at auction. Under the LIPSP employees could also use vouchers to buy shares in their enterprise at concessional rates.[98] Moreover, because of only partial indexation of the price of the assets and the value of the vouchers, the real advantage enjoyed by employees increased over time.[99] This made it possible for employees to gain significant ownership even in highly capital-intensive enterprises. Whilst the 20 per cent extra shares reserved for employees after 1993 initially came without voting rights, it was later possible for the company in general meeting to convert these shares into normal voting shares.

All countries built-up significant contingent liability in outstanding vouchers. To alleviate this pressure Estonia focused on the tradability of vouchers and opening the door to FDI. In contrast, by February 1994 about 30 per cent of the vouchers in Lithuania were still not used. The government took action to move the date at which outstanding vouchers would be automatically converted to sovereign bonds (originally July 1995); at the revised deadline some 7 per cent of vouchers were still outstanding.[100] The validity of these vouchers subsequently expired. Latvia used a similar approach to Estonia and redeemed nearly LVL 1 billion nominal value in vouchers by the end of 1998 through public offerings.

Both Latvia and Estonia explicitly favoured insiders (i.e. employees, including enterprise management) during the privatisation of "small" enterprises, especially during the early years, although this policy did not rely on the use of vouchers. By contrast, while de jure there were fewer formal advantages to Lithuanian employees in small privatisation, as small enterprises were generally sold at public auction,[101] insiders did retain considerable power. Sales were subject to special conditions designed to secure continuation of existing activity for at least three years, and redundancies were restricted to a maximum of 30 per cent of the workforce over the same period. Employees also took advantage of inside information on the true value of the assets for sale, and used their vouchers to buy shares. At this stage privatisation in Lithuania was also faster than in the other two countries, and faster indeed than throughout the former CMEA countries: by end-1992, 56 per cent of all assets had been privatised. But speed of privatisation especially in the case of large enterprises entailed much greater reliance on voucher privatisation and employee-ownership; direct sale and foreign investment had a negligible role at this stage. Privatisation policy was also caught up in the struggle for independence. Once this had been achieved a comparatively homogeneous and less divided workforce was able to win a bigger role in privatisation decisions.

Privatisation of small enterprises in Estonia began in March 1991, supervised by the Department of State Property (a unit within the Ministry of Economy) in co-operation with local municipalities. Legislation in 1991 had given priority to restitution and voucher privatisation, but implementation was postponed. Thus privatisation in the early years of transition concerned mainly small firms. About 80 per cent of the first wave of 450 small enterprises were taken over by insiders,[102] who had the right to buy enterprise assets at an "initial price" that was in most cases reckoned to be far below market value.

A break in privatisation policies: reducing insiders' advantages

As already noted, the political climate in Estonia turned against employee ownership in May 1992. The relevant legislation was amended to remove the formal advantages enjoyed by insiders, and to widen the circle of potential participants in privatisation to include foreigners. Insiders retained the right to match the highest bid prior to its acceptance, but even this right was removed in June 1993 when control of all privatisation was taken over by the Estonian Privatisation Agency (EPA). Small privatisation then proceeded mainly by auction, in contrast to the direct sale method favoured for large enterprises.[103] In 1991 more than 90 per cent of the enterprises in the service and trade sector had belonged to the state or municipalities; by 1994 83 per cent of activity in the service sector, 90 per cent of wholesale and 94 per cent of retail sales was in private hands.[104]

These steps were followed by Latvia, though in slower time, while the *status quo* was maintained in Lithuania. Latvia devolved a considerable amount of the responsibility for small privatisation. The privatisation method and initial price were decided by local privatisation commissions, on which sat representatives from the state, municipality, trade unions and specialists. Small privatisation started in earnest from November 1991 through either sale to employees, auction to an invited group of potential buyers, open auctions or sale to a selected buyer. Foreigners were excluded,[105] and some of these options opened the door to substantial abuse:[106] high price differences were recorded between auctions and direct sales. Direct sales either to employees or a 'selected buyer' were by far the most frequently used methods;[107] and of these more than half were sold by instalments. In any case, employees who had worked a minimum of five years in an enterprise had a pre-emptive right to buy at the initial price. This right was removed early in 1992, and the rules were changed to allow foreigners to partici- pate in privatisation. But, in practice, advantages for insiders persisted as local privatisation commissions simply continued to give preferences to insiders.[108] Small privatisation in all three Baltic States was essentially complete by the end of 1994.

Privatising large enterprises

Although the Baltic countries started privatisation of large enterprises in different ways, they eventually all adopted the German "Treuhandanstalt" (Treuhand) model. This method of privatisation usually sought to sell enterprises by international tender to a core investor (see Table 14b). Price was not the only criterion. Potential buyers had to submit business plans setting out their strategy, proposed investment and expected employment. The privatisation agency had wide powers to restructure and/or break up existing state-owned enterprises to facilitate a sale. Existing employees and managers were not given preferential treatment, but were equally able to submit bids.

Estonia adopted this model very early: the Estonian Privatisation Agency (EPA) was established in 1992 and a privatisation law of June 1993 strengthened its authority. The Latvian Privatisation Agency (LPA) was set up in spring 1994, and privatisation of large enterprises took hold a year later. A Lithuanian Privatisation Agency had been created in 1995, as a successor to the Law on the Initial Privatisation of State Property (LIPSP), though was in practice little different. Considerable authority continued to rest with local government and central line ministries and privatisation ground to a halt. It was not until November 1997 that a new law on privatisation established the Lithuanian State Property Fund (SPF). It has similar functions and authority to the EPA and LPA though the ministry of European affairs retained responsibility for implementing some of the largest privatisations oriented towards international investors.

The Treuhand model delivered rapid privatisation, though larger enter- prises tended to be sold later in the process. These were typically large energy- intensive enterprises in heavy industry, often with close relations to the former Soviet Union. Most Estonian privatisation deals were carried out in 1994, and by the end of 1995 most large enterprises had been privatised; the private sector share of industrial sales had increased in two years from 34 per cent to 65 per

Table 14b. **Different types of privatisation of large enterprises, end-1998**

	Leasing, mainly to insiders	Buy-outs, mainly by insiders	Tender to core-investor	of which: minority public offer	Restitution liquidated/other	Remaining under state-ownership	Total
Estonia							
Number of firms	100¹	7	483	39 (for 1997)	40¹	10	640
Per cent of total	16	1	76		6	2	100
Latvia							
Number of firms	237	6	1 009	82	–	100¹	1 352
Per cent of total	18	–	75		–	7	100
Lithuania							
Number of firms	60	2 940	100¹	300	–	200	3 300
Per cent of total	2	89	3		–	6	100

1. Estimate.
Source: Mygind (1999).

cent.[109] Owing to the role of the EPA, 84 per cent of industrial sales were in the private sector by mid-1999, only a few, though quite large, enterprises remained state-owned.[110]

The ability of managers and employees to submit successful bids depended crucially on their ability to raise finance. Hence the speed with which the banking sector developed determined the extent to which insiders gained control of large enterprises. This also influenced whether insider privatisations were to a broad coalition of managers and employees, or whether there was scope for managers to buy out the company on their own. Better access to capital tended to give foreigners an advantage, which only increased as they became entitled to use vouchers to meet the purchase price or pay by instalment.[111] Only in rare cases did broad groups of Estonian employees manage to take over their enterprises.

In Latvia, the main privatisation authority in Latvia had been the Department of State Property Conversion (a division within the Ministry of Economy) until 1994, but responsibility for privatising large enterprises rested with individual line ministries. Progress was comparatively slow as ministries sought to retain control over their sector of the economy: of 712 enterprises listed for privatisation[112] only 312 were privatised during 1992-94, mostly through lease by-outs to insiders. Only about 50 companies ended-up in the hands of outsiders. A further 78 had been legally transformed into companies in preparation for privatisation before the LPA took over. Few enterprises were liquidated. Insiders, especially managers, had been rather more active in exploiting the advantages of lease by-out agreements. Over the same period nearly one-third of firms on the list had been "privatised" in this way.[113] Most of these have subsequently been sold to the leaseholder at prices equivalent to that in tender privatisation.[114] Take-overs by insiders practically ceased after 1994, though employees retained some pre-emption rights where companies made initial public offerings.[115]

In Lithuania the LIPSP programme started in September 1991 had conferred considerable advantages to insiders, and particularly broad groups of employees. This flowed from the wide use of voucher privatisation and only rather limited amount of restitution. Data from the Privatisation Department in the Ministry of the Economy clearly shows how the LIPSP boosted insider ownership. Soon after the start of privatisation, at the end of 1992, 67 per cent of enterprises had no employee ownership.[116] By 1994 more than 95 per cent of the privatised firms in the LIPSP programme had some employee ownership. The percentage of enterprises where employees took the majority of assets increased from 3 per cent in 1992, to 65 per cent in 1993 and to 92 per cent in 1995. Although the central privatisation commission approved the overall plans and local commissions the details, most sales were conducted by local privatisation offices.[117] Unlike in other Baltics, insiders had a greater advantage in privatisation of large enterprises than in "small" privatisation. Lithuania had intended that privatisation following the end of the LIPSP programme[118] should be for "cash". But progress was slow until 1997, when the new Lithuanian government announced the privatisation of 14 major state enterprises in communication, energy, airlines and shipbuilding with a total capital of LTL 2.3 billion[119] and about 10 800 employees.[120] By 1999, the government had approved an additional list which leaves over 2 800 entities with state capital to be privatised, but the state only held a controlling interest in about 240 of these enterprises. Of the total, more than 1220 represent interests in property.

The Treuhand model has not precluded development of local stock markets. For instance, the LPA has sold minority stakes (on average 25 per cent) in the largest 82 companies after selling a controlling stake to a core investor. The price is generally set by auction, though in some cases a "people's round" fixes an initial price[121] to reduce uncertainty and hence attract a broader group of investors. This method was used in an offering of 6 million shares in Ventpils Nafta at the end of 1997.[122] Offerings for cash have been less widespread in the Baltic markets as capital availability has fallen in the wake of the Asian financial crisis.[123]

There is no systematic way to assess the role of investment and employment guarantees in the privatisation of large enterprises. In Estonia, foreigners seem to have provided high investment guarantees compared to domestic purchasers. But foreigners made few commitments to guarantee employment, and generally assumed lower levels of debt. Latvian purchase agreements involved different combinations of payment in the form of cash, vouchers, instalments and assumption of debt, as well as guarantees on a certain volume of investment and level of employment. Purchases were financed using mainly vouchers[124] (worth only around 10 per cent of their face value); but the buyers had to assume a relatively high volume of debt: some LVL 244 million in total (or around USD 400 million). Investment guarantees amounted to LVL 127 million (around USD 211 million) up to 1998. Employment guarantees were provided for a total of some 48 000 jobs (on average, about 50 jobs per firm).

The critical role of foreign direct investment

Capital inflows from abroad have been important to all the Baltic States given the size of their current account deficits (see Chapter I). But foreign investment has also been particularly important in the privatisation process in Estonia and less so, but increasingly, in Latvia. Lithuania had the lowest level of cumulative foreign investments per capita in the Baltics (see Table 15). Foreign investment also tended to be in joint ventures (70 per cent of cases compared with 30 per cent wholly owned). During the early programme, in parallel with the LIPSP, of those enterprises sold for cash only 4 out of 48 were taken over by foreigners. Subsequently, foreign involvement has become more frequent.

Table 15. **Role of foreign investors in large privatisation, 1998**

Millions of local currency

	Estonia	(In % of total FDI)	Latvia	(In % of total FDI)	Lithuania	(In % of total FDI)
FDI stock, end 1998[1]	20 623	100	886	100	6 501	100
Privatised firm purchases	1 439	7	111	13	2 250	35
As share of total privatisation revenue	31					
Debt taken over	495	2	150	18		
As share of total large privatisation	23					
Investment guarantees	2 364	12	87	10	1 200	18
As share of total large privatisation	51					
Memorandum item:						
FDI stock per capita, US$	1 130		638		439	

1. Estonia 1993-1998; Latvia and Lithuania refer to end 1998. Lithuania's FDI stock is dominated by foreign investment in Telecom where the purchase price was 2 040 million litas and investment guarantees of 884 million litas.
Source: Mygind (1999) and OECD.

By contrast, foreign dominated take-overs played an important role from the beginning of Estonian privatisation. In both 1997 and 1998 foreign capital contributed more than 50 per cent of the EPA total revenue, and over the 5 years to 1998 investment from overseas constituted 31 per cent of revenue. This proportion would almost certainly have been higher if foreigners had been able to pay by instalment and use vouchers in the same way as domestic investors were able to do.[125] Early FDI tended to be in greenfield sites, but over time take-overs have become increasingly important. Data from the Bank of Estonia and EPA suggest that privatisation-related FDI made up around 34 per cent of FDI in existing enterprises (and 18 per cent of total FDI) between 1993 and 1998. It is worth noting that privatisation carries particular weight since its impact on FDI includes both the purchase price and subsequent investment plans. Privatisation may also open the door to future FDI inflows. For instance, the steep increase of FDI in 1998 is largely explained by the sale of the two largest private banks in Estonia to Swedish/Finnish investors, though this took place sometime after privatisation.

Although press interest tends to be centred on very large investments, most foreign owned enterprises are quite small including many sales outlets and service entities established to facilitate access to the Estonian (and Baltic) market. Out of 6 per cent of all active enterprises registered as under "foreign ownership", half of them were in trade and 19 per cent in manufacturing.[126] These investments were strongly concentrated in the area around Tallinn.[127] Although average foreign investment was quite small, large energy and utility companies were sold to foreign investors.[128] Where appropriate, these were subsequently subject to government regulation.

Foreign involvement in Latvian privatisation was slower to take hold. LPA issued its first international tender at the end of 1994, and this form of privatisation peaked in 1997 with the privatisation of 313 enterprises for a total of LVL 82 million. Most sales were to domestic outsiders but some of the largest went to foreign owners, including Latvian Gas (sold to a consortium of German Ruhrgas and Russian Gazprom). Overall between 1995 and 1998 foreign capital provided 35 per cent of the total purchase price, 67 per cent of assumed liabilities and 64 per cent of investment guarantees. However, FDI is concentrated in a few of the largest enterprises in manufacturing, energy, transport, telecommunications and the financial sector. The role of foreign investment in Lithuania has been rather muted. The government published a list of 114 companies in August 1992 for "unrestricted" sale for foreign currency. By July 1995 this list had been reduced to 71 enterprises; 48 of these were sold for LTL 99 million, but only four went to foreign investors. There was considerable hostility to selling "strategic" enterprises to foreigners, but in the end this opposition was relaxed in the face of a more immediate need to pursue greater integration with the EU.[129] Foreign participation increased once privatisation began to take place through tenders. During 1997-98, thirteen large companies were sold to foreigners for a total of more than LTL 2 billion, though this is mostly accounted for by the sale of 60 per cent of Lithuanian Telecom to a Swedish/Finnish consortium for USD 510 million and guaranteed investments of USD 221 million.

Establishing the links between privatisation and corporate governance

The experience of transition countries shows that there is a clear connection between different methods of privatisation and subsequent ownership structure in privatised enterprises. Owners and stakeholders are a varied group, often with different objectives. The members of the group are also distinguished by their respective access to capital, technological knowledge, and managerial skill. In this regard, foreign investors play a significant role. Ownership structure depends not only on the chosen method of privatisation, but also on how, or indeed whether, ownership rights are tradable, and whether rights, acquired either at the time of privatisation or subsequently, are actually enforceable. As noted above, rules on bankruptcy are especially relevant to enforceability, the development of capital markets to tradeability (see Box 6). The banking sector is central to enterprise restructuring as it both contributes to enforcing hard-budget constraints and participates in the ownership structure, depending on the type of corporate governance model (see Chapter IV).

There have been important differences in the political development in the three countries which have meant that they have chosen different paths of changing the ownership structure from a planned system to a market system based on private ownership (see Mygind 1994, 1995, 1996). In Estonia and Latvia, the nationalist-oriented policies in relation to the large Russian-speaking minority meant that the period of broad employee take-overs of enterprises was very short. Before independence, employee take-overs had implied that control was taken away from central authorities in Moscow to the Baltic Republics. When this goal was accomplished the goal was to strengthen the position of the titular population and to find the most efficient ownership structure. In Lithuania, with only a negligible Russian minority, the workers and employees in general had a much stronger political role. Therefore, the early ideas of insider take-overs were further developed in the early years of transition with the implementation of the LIPSP programme. At the same time, Lithuanians feared Russian take-overs in the form of Russian FDI into Lithuania. Thus, the Lithuanian policy on FDI was quite restrictive for a long period, in sharp contrast in particular to Estonia which implemented very liberal rules for opening up to foreign capital with strong inflows especially from Finnish and Swedish investors.

Box 6. Principles of corporate governance: developments in the Baltics

Corporate governance is largely about establishing a legal and regulatory framework that promotes the emergence of credible and effective governance practices. It has received increasing attention for a number of reasons. The turbulent political and economic events in Asia and Russia during the past two years have stressed the link between sound structural reforms and economic stability. The financial crisis has made clear how poor corporate governance can harm company performance, national economies and ultimately global financial stability. To complete enterprise restructuring, corporate decisions in the Baltic countries are increasingly driven by the need to access financing in international markets. In a competitive investment environment, corporate governance has become a vital part of foreign investment decisions. Improving governance mechanisms is also fundamental to enhancing the confidence of domestic investors in their corporations and capital markets. A sound governance framework will be increasingly important for the development of capital markets and for the attraction of long-term, "patient" capital.

Shareholder rights and protection

In view of harmonisation with EU directives, a number of legal reforms are underway in the Baltic countries, including efforts to improve the legal basis for shareholder protection. Amendments and changes to company laws have been proposed which seek to facilitate recourse to legal action, improve registration, dispute settlement, and voting procedures. Measures have been taken to simplify and harmonise often inconsistent and outdated laws.

However, due to frequent amendments, implementation has been difficult. The judicial systems in the Baltic countries are in their early stages of development, with very limited resources and capacity. Judges have little training and experience in solving complicated commercial cases. As a result, shareholders often lack confidence in the commercial courts. There have been a few cases, reported in the press, where shareholders brought disputes to court. However, more precise quantitative evidence is not available.

In the Baltic countries, there have been cases where management has changed the capital structure or the balance of powers among existing owners without the consent of the shareholders. These practices dissuade external investors. On the whole, the capacity of the capital market regulators to exercise fully their regulatory function is limited due largely to the lack of clear, legal responsibilities, resources and experience. However, in Estonia some steps are being made to strengthen their influence by redrafting securities legislation to reflect the need for better regulation on abusive market conduct.

Minority shareholder protection is important in any governance regime. Shareholder protection warrants particular attention in the Baltic region. In order to support the development of capital markets in the Baltics, it is important to protect the rights of non-controlling shareholders. There is some evidence from the Securities Commission that minority shareholders in the Baltic countries have encountered a range of abuses including restricted access to shareholder meetings, insider trading and self-dealing.

(continued on next page)

(*continued*)

The legal provisions intended to protect minority shareholders are generally weak and enforcement is problematic. In Estonia and Lithuania, the law requires a two-thirds majority for basic decisions such as approval of an increase of share capital. However, according to the Institute of Future Studies in Estonia, there have been several cases of small shareholders learning about the transfer of controlling interests in the company to new owners only through the press. In other cases, minority share-holders have been offered the option of selling their shares, but at significantly lower prices than paid to controlling shareholders. Enhancing transparency in the distribu-tion of voting rights among categories of shareholders and the ways in which voting rights are exercised could help resolve this problem. Strengthening the capacity of relevant institutions would also improve the situation.

Disclosure and transparency

Disclosure can be a powerful tool both for influencing the behaviour of companies and for protecting investors. Shareholders and potential investors require access to regular, reliable and comparable information in sufficient detail for them to make informed decisions about the acquisition, ownership and sale of shares. In the Baltics, efforts are being made to bring accounting and audit standards in line with interna-tional standards and European Union directives. Practical implementation has, how-ever, proven difficult. Some contradictions exist between the laws as they are regularly amended and related regulations are not always adapted. Current requirements for audit in Lithuania are specified in several laws; their implementation is not always adequate. In Latvia, accounting standards are being revised on a regular basis. Many local accountants are unfamiliar with the function of a market economy and perceive the adoption of market-driven accounting practices as a major challenge. Company managers have not yet embraced the new reporting and are frequently concerned about the possible tax implications of restating their accounts under a new system. Enforcement by regulatory authorities has been problematic, as they have encoun-tered difficulties in keeping up with the rapidly developing and changing demands of the private sector.

In OECD countries, securities market regulators usually play an important role in disclosure. In the Baltic countries, the Stock Exchanges have taken the lead in intro-ducing international standards and practices, both in terms of regulations and enforce-ment. They are taking an active role in promoting disclosure by introducing more stringent trading rules. For example, in order to be listed on the Lithuanian Stock Exchange, since 1998 companies have to be audited by an international auditor and financial statements must be presented in accordance with international standards. In reality, however, their influence could be limited because the market is still underde-veloped as a means of corporate finance.

Role of boards and stakeholders

The board is an important mechanism for monitoring management and providing strategic guidance. Board structures differ significantly in the Baltic countries depend-ing on the legal framework. Estonia has adopted a two-tier corporate oversight struc-ture, largely based on the German model although no labour representation is

(*continued on next page*)

(*continued*)

required. In Latvia, the Joint-Stock Company law allows for either a one or two tier board structure. A management board is mandatory and supervisory board must be established when there are at least fifty shareholders and for all joint-stock companies in the financial sector. In Lithuania, the general shareholder meeting determines whether a one or two-tier board structure should be formed.

The exact definition of the role and responsibility of the corporate governance bodies in the legislation need to be made more consistent. In Lithuania, members of the management board are elected at the annual general meeting or by the supervisory board when it exists. In practice, there appears to be one board consisting of managers and majority owners that actually conduct the daily management. In cases where companies have foreign strategic investors, these investors may choose to create a supervisory board to reflect their interests through its supervision over management. Weak sanctions have not prevented managers from acting in their own interest to the detriment of shareholders. The company law in each Baltic country specifies whether or not stakeholders have legally recognised governance rights, *i.e.* representation on the boards. There are no legal hurdles to the representation of creditors or labour on boards, but in practice such cases are rare.

Ownership structure after privatisation and creation of new firms

The present ownership structure in the Baltic countries results from both the privatisation process and the start-up of new enterprises, as well as from the dynamics of ownership change after privatisation.[130] It is seldom possible to make a clear distinction between *de novo* and privatised enterprises. But, in general, most small enterprises (with less than 20 employees) are started from scratch although often with some privatised assets. On the other hand, most large private enterprises (with 100 or more employees) result only from privatisation. It is harder to make this distinction for the medium size enterprises.

The general trend in all three countries is that management ownership dominates in small enterprises, both for *de novo* and privatised. A sole proprietor has started most small enterprises in trade and light manufacturing. As discussed above, new co-operatives have been a transition-specific way to give broader group of employees a more formal role in the ownership structure. But, it seems that most of these enterprises quickly transformed to management ownership. In the early period of transition, managers in all three countries had good opportunities to take-over their units. This was particularly the case for small enterprises or small branches of large enterprises.

As a result, Estonia and Latvia have a very high proportion of manager-owned small enterprises. The proportion is somewhat lower in Lithuania. Employee ownership is also found in small enterprises, but to no greater extent than for medium and large-sized enterprises. Overall, it was estimated that in January 1995 30-60 per cent of the private companies had majority ownership by insiders. Employee ownership appears highest in Latvia and lowest in Lithuania. However, in Lithuania employee ownership is concentrated in large companies, with insiders owning shares in nearly all companies, and nearly all enterprises have at least an element of employee ownership; in industrial enterprises around 75 per cent of employees own shares. Employees have a quite strong position versus management, and there are fewer non-owners among the employees than in Estonia and Latvia, this is particularly true for industry. In Estonia and Latvia the two types of ownership had about the same weight in January 1995. The incidence of employee share ownership is lower in Estonia, where only one in four employees owned shares in privatised firms in 1995. Foreign ownership has been most important in relation to large privatisation in all three countries.

Regarding the concentration of ownership, by 1996, Lithuania had a relatively high proportion of enterprises categorised as "no majority" owners (i.e. less than 50 per cent). This is mainly because the state kept a substantial minority stake in many enterprises in the LIPSP privatisation, and has been slow to sell its residual holdings up to 1998. In contrast, in both Estonia and Latvia there is considerable concentration of shares, leaving only 2-6 per cent of privatised enterprises having "no majority".

Ownership dynamics after privatisation or start up

The initial ownership structure following privatisation is most unlikely to be optimal for the reasons discussed above. However, a degree of inertia characterises all three countries. Except for continuing privatisation, there is little movement between insiders, and domestic and foreign outsiders. In this respect, Estonia appears somewhat more dynamic than the two other countries. The main trend has taken place within the insider group, with ownership transferring from employees to managers. For the sample of enterprises used in this study, this change is particularly pronounced in Estonia and Lithuania, somewhat less so in Latvia, possibly because of the smaller sample of firms. This is reinforced by the finding that the number of non-share owning employees is increasing in all three countries. It is also significant that the group of enterprises with "no majority" is falling in all three countries. Concerning foreign ownership, there is some indication that foreign investors increase their stake gradually over time rather than in one go (Mygind, 1999).

Ownership structures and performance

The literature gives limited guidance on the relation between type of ownership and economic performance.[131] Predictions from evidence in transition countries are summarised in Table 16. It suggests that insider ownership, and

Table 16. **Some observations of efficiency by ownership group**

State	Employee	Manager	Outside domestic	Foreign
Lack of incentive, information problems.	Lack of skills and capital, specific goals.	Problems between employee and outside.	Specific barriers in transition.	Profit-maximisation, capital, management skill and networks.
	Specific barriers on the domestic market and lack of efficient financial market.			Access to well functioning international markets.

Source: Mygind (1999) and OECD.

especially employee ownership, has specific disadvantages since employees may have objectives, such as the stability of employment and higher wages, that differ from profit maximisation. Foreign ownership, in contrast, has delivered better performance through restructuring. This is due to better access to capital, management skills, including corporate governance abilities, and access to international business networks.

In order to assess the actual performance of the separate ownership groups different starting conditions should be borne in mind. For example, it is rare that employee ownership results from a new start-up. There are also striking differences in enterprise size and capital-intensity between ownership groups. Management ownership is especially found in small enterprises, while employee ownership is more frequent in large firms. Insider-ownership tends to be associated with lower levels of investment than foreign ownership; this applies both to privatised and *de novo* firms.

An important point to evaluate performance is the direction of causality between ownership and performance. In other words, particular ownership groups may appear to perform better at a given point only because they systematically acquired the better performing enterprises. Data are not very reliable, but those indicators which are available show that there is no significant variation in the level of pre-privatisation profitability between ownership groups. Insiders may, however, have been able to acquire their shares at less than market value.

Taking into account these qualifications, there are some quite strong trends in performance by different ownership groups in the Baltic countries (see Table 17). It stands out that foreign ownership is associated with relatively higher performance. Among other characteristics, foreign-owned firms have higher capital-intensity, sales per employee and growth rate of sales from the start. They also

Table 17.   **Results on the relation between type of ownership and performance**

	Estonia	Latvia	Lithuania
Initial conditions			
Size	FO low, EO average, MO low.	FO average, IO smaller.	FO average, MO smaller, EO average.
Capital intensity	FO very high, EO and MO low.	FO very highIO lower.	FO high, EO and MO average.
Profitability	IO average, FO.	No information.	EO and MO average, FO and IO average.
Growth in sales	FO high.	FO high.	FO and MO high, EO average, OO low.
Export share	EO, FO higher.	–	–
Employment change	FO highest growth, EO less reductions, EO and MO higher growth.		FO high growth, EO sluggish adjustment.
Labour productivity	EO average.	FO highest.	FO highest, EO and MO high.
Wage level	EO and MO lower, FO higher.	FO highest, PO lower than SO.	FO highest, EO and MO high.
Profitability (return on assets)	FO lower, EO and MO higher.	FO lower, IO higher.	FO low, later high, EO high, MO average.
Finance			
Debt/Equity	EO and MO higher.	FO average, IO high.	FO higher.
Bank loans/employee	FO higher, EO and MO lower, SO lower.	FO highest, IO low, SO lowest.	FO higher, EO and MO lower.
Investment/employee	FO highest, EO and MO average.	FO highest, IO higher than OO.	FO highest.
Special note			Financial-owned firms have relatively worse performance.

Note: These results are based on a survey of enterprises in each country.
    FO = foreign ownership; EO = employee; MO = management; IO = insider; OO = outside domestic; SO = state;
    PO = private.
Source: Jones and Mygind (1999a, b, c) and Mygind (1997a, b).

have higher investment levels and better access to bank loans. These conditions make them more likely to engage in a process of pro-active restructuring, that is developing new markets, new products and new production methods. They also have higher labour productivity (measured by output per worker) and pay relatively higher wages. In counterpart, they have higher capital costs, entailing a relatively lower return on assets. Hence, present profitability is also lower, but could be matched by higher and more sustainable growth in the future.

Insider-owned enterprises tend to display more defensive restructuring. In relative terms, they adjust employment more slowly, pay lower wages, have lower investments, and find it more difficult to access bank loans. Partly as a consequence, they have higher levels of profitability. While this is related to relatively low capital-intensity at the starting point, it may also indicate that they have done some restructuring and improved the use of scarce resources towards higher efficiency. The most notable exception to the general pattern is a some-what higher capital-intensity of employee-owned enterprises in Lithuania. This resulted from the first stage of the privatisation programme that enabled employees to buy relatively expensive enterprises with vouchers. Employee own-ership may explain comparatively higher wages in these enterprises, although still significantly lower than in the foreign owned enterprises. Sectoral evidence for Latvia and Lithuania (Mygind, 1999) suggests that managers tend to establish control of the most profitable sectors (e.g. trade and construction), while employee ownership appears more frequently located in sectors or segments of the manufacturing sector with less favourable business developments. It is impor-tant to note that domestic outside ownership does not appear to provide any specific advantages compared to insider ownership.

The impact of privatisation on the growth of the capital market has varied. In Estonia it was minimal. While the public offering of minority shares through vouchers facilitated the development of the Stock Exchange, the biggest listed firms are commercial banks, which started as private entities. The Latvia Stock Exchange developed quite rapidly during the past few years largely in close connection with the acceleration of large-scale privatisation and public offerings. The speed of privatisation in Lithuania during the early years facilitated the early establishment of the Exchange as many of the large enterprises were listed.

Continued interplay between insider and foreign ownership should improve corporate governance

The most important change in the dynamics of ownership has been the taking over by managers of employee-owned firms, especially in small and medium sized enterprises. Although this process will probably develop further, in the foreseeable future, a strong element of employee ownership will continue to prevail. At the same time foreign ownership will play an increasingly strong role in these small open economies.

How are the perspectives for restructuring under these conditions? Eco-nomic performance suggests that foreign companies implement active restructur-ing, whereas insider owned enterprises tend to restructure in a more defensive manner. Therefore, the challenge for the Baltic economies is not only to develop further co-operation with foreign investors, but also to improve conditions for domestically owned enterprises so that they match the advantages and standards provided by foreign ownership. This could be the case in relation to access to capital, management training, building networks for exports etc. Certainly, the development of domestic businesses would be stimulated by the development of financial markets. These, in turn, benefit from the openness of the economy. Also the development of institutions for management training, management consulting and activities promoting exports and international networks for SMEs could be important elements in restructuring the Baltic economies. Employee-owned enterprises also have the chance to develop in certain cases, if firmly profit-oriented. Finally, a competitive environment enhances motivation and alignment of the interests of owners and employees.

Regional and sectoral dimensions of enterprise restructuring

One particular aspect of enterprise reform pertains to the regional and sectoral dimension. Indeed, following the restoration of the Baltic countries' independence regional disparities have emerged from the transition process (Ryder, 1998). New enterprises are being developed around capitals and major cities, while remote and rural areas, dominated by farming or by one single industry or sector (so called *mono-enterprise regions*) appear in some cases to be lagging behind. In several cases the mono-enterprise regions were, before the restoration of independence, part of the military-industrial complex of the former Soviet Union. These large enterprises were often "All-Union enterprises", supplying the entire Soviet market and were under the control of national ministries based in Moscow. They were given output targets, operated independently from local governments and usually paid above-average wages. Moreover, they were highly vertically integrated and supplied social services, such as health care, housing and education.

Following the collapse of the Soviet Union, the markets for these enterprises vanished. Raw materials and other intermediate products supplied at low cost through the internal Soviet market also became unavailable. These conditions created a particularly difficult and painful restructuring problem. Moreover, the disparity between these mono-enterprise regions, on the one hand, and the more dynamic, expanding cities on the other, tends to be self-reinforcing. Indeed, there are important externalities associated with the concentration of economic activity. While in some regions, there is a positive feedback between enterprise development and entrepreneurial environment, other parts continue to stagnate. The best predictor for the creation of new small and medium enterprises is strongly dependent on the number of the existing firms. The greater number of small firms the greater likelihood of new small firm creation. Under these conditions, not only it is politically very sensitive to tackle enterprise restructuring problems in mono-enterprise regions, but also policies using subsidies or other forms of support tend to perpetuate the existing structure. Therefore, these policies often delay the adjustment process and, at best, avoid excessive unemployment only in the short-run. Given these particularly difficult legacies, there has been an impressive amount of structural change during the first decade of transition, but there are also relatively well identified areas where enterprise and sectoral restructuring is lagging.

The industrial sector has contracted in all three countries

In Estonia the share of total industry dropped from 39 to 28 per cent of GDP between 1991 and 1998 (see Figure 32). This fall was concentrated in 1991-92 thereafter the share of industry in GDP has remained stable. Mining and electricity production remains important and geographically concentrated. Declining production in these sectors has had, and will continue to have, a pronounced regional impact as they are dominated by a few large enterprises. In Latvia, the industrial sector accounted for 38 per cent of GDP in 1991 and a little less than one third of employment. The heavy industrial sector was more important in Latvia than in Estonia. The central Soviet authorities had emphasised development of sectors such as engineering, chemicals and electrical power. Traditionally, more than 70 per cent of production was directed to the former Soviet Union, and a further 18 per cent to other CMEA markets. With the loss of these markets, industrial production had fallen to 29 per cent of GDP by 1998, and manufacturing from 36 to below 20 per cent of GDP. In Lithuania, the decline of food processing and light industries in favour of heavy industries under Soviet rule brought about the rapid development of machine building and chemical industry. As in Estonia and Latvia, the bulk of these heavy industries were severely affected by transition. Between 1991 and 1998, the share of total industry dropped from 51 to 32 per cent of GDP; of which manufacturing dropped from 45 to 19 per cent.

The problematic regions and sectors

Estonia illustrates well the contrasts existing at the regional level and how they are related to sectoral or enterprise restructuring problems. Indeed, Estonia can be roughly divided into three types of regions (see Figure 33a). First, the city of Tallinn and its vicinity has had an extremely rapid growth. Then mono-enterprise regions, such as the Kothla-Jarve/Narva agglomeration and former Soviet military bases, with heavy industrial enterprises still in need of reorganisation and restructuring. Lastly, the regions mostly dependent on agriculture, fishing and forestry. The three different types of regions are to some extent mirrored in the distribution of non-native Estonian speakers in the population. In particular, Russians were typically concentrated in the mono-enterprise regions, dominated before independence by "all-union enterprises". This has persisted, and differences in native language have tended to be reinforced by contrasting experiences

Figure 32. **Activity as share of GDP**
Per cent

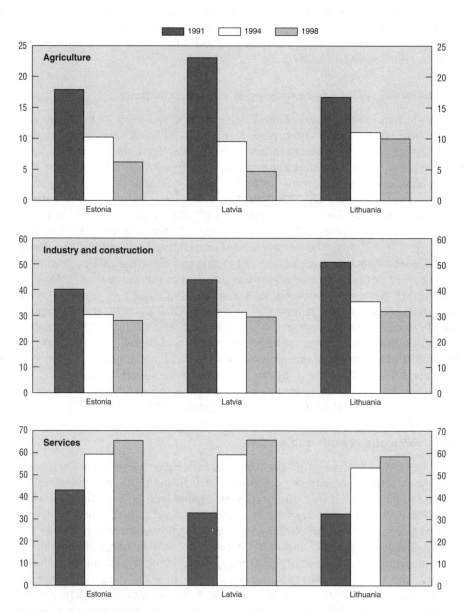

Source: National Statistical Offices.

Figure 33a. **Regions and major cities in Estonia**

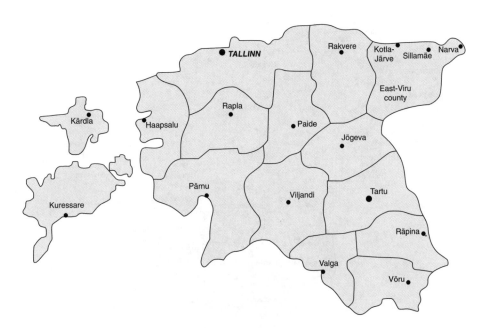

Figure 33b. **Regions and major cities in Latvia**

Figure 33c. **Regions and major cities in Lithuania**

in regional growth, and the painful prospect of the bulk of restructuring yet to come. A similar situation exists in Latvia where almost half of the population lives in the Riga agglomeration and the port city of Ventspils. The rest of the country has a lower standard of living and some 15 per cent of the population live in districts or rural communities that are declared "assisted regions". State budget support to these areas is given mainly as an interest rate subsidy to small enterprises.

Energy and mining are in need of a deep restructuring

A good example of problematic regions, suffering from unrestructured heavy industries, is the East-Viru county in Estonia. Employment is concentrated in three main sectors: mining, energy and transport. The country's deposit of oil shale and the largest power plants using this primary energy are located in this county. Until independence, much of the country's energy production was exported to the Soviet Union, but since 1991 this export market has contracted sharply. The county's largest employers are very large enterprises in the state sector. The mining and energy sectors were traditionally favoured sectors under Soviet rule, and as a result wages were higher than average wages within the republic. This situation persists today, both for state-owned industries and for enterprises in mining, energy and transport, although since 1992 the rate of wage increase in these industries has been below the national average. While the East-Viru County still needs industrial restructuring it is also characterised by an extremely low rate of business creation. By July 1995 it had some 7 per cent of total enterprises in Estonia, about half its share in the population. With an unfavourable business environment, the county has also been neglected by foreign investment. It may well be that the traditionally high wage levels in these areas have inhibited the development of private entrepreneurs.

The mines and quarries, with around 9 000 employees in 1996, are generally loss-making in Estonia. Measures are however being taken to restructure the enterprises. The counsel of the state-owned oil shale mining company, Eesti Polevkivi announced it would merge their largest mine, Estonia, and a loss making mine, Sompa. About one-third of employees of the Sompa mine will be made redundant. The Ahtme mine also faces closure in the near future. The oil shale industry and the associated power plants in the northeastern part of the country are particular heavy polluters. Higher environmental standards, notably related to the EU integration process, will entail high costs for these industries and may possibly hamper their successful privatisation.

In Lithuania, the major restructuring problem also lies in the energy and oil sector, which amounts to more than 20 per cent of GDP and suffers from large over-capacity and inefficiency. Ignalina, the only nuclear power plant in the Baltics was built in the early 1980s with its two 1500 MW reactors which, at that time, were the largest Chernobyl-type reactors in operation. The plant is located some 130 km north east of Vilnius and is producing about 80 per cent of Lithuania's electricity. Concern about safety at the plant is high in the neighbouring countries, and so far USD 100 million has been invested to upgrade the plant's safety. The government maintains that it can not afford to decommission Ignalina without international financial support. It envisages keeping the plant in operation until 2009, though has made a commitment to the EU to decommission one reactor by 2005.

The oil sector and related activities consisting of an oil-refinery, pipelines and a port, alone account for roughly 8-10 per cent of Lithuanian GDP. The major company in this sector, Mazeikiu Nafta in Mazeikiai, whose refinery operations account for 2 per cent of GDP, has long suffered from over-capacity and outdated equipment. However, in an attempt to increase its share of Russian oil exports, the government invested USD 75 million to prepare the Butinge oil terminal for crude oil exports and reorganised the oil sector by merging Mazeikiu Nafta, Butinge terminal and its pipelines. One third of the company was sold in

October 1999 to the American oil company, Williams, which has reportedly promised to invest a further USD 150 million. This transaction led to considerable political differences over the continuing burden on the budget, culminating in the resignation of the Prime Minister. A key problem of the Mazeikiu refinery has been its heavy dependence on Russian oil and the difficulty of obtaining alternative supplies. The interruption of oil deliveries from Russia in 1999 induced a significant drop in energy output and, given the weight of this sector in the economy, had an impact on GDP growth.

Restructuring problems are sometimes aggravated by ethnic problems

The conjunction between economic restructuring and ethnic problems in Latvia is the result of forced large-scale industrialisation, in particular in Soviet military industries that have become obsolete and are undergoing difficult restructuring or liquidation. This drew in immigrants from other Soviet Republics who tended to use Russian as a common language to communicate among themselves. Unlike Estonia and especially Lithuania, Latvians were barely in a majority at independence and were concentrated in rural areas and in the agricultural sector. Of seven major cities and towns in Latvia, Latvians are in a majority in only one, not the capital. Development since independence has left the rural areas at a growing disadvantage in terms of income, life expectancy and employment. This outcome is universal, for instance applying equally to Rezekne, the major town in a rural area in the east of the country where Russians are in majority. Aiming to address the specific problem of the Rezekne region, the government created a free economic zone (see Chapter III). This was supposed to help developing industry and trade in a region heavily effected by unemployment (29 per cent in July 1999) and low rate of business formation. With its strategic location, near the Russian border and at the crossing of international railway and road routes, expectations that the FEZ would bring about industrial growth were high, but results have been modest. The first licence to operate in the zone in July 1998 coincided with the Russian crisis. At end-1998, only three enterprises were established in Rezeke free economic zone.

Contrasting developments in the agricultural sector

The specific problems of the agricultural sector are treated in more detail in Annex I, but some key issues and features are worth stressing here. In Estonia, agriculture has the lowest share of GDP of all Baltic States, with the agricultural sector accounting for 6 per cent of GDP in 1998, a drop of more than half since independence, Estonia has undertaken a large structural change. Employment in agriculture and hunting is only 32 per cent that of its level in 1990 and accounted for 7 per cent of overall Estonian employment in 1998. Production has declined in absolute terms, but labour productivity has increased. However, despite the long lasting restitution process, almost 70 per cent of agricultural land still remains under state control. Out-dated machinery and equipment, and low incomes among farmers are a serious impediment to the restructuring of Estonian agriculture. A new law aiming to develop rural areas was passed by the Estonian parliament in 1998.

In Latvia, the fall in agricultural output together with stable agricultural employment during the transitional period (at around 17-18 per cent of the total workforce) has resulted in over-capacity, declining productivity and profitability. Not helping the restructuring problem is the fact that little long-term credit is available to farmers. In the early stages of restructuring almost the only available source of credit was a World Bank loan administered by the State Credit Institution (Laukkredits).[132] Low farmgate prices have discouraged commercial banks from lending to the sector, although one bank (UniBanka) has been more willing to extend credit. A law on agriculture, which sets out the long-term policy framework for the development of Latvian agriculture, came into force in 1996. It lists several objectives first amongst which is the necessity to implement structural adjustments in order to develop a competitive farming sector, but many of the points in the Law relate to the development of rural areas more generally, notably to maintain employment, rather than restructuring agriculture *per se*.

Lithuanian agriculture's share of GDP was about 10 per cent in 1998, the highest among the Baltic countries despite a drop of 2 per cent from the year before. Because of slow restitution and privatisation of agricultural land, Lithuania has also kept, for several years, stable agricultural employment at 21-24 per cent of total labour force. However, with the restitution process gaining momentum at the end of 1997, agricultural employment has dropped to 19 per cent in 1998. One of the major problems is the payment arrears by the food processing industry. New measures introduced in 1997 set stricter procedures for the payment of overdue debts by processors who are now liable to pay interest on overdue payments to producers and are subject to financial penalties. While this has resulted in a reduction of outstanding debts owed to agricultural farmers, the Russian crisis and its impact on the food processing industry have particularly hit the Lithuanian farmers. The latter is still suffering from a drop in exports to Russia and problems of getting access to the west European markets. It should be noted that the agricultural sector has acted as a social buffer, absorbing the impact on employment of industrial restructuring. This is an additional obstacle to the emergence of more competitive food production and to the structural adjustment in the sector.

The development of cities and East-West transit flows

In contrast to the structural problems of mono-enterprise regions and the agricultural sector, the Baltic cities have flourished, notably in connection with their role as strategic gateways for East-West trade transportation corridors. Competition between the three countries to be the primary link with Russia has actually intensified. In Estonia, Tallinn and its surrounding area have become the engine of growth. The city (which contains about one-third of the population) and the Northwest are the wealthiest parts of the country. The region of Tallinn is the most dynamic measured in terms of wages, turnover per capita, and retail sales per capita. The city is also home to more than 59 per cent of all registered enterprises. Between 80 and 90 per cent of all foreign investment is in Tallinn, which consequently has more than 80 per cent of all foreign enterprises in the country. Private enterprises in Tallinn appear to be more efficient than elsewhere in the country.[133]

Tallinn's position is bolstered by its position as Estonia's main port of entry. The main passenger terminal, Tallinn Kesklinna, handles high Finnish tourist flows. In 1998, the port handled 5.6 million passengers; 91 per cent of foreigners passing through the port were Finnish. Much of the cargo turnover is connected to transit flows to and from Russia. The Estonian ports were designed to supply the needs for the entire Soviet Union, and since the independence they have been suffering from over-capacity and strong competition with the other Baltic ports. However, there are plans to build new terminals: a dry bulk terminal, a container terminal; a coal terminal; and an oil product terminal. All these plans however are heavily dependent on expectations of growth of transit cargo with Russia. According to the port authorities, the traffic through the Tallinn port does not seem to have been severely affected by the Russian crisis. Indeed, during the first three-quarters of 1999, both inbound and outbound cargo transit flows increased respectively by 3100 and 800 thousand tonnes (mainly in bulk cargoes) compared with the same period in the previous year. It seems likely that this is due to an increase in the volume of commodity exports from Russia, following the rouble devaluation. In early 1999, the Estonian authorities created a Free Economic Zone at Sillamae.

In Latvia, the contrast between the major urban area (the capital Riga) and the rest of the country is even more pronounced than in Estonia. Riga has roughly one-third of the country's population. Riga is the major city in the Baltic region, and was chosen by Soviet central planners to be the centre of a fast growing industrialised region. Heavy engineering and chemical plants set up several of the industries were sole suppliers to the whole FSU for products such as dairy machinery, electrical engineering, buses, trams and telephone switchboards. The economic concentration around such a big city can be a great advantage and a source of opportunities for a small country like Latvia, but also exacerbates the regional disparities. In 1998, 54 per cent of all registered enterprises were located in the city of Riga, including 550 of 1262 still existing state-owned firms. Riga also attracted 63 per cent of total investment in 1998. Roughly speaking, the rest of the country is dominated by forestry and farming.

The good transport infrastructure inherited from the Soviet period gave Latvia a specific advantage in relation to its Baltic neighbours. The country has remained the main transport corridor for East-West trade. Latvia has a well-developed ship repair industry, and three major Baltic ports (Ventspils, Riga and Liepaja). The government has tried to use the transportation sector to diversify the location of economic activity, attract foreign investors, create new production sites and improve the business climate in the regions. In 1996-97 it created free or "special" economic zones (FEZ or SEZ) around the three major ports.[134] In addition, Rezekne is the only FEZ located in rural area. Several partial or total tax exemptions are available within FEZs, covering customs duties, excises and VAT. For example, in the Riga FEZ, material used to construct new facilities is exempted from VAT, and there is no customs duty on plant and machinery or construction material brought into the port.

While these policies have a significant impact on the budget (see Chapter III) they have so far produced mixed results. By mid-1999 43 companies were operating in the zone occupying only 7 per cent of the total area made available for the biggest SEZ at Liepaja. Only eight other enterprises have submitted applications to start up activity, creating merely 680 jobs. Explaining part of these modest results is the fact that economic zones and the overall transportation sector have been severely affected by the Russian crisis. The port of Riga lost roughly 14 per cent of its container traffic in 1998. Bulk cargo handling increased by some 32 per cent in 1998 compared to 55 per cent in 1997, and liquid cargo dropped by 67 per cent. On the whole, cargo traffic increased by 19 per cent, compared to 50 per cent increase in 1997. In Ventspils, cargo turnover for 1998 dropped by 2 per cent compared to 1997, with crude oil stable and oil products dropping by 7 per cent. Overall, despite the impact of the Russian crisis, cargo turnover increased in the Latvian ports by 3 per cent in 1998.

Unlike both Estonia and Latvia, Lithuania has not generated a halo of growth around its capital city, Vilnius. This may be partly related to its inner location relative to the Baltic Sea, which did not provide the same advantages for transit trade, as the other Baltic capitals. Economic activity is spread relatively evenly through the country, with a clear-cut separation between areas dominated by agriculture, and those were heavy industry predominates. Nevertheless, the largest shares of FDI are concentrated in Vilnius (61 per cent), Kleipeda port (11 per cent) and Kaunas (10 per cent). However, the fact that Lithuania has three big cities, Vilnius, Kleipeda and Kaunas, a number of other significant urban centres and a good road network may facilitate labour mobility and commuting. Unlike Estonia and Latvia, there is no geographical concentration in Lithuania of minorities. The transport infrastructure in Lithuania along with public investment in this sector has the potential to stimulate increased transit trade. Lithuania has also established in 1996 three Free Economic Zones in the cities of Siauliai, Kleipeda and Kaunas. These are open for domestic as well as foreign investors and offer among other benefits, corporate tax holidays, no custom taxes and no VAT. No information on how they are performing is available.

VI. Labour market and social policy developments

A tremendous transition shock

Workers in the Baltic countries, as elsewhere in the former Soviet Union, suffered a dramatic loss of purchasing power during the initial transition years. It is difficult to make direct comparison of real wages before and during the transition. Notably, the quality and variety of consumption goods increased spectacularly and those should, in principle, be taken into account when assessing changes in real purchasing power. Insofar as real wages using standard CPI inflation can be compared over the period, they may have fallen by as much as two-thirds between 1990 and the end of 1992. But a partial recovery of real wages got underway in 1993 in Estonia and Latvia and in 1994 in Lithuania, after which living standards have continued to increase more or less in line with the trends observed in Central European transition economies. The Russian economic crisis in the autumn 1998 does not appear to have broken the positive development of real incomes, in spite of some job losses.

Estonian workers currently earn the highest real wages in the Baltic region, while the recent improvements have been particularly strong in Lithuania. Nevertheless, due to the large size of the initial output drop, real wages are still barely half of the estimated 1990 levels in any of the three countries, compared with about 100 per cent in Central Europe.

Employment data for 1998 compared with 1990 levels indicate an accumulated job loss of 26 per cent in Latvia, 22 per cent in Estonia and 11 per cent in Lithuania. The bulk of these reductions occurred between 1992 and 1994, but a downward trend in employment has continued to some extent in all three countries. In Estonia and Latvia, the employment decline was initially associated with a wave of net emigration, corresponding to approximately 5 per cent of the previous populations, while migration from Lithuania was much less significant. Above all, however, employment reductions involved a sudden shift towards lower labour-force participation and higher unemployment, affecting women and men in most age groups.

The policy responses to these developments have generally been market-oriented. Few regulatory interventions have been introduced with the direct aim of limiting lay-offs. Nevertheless, to a varying extent, the governments have tried to protect jobs against market forces, for example by demanding employment guarantees from buyers of privatised companies. A number of companies are still in need of restructuring, as discussed Chapter V, implying that further redundancies are still in the pipeline. Social safety nets are in place to deal with this and other contingencies; but their coverage is incomplete, and the benefits are sometimes too low to prevent poverty.

In the present situation, a key policy challenge facing the three Baltic countries is to respond to legitimate demands for better social protection within acceptable budget limits while, at the same time, facilitating labour mobility and not compromising the necessary incentives and freedom of action for business enterprises.

The worst hardships have been overcome, but moderate poverty persists

Several indicators suggest that both the hardships suffered in the early 1990s and the subsequent improvements have been most extreme in Lithuania (see the Statistical Annex, Table A6). A number of developments all recorded within a few years of 1990, bear witness to the severity of the shock. The food share in household consumption rose from 34 per cent to 62 per cent in 1993; annual meat intake per capita dropped from 89 to 50 kg in 1994; male life expectancy declined from 67 to 63 years in 1993 and 1994; infant mortality increased from 10 to 16 per thousand in 1993.

Judging from surveys in 1998 and 1999, the average household budget in Lithuania is still in a state of depression if 1990 is used as a base year for comparison. But life expectancy and infant mortality have returned to their 1990 levels, and some indicators of material well-being – for instance, the numbers of cars and telephones – have risen substantially more.

Developments in Estonia and Latvia have been broadly similar, although the short-term fluctuations were probably not as sharp as in Lithuania.[135] Throughout the 1990s, Estonia's material living standards have been a bit higher than those of the other countries. The particular strength of the recent catch-up in Lithuania is also apparent from Table 18, which shows the estimated development since 1996 in the real value of disposable income, average wages and average pensions.[136]

If a food share exceeding 50 per cent of consumption is taken as a sign of poverty, more than half of Lithuanian households and almost half of Latvian households are still poor (Table 19). Only in Estonia has the incidence of poverty by this measure fallen below 20 per cent. Food produced in private farms or

Table 18. **Personal incomes: key amounts per month**
US dollars at 1998 prices and exchange rates[1]

	Estonia				Latvia				Lithuania			
	1996	1997	1998	1999	1996	1997	1998	1999	1996	1997	1998[2]	1999
Disposable income per person in the average household	121	125	134	132	87	94	106	–	82	92	106	106[3]
Average wage: before tax	255	275	293	282	190	213	226	–	172	201	239	252
Average wage: after tax	200	213	227	218	151	157	165	–	130	149	175	183
Minimum wage	58	65	78	87	73	67	71	83[5]	67	96	104	109
Average old-age pension[4]	82	85	89	107	64	72	87	–	48	61	72	–

1. Average monthly amounts. The averages for 1996, 1997 and 1999 were adjusted for local consumer-price changes compared with 1998. For Estonia, 1999 data is for the 1st quarter.
2. Preliminary data.
3. Data of 1st quarter of 1999.
4. For Lithuania: non-working pensioners.
5. Data for January-March 1999.
All amounts were translated into US dollars using the average exchange rate for 1998.
Source: Statistical yearbooks and Monthly bulletins, various editions and national authorities.

Table 19.   **Food shares in household consumption expenditure**

Per cent

	Deciles									
	1	2	3	4	5	6	7	8	9	10
Estonia										
Total expenditure	55	49	47	48	43	40	38	33	28	17
Monetary expenditure	48	45	42	42	39	36	33	30	26	16
Latvia										
Total expenditure	66	58	54	50	49	45	43	43	37	26
Monetary expenditure	57	49	47	44	42	40	39	37	32	23
Lithuania										
Total expenditure	66	60	57	54	52	52	50	47	42	31
Monetary expenditure	56	50	47	46	44	44	43	42	37	27

Note: Households were distributed into deciles according to total expenditure (including in-kind). Food shares were then estimated for total expenditure and for monetary expenditure.

Source: Estonia: Data for the fourth quarter of 1998 in Estonian Statistics, No. 1, 1999. Latvia: 1998 data submitted by the Central Statistical Bureau of Latvia. Lithuania: Data for the first quarter of 1999 in LS, 1999.

gardens plays a significant role throughout the region, especially in low-income households. However, studies using *relative* as opposed to *absolute* poverty lines, as is common in OECD countries – *e.g.* defining as poor all households with under 50 per cent of the average income – have suggested that less than 20 per cent of the households were poor in any Baltic country during the most recent years.[137]

The income distribution has become somewhat more uneven than before the transition, especially in Estonia. It currently appears less even than in the neighbouring Nordic countries, but it is comparable to the situation in France, Germany or Hungary and not as uneven as in the United States (Table 20). The Gini coefficient, another measure of income inequality, was 0.37 in Lithuania in the early 1990s, but in 1997 it had declined to 0.31, a figure also reported for Latvia (UNDP, 1999, p. 60; Rajevska *et al.*, 1999, p. 7). However, the Gini coefficient reported for Estonia of 0.38 in the fourth quarter 1998 remains high by OECD standards, most Member countries fall in the range 0.25-0.35.[138] Large families and rural inhabitants are generally over-represented among the poor in all three countries, as are pensioners in Estonia.

Taken together, these results show that, while extreme poverty has limited extent, high proportions of the Baltic households are still suffering a moderate degree of deprivation. The evidence suggests a link between progress in transition and increased income inequality. While Lithuania has recorded a trend towards lower income inequality, it is noteworthy that Estonia – where the economic transition has been most successful by several measures – presents the highest degree of inequality.

Table 20. **Income distribution by deciles, 1998**

Disposable income per person as per cent of the average

	Deciles									
	1	2	3	4	5	6	7	8	9	10
Estonia	32	53	62	69	77	87	102	124	158	291
Latvia	23	51	66	77	87	97	109	128	159	279
Lithuania[1]	32	47	58	69	79	89	103	121	151	253
Finland	45	60	69	77	84	93	104	118	141	210
France	33	49	59	69	79	91	104	121	148	248
Germany	35	48	59	70	81	93	106	124	148	237
Hungary	32	53	63	73	83	94	106	120	143	234
United States	18	36	49	62	74	89	106	129	165	272

1. Expenditure.
Source: Data for 1998 submitted by the Statistical Office of Estonia and the Central Statistical Bureau of Latvia, and of Lithuania; Lithuanian data for the third quarter of 1998 in Labour Force Survey, 1999. OECD data for 1994 (France and Germany), 1995 (Finland and the United States) and 1997 (Hungary).

Baltic labour markets are relatively flexible

Significant movements between agriculture, industry and services

To a large extent, the dramatic change in social conditions since 1990 can be attributed to the labour market impacts of three distinct phases of the economic transition. First of all, the breakdown of the Soviet economy led to a precipitous fall in real wages. Shortly thereafter, a wave of massive job losses occurred in industry and agriculture. In a third phase from the mid-1990s on, gradual productivity improvements have permitted a partial real-wage recovery, while employment has been mostly stagnant in aggregate terms (Figures 34 and 35). Significant parts of the necessary restructuring have been achieved, but the effects of the Russian crisis that started in the Summer 1998 have demonstrated the fragility of a number of enterprises whose products are still not competitive on western markets.

Until now, Latvia has experienced the strongest employment adjustment and the least dramatic real-wage fluctuations. The opposite pattern occurred in Lithuania, where high real-wage volatility was associated with a moderate and somewhat slow pace of employment adjustment. Estonia recorded adjustments of both real wages and employment at early stages of the transition, a fact that appears to have helped the country to take a leading position in the subsequent recovery.

Figure 34.   **Real wages**[1]

1990 = 100

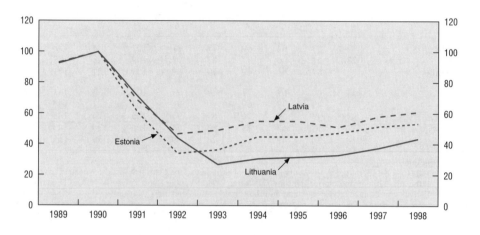

1.   An index of after-tax wages divided by the consumer price index.
Source: Official statistics. The estimates of trends are approximate, as the methods of data collection have been changed in several respects.

Figure 35.   **Employment**

1990 = 100

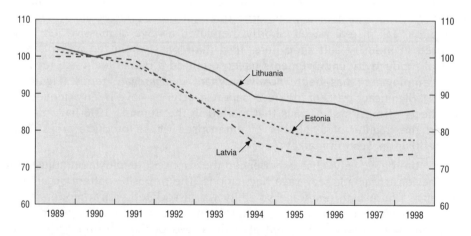

Source: Official statistics produced by the respective governments. The estimates of trends are approximate, as the methods of data collection have been changed in several respects.

Large parts of the employment reductions occurred in *industry* (see Table A7), and the distribution of jobs across industrial sectors has also been profoundly transformed (Table A8 and Chapter VII). In connection with the re-orientation of trade towards western markets, companies producing wood products in particular have created many new jobs. Other consumer-oriented sectors – for instance food and clothing – have increased their employment since 1990 in relative, if not in absolute, terms. In the *service-sector* employment is buoyant in Estonia and Lithuania (Table A7). Latvia's service sector has reduced its employment in absolute terms, though not as much as industry, leading to a moderate increase in relative terms.[139] As a proportion of total employment, the service sector's share has risen above 50 per cent after 1990 in all three Baltic countries, as it has in many medium-income nations including the Czech Republic, Greece, Hungary, Korea, Mexico and Portugal – but not yet in Poland, Romania or the Russian Federation. However, it is still below the 60 to 75 per cent reported for most OECD countries.

The private sector in 1998 accounted for almost 70 per cent of total employment in each country. Nevertheless, the Labour Force Surveys classify relatively few people as *employers* or *self-employed*, other than farmers. Apart from rural self-employment – principally farming – only 5 to 7 per cent of the employed persons in any of the three countries belong to these groups (Table 21). The corresponding proportion in most OECD countries is over 10 per cent.

Table 21. **Employed persons by type of activity, 1998**

	Estonia	Latvia	Lithuania
Employees	91.1	83.0	80.1
Employers	2.7	3.0	3.5
Urban self-employment	2.6	1.7	2.9
Urban unpaid family workers	0.1	0.2	0.3
Rural self-employment	2.7	6.8	9.4
Rural unpaid family workers	0.8	5.2	3.8
Total	100.0	100.0	100.0

Source: Labour Force Surveys, 2nd quarter 1998.

Agriculture – which previously employed about one-fifth of the workforce in the whole region – has contracted to about 10 per cent of employment in Estonia, while apparently declining much less in relative terms in the other two countries. This latter outcome is surprising because the economic conditions for agriculture have undergone largely the same changes in all three countries, including major output reductions and the successive dismantling of industrialised grain and meat production for the Russian market (see Annex I). Many of the workers concerned are currently active on peasant farms or cultivating small family plots, especially in Latvia and Lithuania. But the precise extent of such activity is difficult to assess, given the likely variations in working time and the non-market character of large parts of the output. For some households, farming probably serves mainly as a complementary source of income or as an employment opportunity of last resort.[140]

Labour supply and employment decreased...

Both demographic developments and changing work habits have contributed to a declining labour force. The populations of Estonia and Latvia diminished by 8 per cent from 1989 to 1998 and fell below 1.5 million and 2.5 million, respectively, while Lithuania's population has been stagnant at 3.7 million (Figure 36). Most of the reductions in the two former countries were due to emigration by ethnic Russians, but the natural population increase has also become negative. The working-age populations are set to increase in all three countries in the near future, but they could begin to contract again by about 2010.

Figure 36.   **Population**
1990 = 100

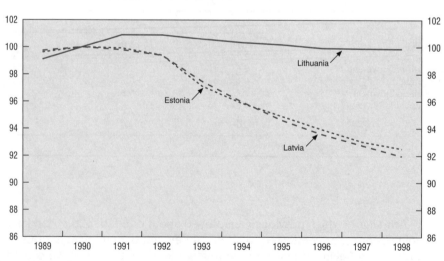

Source: National Statistical offices.

Estonian labour-force data indicate a persistent decline since 1989 in *labour-force participation* and in the numbers of persons *employed* (Table A9).[141] This concerns both men and women and all age groups. The greatest accumulated reductions concerned teenagers and persons aged over 64, whose employment-population ratios declined by almost two-thirds. Strong reductions also affected the age group 50 to 64 in the early 1990s, but here a partial reversal has occurred since the mid-1990s, as the effective age of retirement has begun to increase again (see below).

Data from Latvia and Lithuania do not permit such detailed analysis of the transition period, but the situation in 1998 was strikingly similar (Table 22). The labour-force participation rates for most age and gender groups were then almost identical in all three countries, albeit with a tendency to be lowest in Latvia. But the employment-population ratios for most groups were significantly lower in both Latvia and Lithuania than in Estonia, resulting in correspondingly higher *unemployment* rates, especially for youths. Another difference is that Estonia's employment-population ratio was higher in urban than in rural areas, while the opposite held for all age groups in Latvia and for youths in Lithuania – reflecting, apparently, the greater role of small-scale farming in the two latter countries (Table A10).

Estonia's overall employment-population ratio of 65 per cent corresponded to the OECD average, while at about 60 per cent Latvia and Lithuania were close to the EU average (Table 23). All three figures are low compared with the United States, the United Kingdom and Scandinavia, however. In several respects, employment in the Baltic countries seems to follow a pattern currently found in large parts of Continental Europe, characterised by low work activity among students and in the age group of 50-64 (*Employment Outlook*, 1999, Annex Table B).

The average *educational attainment* of the Baltic populations is relatively high. Individuals with upper-secondary education or more represent 80 to 90 per cent of the respective labour forces, compared with about two-thirds on average in OECD countries (Figure 37). The proportion with tertiary education also exceeds the OECD average in Estonia, but not in the other two countries. As discussed in Box 7, the existing educational provisions may not always be as well adapted as desirable to the present needs. Nevertheless, in all three countries, groups with relatively long education generally perform better in the labour market than those with less education, as shown by higher labour-force participation rates and lower unemployment risk (Table A11).

... but unemployment also went up

Unemployment increased until 1996 when it reached peak levels of over 20 per cent in Latvia, over 15 per cent in Lithuania and over 10 per cent in Estonia, using *labour-force survey* (LFS) definitions. The unemployment rates

Table 22. **Labour force participation, employment and unemployment by gender and age, 1998**

Country, age	Labour force participation Per cent of age-group population			Employment Per cent of age-group population			Unemployment Per cent of the labour force		
	Total	Women	Men	Total	Women	Men	Total	Women	Men
Estonia									
15-24	43	38	49	37	34	41	15	12	17
25-49	88	83	93	79	75	84	10	10	10
50-64	62	55	71	59	53	66	6	4	8
65-	6	4	10	6	4	10	2	3	1
15-64	72	66	78	65	61	70	10	9	11
15-	61	53	70	55	48	62	10	9	10
Latvia									
15-24	37	32	42	26	23	29	30	30	31
25-49	88	84	92	76	73	80	13	13	13
50-64	58	49	70	51	45	60	12	10	14
65-	10	8	15	9	7	14	8	8	8
15-64	70	64	76	60	55	64	15	14	16
15-	59	52	68	51	45	58	15	14	16
Lithuania									
14-24	42	34	48	32	26	37	24	22	26
25-49	92	90	94	80	78	81	14	13	14
50-64	57	47	70	52	43	63	9	9	10
65-	6	4	9	6	4	10	1	–	1
14-64	72	66	78	62	58	66	14	13	15
14-	62	54	70	53	47	60	14	13	15

Note: Small values may not be statistically significant.
Source: Labour Force Surveys, 2nd quarter 1998.

Table 23.   **Labour force participation, employment and unemployment rates:
international comparison, 1998**

Per cent of the population aged 15-64[1]

	Labour force participation rate	Employment-population rate	Unemployment rate
Estonia	72.1	65.1	9.7
Latvia	69.9	59.5	14.9
Lithuania	72.1	61.8	14.2
Czech Republic	72.2	67.5	6.4
France	67.4	59.4	11.9
Germany	70.1	64.1	8.6
Hungary	59.8	55.3	7.6
Italy	57.8	50.8	12.2
Poland	66.1	58.9	10.9
Sweden	78.1	71.5	8.4
United Kingdom	75.9	71.2	6.2
United States	77.4	73.8	4.5
European Union	67.9	61.1	9.9
OECD countries	69.8	65.1	6.8

1.   The data refer to the age group 14-64 in Lithuania and 16-64 in the United Kingdom and the United States.
Source: Estonia, Labour Force Survey, 1998. Latvia, Labour Force Survey, May 1998. Lithuania, Labour Force Survey, May 1998. OECD countries, *Employment Outlook,* 1999.

Figure 37.   **Educational attainment of the labour force[1]**

Per cent of the total

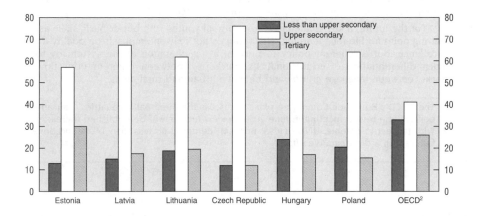

1.   Age 15-74 in Estonia, 15 or more in Latvia, 14 or more in Lithuania, 25-64 in OECD countries.
2.   Unweighted average of Member countries.
Source: Labour Force Surveys, second quarter 1998. For OECD countries, 1996 figures from the Education At a Glance database.

Box 7.   Issues in education policy

As in all transition countries, the change of economic and political systems has called for a variety of adjustments in the area of education. The scope of possible reform remains limited by scarce funding, however, and also by a shortage of some expertise. The financial constraints are most severe in Lithuania, where educational spending as a proportion of GDP has been less than the OECD average of 5 per cent for most of the 1990s, but they also affect Estonia and Latvia where it exceeds 6 per cent (Unicef, 1998).

Judging from preliminary results of OECD reviews of education policy in the Baltic countries,[1] there can be wide discrepancies between the intent of various reforms and their practical application. Several pilot projects have been initiated about educational standards, curriculum and assessments, often with support from the European Union or Nordic countries, but they have not always been followed up on a larger scale in the Baltic countries.

A structural obstacle to change is associated with the existence of many small schools, especially in rural areas, which often lack sufficient resources and experience to adjust to new demands. Teacher training needs to be enhanced, with more emphasis placed on the professional flexibility to adopt new curricula and teaching methods and to assess achievements. Special attention must be paid to linguistic minorities, which may have legitimate claims on instruction in their languages, while there is also an urgent need to enhance their skills in the respective national languages.

Most youths enter some form of upper secondary education, with courses of general academic orientation accounting for over 50 per cent in Estonia and Lithuania and almost 50 per cent in Latvia. But current trends involve a risk of increasing discrepancies in the content and quality of education.[2] Policy makers have recently paid much attention to developing more selective types of academic upper-secondary schools (*gymnasium*), designed as a fast track to university for high-performing youths, while other schools have more often been neglected. Rural vocational schools, for example, tend to be too narrowly specialised, sometimes in skills of questionable labour-market relevance for which they happen to have teachers.

For the future, a key challenge is to equip all youths with better basic skills as a starting point for life-long learning. This requires not only an emphasis on quality and excellence, but a coherent policy to prevent a fragmentation of the system by too much differentiation of educational standards, *e.g.* between different educational tracks, between language groups and between urban and rural areas.

---

1. The OECD's Education Committee plans to discuss the three Baltic countries' education policies at a review meeting in June 2000. Review reports will be published thereafter.
2. With respect to Estonia, UNDP (1998, Box 1.6) identified no less than 14 "educational factors with a disintegrative effect".

---

declined in 1997 and 1998, especially in Latvia. Any increase relating to the Russian crisis is not yet reflected in LFS data. However, an upward trend has been noted in *register-based* unemployment rates, partly reflecting a higher propensity among the most recent job losers to register at the public employment service.[142]

The LFS-based unemployment rates in early 1999 were still almost 15 per cent in Latvia and 13 per cent in Lithuania, which is high by the standards of almost all OECD countries, while the 10 per cent reported in Estonia in 1998 was near the EU average. The incidence of *long-term unemployment* is also high in Latvia and Lithuania by international comparison, but moderate in Estonia (Table 24, Panel A).

Table 24. **Unemployed persons, 1998**

Per cent distribution

	Estonia	Latvia	Lithuania
A. Duration of unemployment			
0-6 months	42	26	31
6-12 months	14	17	32
Over 1 year	43	56	38
Total	100	100	100
B. Reason for unemployment[1]			
Lost a job	59	45	68
Dismissed	45	38	57
End of temporary job	14	7	11
Quit a job	20	19	14
Other	21	36	19
Total	100	100	100

1.   The figures for Latvia exclude persons out of work since over 3 years, representing about 30 per cent of the unemployed.

Source: Labour Force Surveys, 2nd quarter 1998.

Most of the LFS-unemployed are *job losers* rather than new entrants to the labour market (Table 24, Panel B). The highest unemployment rates are nevertheless recorded for youths, a fact that must be considered against the background of their low labour-force participation rates.[143] At the other end of the age scale, the moderate unemployment rates for those aged over 50 may suggest a tendency for the elderly to leave the labour force if work is not available ("discouraged workers").

Foreign ethnic groups are more exposed to unemployment (Table 25). In Estonia, more than in the other countries, the high unemployment among non-nationals appears to owe much to their predominance in non-agricultural manual jobs (53 per cent of the employed non-Estonians compared with 35 per cent for ethnic Estonians).

Table 25. **Unemployment rates by ethnic group, 1998**

Per cent of the labour force

	Estonia	Latvia	Lithuania
Nationals	7	11	13
Non-nationals	14	19	20

Note: For Latvia, November 1997.
Source: Labour Force Surveys, 2nd quarter 1998.

Weak trade unions and decentralised wage-setting...

The predominant form of employment status in the whole region is that of *permanent full-time employee*, having normally a five-day working week of 40 hours. Only 7 to 8 per cent of the dependent employees had part-time work in the second quarter of 1998, while similarly low proportions were classified as temporary or seasonal workers.[144]

Indeed, it is substantially more common to work 50 hours per week or more than to work less than 30 hours. Latvia's workers have the longest average working time, and they also stand out by other measures of "hard-work" habits, *e.g. overtime* and the extent to which it is freely chosen and/or unpaid (Table 26).[145] In most of these respects, Estonia appears to take a second place before Lithuania.

Secondary jobs and various forms of unreported economic activity are also significant. According to the *Working Life Barometer in the Baltic States,* 15 per cent of the workers in Estonia and Lavia had secondary jobs, while the proportion in Lithuania was 8 per cent. The labour force surveys in the three countries report

Table 26. **Working time**

Per cent of interviewed workers

	Working days per week		Working hours per week		Overtime				
	5 or more	6 or 7	40 or more	50 or more	Of any kind	Unpaid	Paid	Voluntary	Involuntary
Estonia	83	23	78	16	34	11	23	7	27
Latvia	85	25	81	22	43	18	25	11	32
Lithuania	86	23	76	12	29	16	13	6	23

Source: Antila and Ylöstalo, 1999. The figures represent replies by workers interviewed in surveys.

substantially lower proportions, probably reflecting the informal nature of many such jobs. The Lithuanian Ministry of Social Security and Labour, while under-lining that information about the "black" or "grey" economy is intrinsically unreli-able, has estimated that it may concern as much as one-fifth of the workforce.[146] The *Working Life Barometer* suggests similar proportions of about one-fifth for the other two countries, but gives a lower figure for Lithuania.[147] In any case, much of the work covered by such estimates is likely to include more underreporting of incomes than of employment. There are indications of a widespread practice by employers to report paying the minimum wage while actually paying more to the workers, presumably to lower their payments of taxes and social security contributions.[148]

As in most transition countries, *trade unions* have a weak position in the emerging private sector: their membership may cover only about 10 per cent of the workforce in private firms in all three Baltic countries (Table 27). Their role is stronger in the public sector, especially in Latvia. Less than one-fifth of all workers are aware of being concerned by collective agreements, according to these surveys, while the actual coverage may be somewhat higher – for instance about 25 per cent in Latvia according to the trade unions.[149] More generally, the surveys suggest that most workers regard wages and other employment conditions as being determined essentially by "individual" rather than "collective" procedures (with or without trade unions).

Table 27. **Industrial relations**

Per cent share of workers concerned by the features mentioned

	Trade union membership			Trade unions in the enterprise	
	Public sector	Private sector	Average	Represented (with or without collective agreement)	Represented and have collective agreements
A. The role of trade unions					
Estonia	20	8	12	22	12
Latvia	42	10	25	33	18
Lithuania	21	11	15	27	18
	Wages	Employment contracts	Vacations	Work safety and health	
B. Collective negotiations[1]					
Estonia	30	23	37	54	
Latvia	28	27	45	53	
Lithuania	52	44	44	64	

1. The percentage of workers who perceive that the cited matters are determined by collective rather than individual negotiation. Excluding "don't know" answers.
Source: Antila and Ylöstalo, 1999. All figures represent replies by workers interviewed in surveys.

The resulting wage systems often include an element of performance or profit-related pay. About one fifth of the workers in each country earn only contract fees, sales commissions etc., while many have various combinations of fixed and performance-related pay, especially in Estonia. A significant minority of workers report delays in receiving their wages (Table A12).[150]

... have increased wage dispersion

The reported average monthly wages in 1998 were between USD 200 to USD 300, with the highest amount in Estonia (Table 28). Allowing for the underreporting noted above, actual wages are probably somewhat higher. The tax deductible from an average wage is about 25 per cent in each country, while the social security contributions are highest in Latvia (37 per cent, of which 9 per cent is paid by the worker, compared with a total rate of 33 per cent in Estonia[151] and 31 per cent in Lithuania).

Table 28. **Average pre-tax wage, 1998**
US dollars per month at current exchange rates

Estonia	**293**
Latvia	**226**
Lithuania	**239**
Bulgaria	107
Romania	153
Slovakia	284
Slovenia	952
Ukraine	68

Source: National authorities and OECD.

Above-average wages are reported mainly in the finance sector, public administration and some other sectors with significant public ownership, especially energy and water and transport and communications (Table A13). By contrast, relatively low wages are frequently reported in agriculture, trade and tourism. However, given the likely extent of underreporting, the actual relative-wage situation may well be different.

The surveys conducted for the *Working Life Barometer* suggest that *new* enterprises in general pay higher wages than those in operation since before the transition (Figure 38). This difference is generally greatest for men, and in Lithuania it only seems to concern men. The gap separating female from male wages appears extraordinarily wide in Estonia's new enterprises, judging from these surveys. There is also some evidence that *foreign-owned* enterprises pay more than domestic ones.[152]

Figure 38. **Average wages after tax by gender and type of enterprise**
US dollars

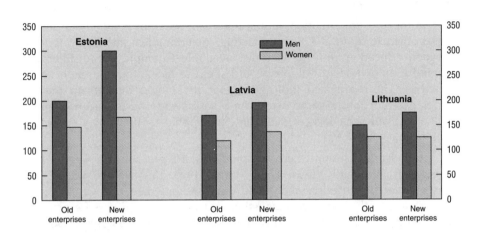

Note: The bars represent median values. "Old" enterprises were in operation before 1988. Some reorganised
enterprises with intermediate wage levels are not represented in the chart.
Source: Antila and Ylöstalo, 1999.

Official statistics are especially unreliable with respect to the relative wages of *public* vs. *private* sectors, the reported public-sector wages being on average over 20 per cent higher in Estonia and 10 to 15 per cent higher in Latvia.[153] But it appears possible to conclude that private-sector wages in general are more unevenly distributed. Both very high and very low wages are likely to be most common in private enterprises, but the difference is probably not as great as official data suggest.[154]

The wage premium attached to *education* has likely increased during the transition, as in other countries, although available data from the Baltic area do not permit detailed analysis in this respect. In Estonia, data from 1995 and 1997 indicate a wage premium of only about 10 per cent for upper secondary compared with lower education, rising sharply to 60 per cent for tertiary compared with upper secondary education (Philips, 1999, p. 50).

Are current labour market conditions favourable to economic growth?

A well-functioning labour market should permit not only full employment, but an efficient allocation of labour. Workers need opportunities and incentives to use their skills to the maximum and to invest in upgrading them when necessary.

Conversely a labour market is too rigid if it does not give sufficient opportunities and incentives to move to better jobs, or if labour shortages constrain the growth of expanding enterprises.

In the present situation, labour shortage does not generally appear as a principal obstacle to growth. Several factors, including high unemployment, relatively good education and the flexibility available to employers to differentiate wages and employment conditions would seem to facilitate recruitment in most occupations. There are also indications that the labour markets in the three countries can function to some extent on a nation-wide basis, and not only in a local context, although lack of sufficient geographic mobility may represent a limiting factor.

At least in Estonia, there is some upward pressure on wages in jobs requiring certain qualifications. Thus, during 1998, the average wages in the country's finance, education and health-care sectors rose by over 5 per cent relative to most other sectors, suggesting that employers in these sectors have found it difficult to recruit qualified workers at existing relative wages (SOE, 1998b, Table A). A similar situation could soon emerge in Latvia and Lithuania as well, given the tendency for economic trends in these countries to follow somewhat after those in Estonia.

A risk of future recruitment difficulties may also face businesses depending on low-cost unskilled labour – especially, perhaps, when the job tasks are not so attractive. In Estonia, again, above-average wage increases were recorded between 1995 and 1997 for unskilled and semiskilled manual workers (machine operators, assemblers and "elementary" occupations), while below-average increases were recorded for craft workers (Philips, 1999, p. 50). This applies mainly for the area around Tallinn.

Such relative-wage trends may reflect a general inadequacy of the prevailing financial incentives for work in the formal sector. However, unemployment benefits and social assistance are unlikely to cause significant incentive problems in the Baltic countries – as they possibly do in some OECD countries – because these benefits are substantially lower than the common wages in most cases (see below). Other factors are probably more important, e.g. an attachment to particular localities and the option to satisfy part of the consumption needs from private land plots. Such factors add to the opportunity cost of accepting jobs, especially when it would require moving house. The following two sub-sections look at the prevailing patterns of regional disparity and labour mobility in such a perspective.

Modest regional variations...

As discussed in the previous chapter, regional disparities are mainly between the largest urban areas and the remaining towns and countryside. Only a few regions with relatively small populations can be said to display labour market problems of an extraordinary nature. Contrary to the experience of other transition countries, the regional differences in survey-based unemployment rates are generally not very great, but average incomes differ. Rural living standards are estimated to be on average 20 to 30 per cent lower than the urban levels, or even more below these levels if only cash spending is counted (Table A14). This shortfall in rural areas depends mainly on lower wages and other work incomes (Table A10), not on lower employment.

However, some rural districts in each country stand out with both relatively high unemployment and below-average wages (Table A15). They are located essentially in south-eastern Estonia, eastern and south-eastern Latvia (Latgale) and some parts of Lithuania (e.g. Alytus, in the South). Latgale's population includes a high proportion of ethnic Russians, while many of its ethnic Latvians are Catholic (contrary to other Latvian regions, which are predominantly Protestant). In spite of their rural nature, all these districts are influenced by employment problems originating in neighbouring towns, which may have pushed many to engage, or to remain engaged, in low-productive forms of farming. Indeed, some of the registered unemployed – who perhaps collect unemployment or related welfare benefits – are probably working at least part-time on private farms.[155] This may explain a tendency for unemployment statistics based on official registers to exaggerate the regional variations compared with the LFS, especially in Latvia. Relatively severe labour-market problems of a more industrial nature are found in Estonia's Ida-Viru district, related to the concentration of employment in the energy sector (Chapter V).

In the future, the largest cities and their diversified labour markets are set to play an increasing role for job seekers throughout the Baltic countries. Daily or weekly commuting is often possible, although it may not be so attractive when the wages are low. Estonia's 1998 LFS reported that 7 per cent of the employed men lived 20 to 50 km from their workplaces, while 4 per cent commuted over 50 km each way. The chances of finding work within such distances are probably better on average for the inhabitants of Lithuania, which has more cities spread across its territory. Although the extent of commuting in Lithuania is not known from statistics, it undoubtedly plays a role in reducing the regional variations in employment opportunities. Furthermore, it is striking that the problematic districts in Estonia and Latvia are all located relatively far from the capitals. Perhaps many of their problems can be alleviated by better means of travel and transport infrastructures.

... with little regional labour mobility

Labour mobility has been relatively low in many transition countries during the 1990s. The Baltic countries are no exception to the rule, although

Estonia's labour force is more mobile than those of Central Europe are by some measures (Eamets, 1998). Internationally, labour mobility has frequently declined during periods of macroeconomic contraction, and expanded during upswings, reflecting its tendency to be driven more by "pull" than "push" effects in the labour market. Thus, in most countries, job separations are more often initiated by the workers than by their employers, and the workers are most likely to quit jobs in periods when there are many vacancies.[156] In the early transition years, many Baltic workers undoubtedly chose to stay where they were in the absence of attractive alternatives.

Information reviewed below suggests three tentative conclusions about the patterns of labour mobility. First, labour turnover (mobility by individuals to and from particular jobs) appears to have increased, although such data are available only for Estonia. Secondly, many of the long-term unemployed seem to represent a stagnant pool of people in all three countries, having too little contact with the labour market. Thirdly, geographic mobility is markedly low in all three countries, apart from commuting.

The Estonian LFS in 1995 indicated a *job-separation* rate as high as 25 to 30 per cent per year, up from 10 to 15 per cent in the early transition period (not counting emigrants). About half of all the separations were job-to-job changes, with a predominance of workers having relatively high education. Most of the other half were accounted for by persons, often with little education, who left the labour force, while a smaller number became unemployed (Eamets, 1998, Table 4). Similarly, most *hires* concerned persons who changed jobs or entered the labour market, while relatively few vacancies were taken by unemployed persons. By OECD standards, mobility has been found quite low both into and out of the state of unemployment (for evidence for Estonia and Latvia, see Lemaitre and Reuterswärd, 1998, Table 1). In other words, while most people did not become unemployed, those who did so were at high risk of staying out of work for a long time. Against this background, the declining incidence of long-term unemployment since 1996 in the three countries is an encouraging sign.

Geographic mobility, leaving aside commuting to work, is low by OECD standards. It concerns less than 2 per cent of the population annually in any Baltic country, if moves over very short distances are excluded (Table A16). Housing markets are essentially liberalised, but their development is constrained by the low purchasing power of most households, and also – at least until recently – by the difficulty of obtaining bank loans using homes as collateral (UNDP, 1996, p. 71, and 1998b, p. 37). In addition to the market-driven housing provisions, municipalities in all three countries provide some low-cost rental accommodation; but access to this is limited and not primarily governed by the objective of promoting labour mobility.

International migration has declined to insignificant levels, as emigration to CIS countries has subsided during the second half of the 1990s. Most notably, there has not been any quantitatively important exchange of migrant workers between the three Baltic countries, nor between these countries and the neighbouring Nordic region or Poland. From a policy perspective, the low internal mobility of the unemployed is more preoccupying. Their job-search activity is apparently neither as regular nor as effective as it ought to be. To some extent, however, insufficient job search can reflect a situation where people do not find available vacancies attractive – a problem likely to subside gradually over the coming years as real wages become more competitive, *e.g.* compared with work in the informal sector or private farms. To promote job search in the formal sector, it may be desirable to improve the capacity for job counselling and placement in the public employment service. Such job-search assistance is provided mainly to registered job seekers, a much smaller group than the LFS-unemployed, and available resources may not always permit adequate assistance even for them.

High social contribution rates, but limited coverage

Social income transfers to households amounted to around 10 per cent of GDP in Estonia and Lithuania and 13 per cent in Latvia in 1997. These proportions are similar to those found in many countries at various income levels – including the Czech Republic, Romania and the United States, for example – but modest compared with the 18 to 20 per cent reported for several EU countries (Table 29). The difference compared with western Europe results both from incomplete coverage of the social insurance and from lower levels of income replacement in several programmes.

Social insurance is compulsory for all employees and the self-employed, and other groups such as mothers taking care of children are also covered. To support the administration of income-related benefits, the three countries have recently taken a number of steps to develop individual records, in principle covering all incomes including secondary jobs. However, only in Estonia do practically all employees and self-employed persons actually seem to be covered at the moment, paying contributions a least for some of their incomes. In Latvia – where reported incomes make most difference for the potential benefits[157] – many employees have incomplete insurance coverage, and as many as 200 000 are not insured because their employers fail to pay contributions, perhaps without informing them.[158] In Lithuania, large numbers of farmers and other self-employed persons do not pay any contributions, and so have only some minimum entitlements (unless they have other jobs or are pensioners). To encourage better compliance, Lithuania's authorities decided in 1995 to permit the self-employed to be insured for an income corresponding to the minimum wage, any additional coverage being optional.[159] Nevertheless, only 2 per cent of the

Table 29. **Public expenditures on social programmes**

Per cent of GDP

Type of programme	Estonia	Latvia	Lithuania	USA	Sweden	Netherlands	Germany	France	Czech Republic	Romania
Pensions	7.1	10.4	7.3	7.2	11.4	11.5	12.0	13.3	7.9	6.5
Child and family allowances	1.7	1.6	0.8	0.3	2.1	1.0	1.3	2.2	2.0	1.4
Child allowances	1.6	1.4	0.4							0.1
Sickness benefits	0.9	0.1	0.9	0.3	1.5	2.2	2.0	0.5	1.2	0.2
Unemployment benefits	0.1	0.4	0.1	0.4	2.3	2.9	2.4	1.8	0.1	1.1
Active labour market programmes	0.1	0.2	0.2	0.2	2.4	1.2	1.4	1.3	0.1	0.1
Social assistance benefits	0.6	0.4	0.2	0.6	2.2	1.0	0.8	1.4	0.4	0.3
Total	**10.4**	**13.1**	**9.6**	**9.0**	**22.0**	**19.7**	**19.8**	**20.6**	**11.8**	**9.5**
of which: Income transfers to households	10.3	12.9	9.3	8.8	19.6	18.5	18.4	19.3	11.6	9.4

Note: Health care, insurances for occupational injury and disease and in-kind services to households are not included.
Data for the Latvia, Lithuania and Romania refer to 1997, with indicated exceptions. Estonia: 1998; the Netherlands: 1996. Other OECD countries: 1995.
Housing benefits, if relevant, are included under social assistance in Estonia and OECD countries.
Source: *Statistical Yearbook of Estonia*, 1998; MOW, 1998; MOSSL, 1998; OECD-SOCX database.

74 000 registered farmers paid contributions regularly during 1998. Two-thirds of registered farmers did not have to make payments to the Social Insurance Fund because they were retired or working under contract.

Between half and three-quarters of spending on social income transfers is devoted to *pensions* (including disability and survivors' pensions). The public pension systems in all three countries are either undergoing reforms or reforms are under active consideration (see Box 8). Most of the reforms are expected to be phased in gradually over relatively long periods, however. In 1998, the average old-age pensions were only about as high as the minimum wage, or barely half of the average after-tax wages (Table 18). As an ultimate floor, the governments guarantee certain minimum pensions – in 1998, USD 39 per month in Estonia, USD 53 in Latvia and USD 34.5 in Lithuania, or lower than any conceivable poverty line (see above).[160] Significant numbers of pensioners receive only these minimum amounts.

In addition to pensions and unemployment benefits (see below), the social insurance programmes in the Baltic area – as in most OECD countries – cover *sickness, child birth* and some further contingencies. Spending on sickness pay is relatively low in Latvia, reflecting an obligation on employers to pay wages during up to two weeks of sickness – a solution also under consideration in Estonia. Only Latvia of the three countries has a public insurance for *occupational accidents and diseases*, a type of contingency for which individual employers may be made responsible in the other two countries.

Existing provisions for *family support*, paid from general revenue, include a monthly *child allowance* of about $15-25 per child, with lower amounts for small families. This is paid until completion of secondary school in Estonia and Latvia, but only up to the age of three in Lithuania, where the allowances beyond this age are reserved for families with three or more children. On the other hand, Lithuania offers relatively generous support in connection with childbirth, when the mother or the father can receive 60 per cent of the lost income or the minimum wage during a year. The Latvian authorities, concerned about the low birth rate, decided in 1998 to more than double a childcare allowance paid for children under 18 months, henceforth amounting to USD 36 per month.

Social assistance of last resort is means-tested and falls under the responsibility of municipalities. National regulations specify certain minimum incomes which households must be guaranteed – generally in the range USD 30-35 per month for one adult in 1999.[161] Estonia integrated this assistance with housing allowance in 1997. But in Latvia, many municipalities seem to prefer covering specific costs, such as heating, housing or lunches, rather than paying the guaranteed minimum in cash (MOW, 1998, Table 6.8). In Lithuania low-income families receive additional support to cover heating and water.

Box 8.   Reform of pension systems

The standard pension age was only 55 years for women and 60 for men in the Soviet Union, and several groups with hard working conditions could retire even earlier. But the combination of demographic pressures and falling employment has rendered the inherited pension systems increasingly expensive in the Baltic States. By the mid-1990s, when the need for a change was widely recognised, the dependency ratio (the number of pensioners relative to the working population) was over 50 per cent in Estonia and Lithuania and over 85 per cent in Latvia. The average pensions paid out in 1998 were barely sufficient for a minimum basket of consumer goods. Nevertheless, the ratios of income replacement (average pensions as a proportion of gross average wages) were comparable to the levels existing in some OECD countries,[1] or in 1998 over 38 per cent in Latvia, about 30 per cent in Estonia and Lithuania. Compared to after-tax wages the net replacement rates were respectively 52 and 40 per cent. Reforms now underway include different combinations of statutory pension-age increases and systemic changes, many of which are aimed to create incentives to work longer.

The statutory or minimum pension ages have not been raised by more than a few years until now, but further increases are scheduled over the coming years.[2] This will also reduce the difference in pension ages for women and men and limit the number of occupational groups with especially favourable pension regimes.[3] However, as in many European countries, a generous awarding of *disability* pensions can have the opposite effect. In Estonia, about 40 per cent of those retiring in 1997 were classified as disabled. This may reflect an increase in the retirement age.

Practically all public pensions paid out in 1999 are part of unfunded programmes of the pay-as-you-go type. But these programmes will henceforth only form the "first pillar" of the pension systems, with complementary second and third "pillars" consisting, respectively, of compulsory and voluntary pension-fund savings. Among various options discussed for reforming the pay-as-you-go "first pillars", Latvia decided in 1995 to adopt one of the more radical solutions, based on the Swedish example, known as the "notional defined-contribution" model.[4] It permits all pensions above a guaranteed minimum to take full account of individual contributions paid during a lifetime (even after retirement). Compared with the more redistributive systems used elsewhere, this creates a stronger incentive to work as long as possible, and it should also make it more attractive for individuals to report incomes to the social-insurance authorities.

By definition, however, "notional defined-contribution" pensions require much more public spending than can be justified by the need to reduce poverty – a potentially undesirable implication, not least in transition countries. In Estonia, the government in 1997 analysed the option of establishing a first pillar on a similar basis. But a new State Pension Insurance Act, adopted in 1998 for implementation in 2000, establishes a pension formula comprising three components: flat rate, years of service and contribution-related, of which the last element will be more limited than in Latvia. Lithuania's government, by contrast, has presented a draft law based on a reformed defined-benefit model, with "first-pillar" pensions calculated to cover 40 per cent of the previous wages in typical cases.[5]

(*continued on next page*)

(continued)

As a "second pillar", all three governments plan to begin implementing mandatory programmes for individual saving in pension funds during 2000 or 2001. Lithuania's government has proposed as a target that the second-pillar pensions should cover 20 per cent of the previous incomes after a normal working life. The government in Latvia envisage introducing the corresponding systems on a small scale initially, with a possibility to devote gradually higher proportions of the social security contributions to second-pillar pension funds in the coming years. In Estonia the government's position in mid-1999 is that the second pillar should be about one-third of the current 20 per cent social tax. This reform will be taken as a single step.

Regulatory frameworks for a "third pillar" of voluntary pension-fund saving are already in place in Estonia and Latvia, and will be in force in Lithuania from 2000. Such private saving is insignificant at the moment, but policy makers believe it can develop in the future as a complement to public pensions and as a potential stimulus for the capital markets.

1. The source for replacement rates is Table 18 and OECD(1998c).
2. *Estonia* plans to raise the pension age by six months annually until it reaches 63 years, which would happen in 2001 for men and in 2016 for women. *Latvia* has until now increased its minimum pension age only for women, also by six months annually. But from 2000 a gradual increase up to 62 years by 2006 has been scheduled for both genders. However, following public criticism of the increases implemented so far, an option has been preserved for women to retire at age 55 with a reduction of their minimum pension by 20 per cent. *Lithuania* has increased its pension age annually by 2 months for men and by 4 months for women since 1995, and plans to continue this process until 2009 when the pension age would be 60 years for women and 62.5 years for men.
3. Nevertheless, in Latvia, the *actual* pension age has increased more for men than for women, reaching on average 64 years in 1997 if disability pensions are excluded (MOW, 1998).
4. Latvian workers and employers pay pension contributions to the state, as in all pay-as-you-go systems, but these payments are "notionally" attributed to individual accounts as a pension capital, which is indexed to average earnings. When an individual retires, the pension is calculated as an annuity depending only on the accumulated capital and the expected remaining lifetime. A certain minimum amount is guaranteed, as in the previous system, while the previous standard retirement age has been replaced by a *minimum* retirement age (60).
5. By definition, however, a defined-contribution scheme cannot be designed to reach such a pension target with any certainty. The returns to invested funds will vary over time and between different alternatives allowed for their investment.

Labour market policies need to support economic restructuring

Economic policies in the Baltics have in general been business-friendly, but various institutional obstacles have continued until now to cause delays in the restructuring at enterprise level. As in all formerly planned economies, the administrative and political constraints facing enterprises planning to dismiss workers were mostly related to state ownership. By now, however, a majority of enterprises have been privatised, their administration has been reformed, and most of the employment guarantees which the new owners may have been required to sign – frequently lasting three years after privatisation – have expired. Companies will need to take many difficult restructuring decisions over the coming years, often involving a need to dismiss workers. In this context, policy makers will need to consider, on the one hand, if enterprises have sufficient possibilities and incentives to take the necessary steps quickly, and, on the other hand, to what extent the risk of lay-offs may justify some improvements of the relevant social protection programmes. Such improvements would involve a budgetary cost that would depend on the rate of employment creation elsewhere in the economy, notably in small and medium-sized enterprises (see Chapter VII). However, this may be preferable if the alternative is to persuade enterprises to slow down their necessary modernisation.

The legislation governing termination of employment contracts, largely similar in the three countries, generally permits employers to dismiss redundant workers on condition that certain procedures are followed. Lithuanian authorities (municipalities) have a formal possibility to stop dismissals, but this provision has practically never been used, and the government is considering a proposal to abolish it. In all three countries, employers can generally select the workers they want to dismiss on the basis of productivity, although they must also take account of social factors such as family size. The employers must pay severance benefits corresponding to one month's pay in Latvia, 2-4 months' pay in Estonia and up to six months' pay in Lithuania.

However, only Latvia of the three countries has an unemployment-insurance programme that can be compared with such programmes in OECD or central European countries. The corresponding provisions in Estonia and Lithuania are minimal, with benefits below any of the poverty levels discussed above, which can be paid for up to six months compared with nine months in Latvia.

Estonia's unemployment benefits are particularly parsimonious, paid at a flat rate of only USD 28 per month in 1999, or about 10 per cent of the average wage; the equivalent benefits in Lithuania range from about USD 34 to USD 63 (13 to 23 per cent of the average wage).[162] Designed in part to encourage working in Lithuania's formal sector, this programme pays benefits only to persons having worked and paid contributions for two years, and the benefit amounts depend on the duration of such previous employment but not on the wages (MOSSL, 1998, p. 40). Latvia's unemployment insurance, by contrast, offers to replace 50 to 65 per cent of the previous income during the first three months of unemployment, depending on the duration of the previous employment, with a benefit ceiling at five times the minimum wage. The benefits are subsequently reduced in two steps, amounting to four-fifths and later to three-fifths of the initial amount until the maximum nine months of benefits have been paid.

Only a minority of the LFS-unemployed in any of the three countries receive unemployment benefits.[163] This is largely a result of the high long-term unemployment and the limited duration of the benefits: a high proportion of the unemployed are not eligible for any benefits, except, possibly, the means-tested social assistance (see above). But other factors may also contribute to a low number of individual benefit claims, including administrative procedures[164] and the fact that some people may find the benefits too low to make it worthwhile to travel to an employment office.

The *public employment service* agencies have offices in all parts of the three countries, with staff numbers ranging from a few hundred in Estonia to 600 in Latvia and 1 300 in Lithuania.[165] But many of the LFS-unemployed are not registered, as noted already, and it is questionable whether the offices would have the capacity to serve them all or to check that they were actively seeking jobs, assuming that they were all to come to the offices. Many clients can benefit from self-service facilities, however – especially in Lithuania, which features a nationwide system for computerised job search based on transparent vacancy information, as well as a computerised self-service system for information on education and vocational training. More intensive job-search assistance is provided in *job clubs*, also most developed in Lithuania, where they enrolled over 25 000 unemployed persons during 1998, compared with 7 700 in Latvia (of whom 2 200 were reported to find jobs). *Private* employment agencies are allowed as well and appear to play a significant role in Estonia and Latvia. In Lithuania, private employment agencies mainly help high-skilled employees to find appropriate jobs, and so affect a relatively low proportion of the working population.

In response to the Russian crisis in the summer 1998, Lithuania's public employment service introduced a series of targeted measures, which apparently have been effective in encouraging redundant workers to seek new jobs already before becoming unemployed. About 2 000 of these employees were enrolled in job clubs, while many were temporarily engaged in public works (LLE, 1998).

Active labour-market programmes such as training and subsidised work play a significant role in Lithuania and Latvia, but less so in Estonia. Lithuania's employment offices try as a rule to offer every newly registered unemployed person a job or a place in programme within 12 months, or within six months in the case of youth. This implicit "job guarantee" seems to have made it difficult – in Lithuania as in several OECD countries – to prevent a perhaps too-heavy reliance on public works as a substitute for market-sector jobs.[166] Such works in Lithuania employed 21 000 individuals for on average two months in 1998, while 16 600 unemployed persons were sent to training.[167] In Latvia, over 16 000 unemployed persons were sent to training while a smaller number were engaged in public works. The corresponding measures in Estonia include a small training programme and a cash allowance for enterprise start-ups.

Altogether, Lithuania's public employment service reportedly helped about 5 per cent of the country's labour force to find ordinary jobs during 1998, while placing 71 000 persons or 4 per cent of the labour force in active programmes. In Latvia in the same year, 3 per cent of the labour force found ordinary jobs with the help of the employment service, while about 1 per cent were admitted to active programmes.

As a general principle, employment offices should give the highest priority to ordinary job search, not to administering temporary measures like public works. Regarding training, OECD experience suggests that courses for the unemployed can be effective on a moderate scale if they address well-defined labour-market requirements, while large-scale training needs may be better addressed in a country's general education system. Above all, OECD reviews of the public employment service in various countries underline the importance of regular counselling and support of the benefit recipients' own efforts to seek jobs. Official systems for providing information about job vacancies can be helpful; at least as important, however, is to encourage the unemployed to seek jobs for themselves using all available information channels including personal contacts, newspapers, private employment agencies and the Internet.

Finally, some increase in the levels of unemployment benefits appears justified in Estonia and Lithuania as a complement to a strong policy commitment to accept lay-offs as a necessary part of the modernisation of the economy. In a longer perspective – depending on economic growth in coming years – it will also be desirable to implement a gradual increase in minimum pensions, child benefits and social assistance benefits up to the levels that would prevent poverty in most households.

VII. Integration in the world economy and regional co-operation

Trade liberalisation has led sectoral adjustment

An early reform was the adoption of liberal trade regimes and the opening of membership negotiations with WTO.[168] Significant reorientation of Baltic trade has taken place during a decade of transition. The proportion of trade with western countries is somewhat below the levels prevailing in central Europe, but given the starting point the change is remarkable. Notwithstanding, the increasing trade gap emerging in the Baltic countries (discussed in Chapter I) raises the issue of their ability to sustain necessarily high rates of export growth.

A revealing way to look at this problem is through a more detailed decomposition of the trade balances. An analysis of revealed comparative advantages (RCA)[169] shows that important strides in the production and trade of new output, compared with the inherited output structure, has been achieved only in Estonia (Table 30). This is very likely related to FDI in the field of transmission apparatus and accessories for radio-broadcasting and telecommunications, whose cumulative share in exports was up to about 12 per cent in 1998 from about zero in 1994. In both Latvia and Lithuania important changes in RCAs are found in commodities related to their natural and human resource endowments, such as forestry in the case wood working and female skilled labour in the case of garments. Therefore, despite the attempt at heavy industrialisation during the Soviet period, the pre-war patterns of trade specialisation have re-emerged. This is a striking example of the law of comparative advantage at work. In some cases, the Baltic countries have reverted to pre-war export composition. Technologically advanced output is still rare. While these developments suggest that a restructuring through market-re-orientation is indeed taking place, they also reveal a serious exposure to business cycles and, with the likely increase in real wages, a possible progressive loss of competitiveness *vis-à-vis* Asian countries.

Changes in trade specialisation have induced structural adjustment, which can be seen through the sectoral shifts in employment and enterprise creation and destruction. In Tables 31*a-c*, sectors are ranked by intensity of respectively net employment creation and destruction. It is notable that the more

Table 30. Comparison of trade structure

SITC code	Main comparative advantages	RCA 1994	RCA 1998	Export share 1998	Cumulative share of exports 1998	SITC code	Main comparative disadvantages	RCA 1994	RCA 1998	Import share 1998	Cumulative share of imports 1998
Estonia						**Estonia**					
24	Cork and wood	6.8	8.6	9.2	9.2	77	Electrical machinery, apparatus and appliances, NES	-2.9	-6.4	9.6	9.6
76	Telecommunication and sound reproducing apparatus	-2.1	6.2	12.2	21.3	78	Road vehicles (including air-cushion vehicles)	-0.9	-4.1	8.2	17.8
84	Articles of apparel and clothing accessories	5.4	4.1	6.5	27.8	74	General industrial machinery and equipment, NES	-2.0	-2.2	3.5	21.4
82	Furniture and parts; bedding and similar stuffed furniture	2.3	2.6	3.6	31.5	67	Iron and steel	-0.9	-2.1	4.5	25.9
63	Cork and wood manufactures	2.0	2.4	3.5	34.9	33	Petroleum, petroleum products and related material	-5.9	-2.0	4.5	30.4
03	Fish, crustaceans, molluscs, aquatic invertebrates	6.6	2.1	3.1	38.1	72	Machinery specialised for particular industries	-2.0	-1.9	3.3	33.6
28	Metalliferous ores and metal scrap	1.8	1.8	2.8	40.9	75	Office machines and automatic data processing mach.	-1.7	-1.5	2.4	36.1
Latvia						**Latvia**					
24	Cork and wood	16.2	26.0	26.4	26.4	78	Road vehicles incl. air cushion vehicles	0.2	-7.8	8.9	8.9
63	Cork and wood manufactures, excluding furniture	3.7	6.7	7.1	33.5	33	Petroleum, petroleum products and related materials	-17.7	-4.7	5.9	14.8
84	Articles of apparel and clothing accessories	2.9	6.5	9.5	43.0	72	Machinery specialised for particular industries	-2.9	-3.5	4.3	19.1
65	Textile yarn, fabrics, made-up art., related products	5.1	3.7	7.6	50.6	34	Gas, natural and manufactured	-6.9	-3.4	3.4	22.5
82	Furniture and parts thereof	2.6	2.9	4.0	54.6	76	Telecommunications, sound recording apparatus	-0.7	-3.3	3.9	26.3
67	Iron and steel	5.0	1.7	5.7	60.2	75	Office machines, automatic data-processing equip.	-1.9	-2.5	3.2	29.5
03	Fish, crustaceans, molluscs, preparations thereof	4.5	1.7	2.5	62.8	74	General industrial machinery and equipment and parts	-0.7	-2.4	4.0	33.5
Lithuania						**Lithuania**					
84	Articles of apparel and clothing accessories	4.3	9.9	11.4	11.4	78	Road vehicles (including air-cushion vehicles)	-2.1	-4.2	11.0	11.0
56	Fertilisers	3.9	4.4	4.9	16.3	72	Machinery specialised for particular industries	-3.9	-2.9	3.7	14.7
33	Petroleum, petroleum products and related materials	-7.1	3.7	14.6	30.9	34	Gas, natural and manufactured	-5.5	-2.6	3.0	17.7
35	Electric current	-0.5	2.9	3.2	34.1	74	General industrial machinery and equipment, NES	-1.2	-2.4	3.9	21.6
24	Cork and wood	2.5	2.7	3.2	37.3	67	Iron and steel	-1.1	-2.0	2.9	24.5
82	Furniture and parts; bedding and similar stuffed furniture	1.2	1.5	2.1	39.4	76	Telecommunications and sound reproducing apparatus	-1.9	-1.7	3.1	27.6
28	Metalliferous ores and metal scrap	1.6	1.2	1.5	40.9	54	Medicinal and pharmaceutical products	-1.5	-1.6	3.1	30.7

Note: RCA = Revealed Comparative Advantage Indicators (see text).
Source: National Statistical Offices and OECD.

Table 31a. **Estonia: net job creation and destruction by enterprise size, 1994-97**

NACE	Sector	Change in number of employees						Change in number of enterprises				
		Total	Total growth rate in %	0-9 employees	10-49 employees	50-249 employees	Over 250 employees	Total	0-9 employees	10-49 employees	50-249 employees	Over 250 employees
Sectors with highest net employment destruction												
17	Manufacture of textiles	-3 941	-31.1	-151	537	-497	-3 830	7	11	-2	-1	-1
29	Manufacture of machinery and equipment	-2 890	-35.1	14	-22	-701	-2 181	-39	-20	-7	-8	-4
40	Energy supply	-2 713	-19.7	419	1 878	896	-5 906	200	86	98	13	3
15	Manufacture of food products, beverages	-2 387	-8.5	126	1 493	1 825	-5 831	109	68	36	12	-7
26	Manufacture of other non-metallic mineral products	-2 059	-29.2	325	-521	-687	-1 176	-12	2	-6	-6	-2
19	Tanning and dressing of leather and manufacture of footwear	-1 700	-38.0	68	-432	120	-1 456	-33	-24	-6	0	-3
31	Manufacture of electrical machinery and apparatus	-1 128	-25.0	20	-135	400	-1 413	-32	-33	-1	3	-1
24	Manufacture of chemicals and chemical products	-982	-12.7	-40	47	94	-1 083	2	2	2	1	-3
34	Manufacture of motor vehicles	-791	-30.4	-57	243	-311	-666	-7	-7	2	-2	0
30	Manufacture of office machinery and computers	-379	-74.2	0	-81	82	-380	-7	4	-7	-3	-1
35	Manufacture of other transport equipment	-365	-10.5	-12	63	-524	108	-53	-54	1	0	0
33	Manufacture of medical, precision and optical instruments, watches and clocks	-291	-10.1	-69	-65	485	-642	18	14	1	4	-1
16	Manufacture of tobacco products	-270	..	0	0	0	-270	-1	0	0	0	-1
27	Manufacture of basic metals	-106	-28.0	21	49	-176	0	5	4	1	0	0
37	Recycling	-68	-36.6	0	-66	-2	0	0	1	0	-1	0
23	Manufacture of coke, refined petroleum products	-29	-17.4	0	42	-71	0	1	2	0	-1	0
	Subtotal	-20 099	-20.8	664	3 030	933	-24 726	158	56	112	11	-21
Sectors with highest net employment creation												
20	Manufacture of wood	3 865	37.0	705	441	4 093	-1 374	156	111	22	26	-3
28	Manufacture of fabricated metal products	1 625	27.2	300	874	921	-470	133	106	18	10	-1
32	Manufacture of radio, television and communication equipment and apparatus	1 432	106.5	15	807	71	539	79	69	10	0	0
18	Manufacture of wearing apparel	1 288	10.1	-132	1 598	1 101	-1 279	70	60	6	7	-3
22	publishing, printing and reproduction of recorded media	1 131	24.8	248	756	-1	128	116	122	0	-6	0
36	Manufacture of furniture and other manufactured goods	707	6.1	556	1 314	1 953	-3 116	124	75	35	19	-5
25	Manufacture of rubber and plastic products	637	41.3	94	528	15	0	16	3	13	1	-1
21	Manufacture of paper and paper products	523	63.3	28	-111	53	553	7	3	1	2	1
10 + 14	Mining of coal and lignite and other	312	3	43	195	180	-106	2	4	0	-1	-1
	Subtotal	11 520	20	1 857	6 402	8 386	-5 125	703	553	105	58	-13
Memorandum items:												
	Total variation 1994-97	-8 579	-5.5	2 521	9 432	9 319	-29 851	866	607	224	70	-35
	Levels in 1994	156 057		6 011	20 986	36 042	93 018	4 448	2 830	1 122	380	116

Source: Annual Industry Survey, Statistical Office of Estonia and OECD.

Table 31b. **Latvia: net job creation and destruction by enterprise size, 1995-98**

NACE	Total	Change in number of employees				Change in number of enterprises			
		Total growth rate in %	0-49 employees	50-249 employees	Over 250 employees	Total	0-9 employees	50-249 employees	Over 250 employees
Sectors with highest net employment destruction									
32 Manufacture of radio, television and communication equipment and apparatus	-5 646	-69.7	48	-113	-5 581	12	18	-2	-4
29 Manufacture of machinery and equipment	-4 657	-37.2	-310	-453	-3 894	-8	4	-8	-4
17 Manufacture of textiles	-3 792	-27.0	-406	-503	-2 883	13	18	-5	0
35 Manufacture of other transport equipment	-3 712	-33.3	400	-229	-3 883	33	36	-1	-2
36 Manufacture of furniture; manufacturing n.e.c.	-2 740	-31.2	307	-954	-2 093	52	61	-8	-1
26 Manufacture of other non-metallic mineral products	-2 543	-39.3	13	-1 462	-1 094	63	74	-10	-1
34 Manufacture of motor vehicles, trailers and semi-trailers	-2 525	-78.7	-47	321	-2 799	-3	-3	1	-1
31 Manufacture of electrical machinery and apparatus n.e.c.	-2 445	-39.9	54	-77	-2 422	25	26	0	-1
24 Manufacture of chemicals and chemical products	-2 435	-27.6	23	-555	-1 903	49	51	-1	-1
19 Tanning and dressing of leather; manufacture of luggage, handbags, saddler, harness and footwear	-2 288	-50.8	15	-204	-2 099	19	27	-3	-5
21 Manufacture of pulp, paper and paper products	-462	-25.5	66	407	-935	29	25	6	-2
10 Mining of coal and lignite; extraction of peat	-315	-22.9	21	-28	-308	11	9	3	-1
41 Collection, purification and distribution of water	-69	-7.3	51	-43	-77	10	10	0	0
14 Other mining and quarrying	-48	-10.6	-14	-34	0	-1	-1	0	0
16 Manufacture of tobacco products	-42	-12.4	12	0	-54	1	1		0
23 Manufacture of coke, refined petroleum products and nuclear fuel	-19	-18.1	-16	-3	0	2	2		0
Subtotal	-33 738	-38.0	217	-3 930	-30 025	307	358	-28	-23
Sectors with highest net employment creation									
20 Manufacture of wood and wood products	7 932	50	2 045	3 515	2 372	355	313	39	3
18 Manufacture of wearing apparel; dressing and dyeing of fur	3 660	38	1 024	488	2 148	101	91	3	7
22 Publishing, printing and reproduction of recorded media	1 444	21	762	335	347	249	245	4	0
28 Manufacture of fabricated metal products	1 087	24	762	266	59	70	64	6	0
40 Electricity, gas, steam and water supply	759	4	432	320	7	29	24	6	-1
15 Manufacture of food products and beverages	134	0	2 950	1 045	-3 861	198	194	16	-12
27 Manufacture of basic metals	93	4	14	25	54	4	4	0	0
30 Manufacture of office machinery and computers	78	107	-29	107	0	7	6	1	0
25 Manufacture of rubber and plastic products	26	1	516	-490	0	10	13	-3	0
33 Manufacture of medical, precision and optical instruments, watches and clocks	24	3	131	-107	0	37	39	-2	
37 Recycling	19	4	147	-128	0	8	9	-1	
Subtotal	15 256	16	8 754	5 376	1 126	1 068	1 002	69	-3
Memorandum items:									
Total variation 1995-98	-18 482	-10	8 971	1 446	-28 899	1 375	1 360	41	-26
Levels in 1995	185 821		27 803	51 737	106 281	3 171	2 554	476	141

Source: Statistical Office of Latvia and OECD.

Table 31c. **Lithuania: net job creation and destruction by enterprise size, 1995-97**

NACE		Change in number of employees						Change in number of enterprises				
		Total	Total growth rate in %	0-9 employees	10-49 employees	50-249 employees	Over 250 employees	Total	0-9 employees	10-49 employees	50-249 employees	Over 250 employees
Sectors with highest net employment destruction												
29	Manufacture of machinery and equipment	-6 014	-27	27	-257	-519	-5 265	-4	8	-9	1	-4
17	Manufacture of textiles	-5 807	-19	24	180	797	-6 808	14	5	11	5	-1
32	Manufacture of radio, television and communication equipments and apparatus	-4 263	-31	10	49	2	-4 324	3	3	3	0	
26	Manufacture of other non-metallic mineral products	-3 455	-23	19	45	-159	-3 360	1	8	4	-4	-7
19	Tanning and dressing of leather and manufacture of footwear	-1 758	-25	0	29	152	-1 939	4	-1	1	3	-3
34	Manufacture of motor vehicles	-1 002	-42	1	3	14	-1 020	-1	-1	2	0	-7
15	Manufacture of food products, beverages	-885	-2	-34	724	-297	-1 278	42	0	31	11	-1
28	Manufacture of fabricated metal products	-841	-12	-22	297	-251	-865	17	2	16	1	0
21	Manufacture of paper and paper products	-830	-18	-4	5	-50	-781	3	-3	2	1	0
31	Manufacture of electrical machinery and apparatus	-736	-11	-29	8	-30	-685	1	3	3	1	-2
30	Manufacture of office machinery and computers	-545	-36	24	-12	161	-718	3	3	0	-1	0
24	Manufacture of chemicals and chemical products	-435	-5	14	237	-226	-460	13	4	10	4	0
14	Other mining	-351	-22	-8	40	-5	-378	-1	-1	2	-1	-1
35	Manufacture of other transport equipment	-219	-3	4	-20	277	-480	8	3	2	4	-1
36	Manufacture of furniture and other manufactured goods	-173	-2	22	643	-136	-702	38	4	30	3	1
37	Recycling	-113	-24	-3	-32	-78	0	-2	-1	-1	0	0
11	Extraction of crude petroleum	-69	-16	0	48	0	-117	-1	0	3	0	0
27	Manufacture of basic metals	-64	-4	-3	68	-71	-58	2	0	1	-1	0
33	Manufacture of medical, precision and optical instruments, watches and clocks	-33	-1	9	-257	-199	414	-15	-2	-14	0	1
	Subtotal	-27 593	-16	51	1 798	-618	-28 824	131	33	97	26	-25
Sectors with highest net employment creation												
18	Manufacture of wearing apparel	2 960	14	62	598	1 115	1 185	44	9	21	21	-7
20	Manufacture of wood	945	7	-26	813	1 363	-1 205	40	-10	38	15	-3
23	Manufacture of coke, refined petroleum products	417	13	0	-27	53	391	0	0	-1	8	-7
10	Mining of coal and lignite	267	23	-8	0	-65	340	0	-1	0	2	-1
22	Publishing, printing and reproduction of recorded media	239	4	64	-74	183	66	17	17	-4	4	0
25	Manufacture of rubber and plastic products	192	6	24	537	11	-380	25	4	22	-1	0
16	Manufacture of tobacco products	82	27	0	0	0	82	0	0	0	2	-2
	Subtotal	5 102	10	116	1 847	2 660	479	126	19	76	51	-20
Memorandum items:												
	Total variation 1995-97	-25 519	-11	157	3 146	161	-28 983	266	52	173	56	-24
	Levels in 1995	3 353		20 206	57 128	159 612	240 299	666	864	490	221	2 232

Note: The information of number of enterprises and employees is prepared only on data received. Data on the number of enterprises and employees represents enterprises, joint-stock and stock companies; sole proprietorships and auxiliary production of non-industrial enterprises excluded.
Source: Statistical office of Lithuania and OECD.

capital and skill-intensive sectors shed most employment during the period 1994-97, whereas jobs were created mainly in low value-added traditional industries, such as wood, wearing apparel, furniture and paper. In Latvia, most of the high technology sectors were largely related to former Soviet military industries, and have decreased employment significantly. The main exception to this reinforcement of traditional industries is in Estonia, which created jobs in radio and communications equipment. Estonia and Latvia also created jobs in the manufacture of metal products, a specialisation in line with strong endowments in technically skilled labour in the engineering industries under the Soviet system, as discussed in Chapter VI.

Job destruction has been concentrated in large enterprises in heavy industries whereas the slack has been taken up by small and medium-size enterprises in light industries. However, the speed of this inter-sectoral adjustment differs across countries. In the 1994-97 period, Estonia replaced around 60 per cent of the jobs lost within the manufacturing sector; the equivalent figure for Latvia is 45 per cent (1995-98) and 18 per cent for Lithuania (1995-97). This illustrates the pivotal role of small and medium-size enterprises in structural adjustment during the transition. This relies on a favourable climate for enterprise creation and an appropriate mechanism to enforce bankruptcy where this is warranted.

The benefits of this significant structural adjustment taking place during transition are reflected in the increase in labour productivity. For example, textile manufacturers shed large numbers of employees but those which survived through this process display amongst the highest rates of productivity growth (see Statistical Annex, Tables A23-25). Overall, trade liberalisation turned out to be a necessary but not sufficient condition for economic and enterprise restructuring. In order to accommodate the trade "shock" other structural reforms have to be in place. In other words, policies are interdependent; any single policy cannot be effective on its own, but relies on links with policies in other areas. Where this is not the case, the labour market is left to absorb the adjustment on its own. Policy interventions may mitigate the effect on the labour market, but this cannot be sustained over the long run.

Economic integration of the Baltic countries

The Baltic countries started from a position where almost all their trade was with the former Soviet Union and socialist countries. Economic integration of the Baltic countries has subsequently developed in three main regional dimensions. Firstly, within the Baltic countries themselves; secondly, with other countries in the Baltic Sea region (Nordic countries); and finally with the European Union. Economic and trade integration at these three different levels is supported by developments in policies and institutions (see Box 9).

Box 9.   Institution of political co-operation between Baltic countries

The Baltic Assembly, the Baltic Council and the Council of Ministers of the Baltic States are the main bodies of political and economic co-operation which evolved after the restoration of independence.

The *Baltic Assembly* was founded on 8 November 1991 and its Secretariat is based in Riga. The Regulations of the Baltic Assembly stipulate that the Baltic Assembly is a consulting and co-ordinating institution founded as a body for co-operation between the parliaments of Lithuania, Latvia and Estonia, to deliberate on general issues and projects. The Regulations of the Baltic Assembly do not specify any spheres or boundaries for possible parliamentary consultations. This gives the Baltic Assembly the right to voice its opinion on all the issues of political and economic activities of the three Baltic States. The Baltic Assembly is comprised of sixty parliamentarians of the Baltic States - twenty parliamentarians from each country. The Baltic Assembly maintains relations with international and regional organisations, notably the Nordic Council, and is of particular importance for regional integration.

In 1993, the Baltic Assembly proposed to create a permanent organisation for international co-operation – the *Baltic Council*, which would act through the Baltic Assembly and the *Council of Ministers of the Baltic States*. The Agreement was signed and the Regulations of the Baltic Council of Ministers were approved on 13 June 1994. At present, the Baltic Council of Ministers carries our intergovernmental and regional co-operation between the three Baltic states through its institutions: the secretariat of the Baltic Council of Ministers, committees, committees of high-ranking officials and co-operation of ministers. Joint sessions of the Baltic Assembly and the Baltic Council of Ministers organised by the Baltic Council are held annually.

Intra-Baltic trade integration has been limited. However, trade reorientation towards European markets took place relatively quickly (see Table 32). In 1998, between 45 and 60 per cent of Baltic trade is with the EU, though weighted towards different EU members by the three Baltic States. In Estonia, trade with the EU is concentrated in the Nordic countries. In Latvia the focus is both on Germany and the Nordic countries, while in Lithuania mainly Germany.

Intra-Baltic trade has not yet responded to far-reaching liberalisation

A Baltic Free-Trade Agreement (BAFTA) for industrial products was agreed between the Baltic Countries at Tallinn in March 1992. The agreement came into force on 1 April 1994. The BAFTA established the principle of free trade in industrial products. Parties abolished substantially all customs duties and other restrictive charges, as well as quantitative restrictions, although some export duties on particular products were maintained for an initial period.[170] The latter

---

Table 32. **Trade structure by partner country**

Per cent of total

	Estonia				Latvia				Lithuania			
	1995	1998	1998 I-VII	1999 I-VII	1995	1998	1998 I-VII	1999 I-VII	1995	1998	1998 I-VII	1999 I-VII
Exports												
World	100	100	100	100	100	100	100	100	100	100	100	100
Baltics	12.1	14.1	14.3	12.8	8.7	12.0	11.6	11.9	9.3	13.7	12.0	15.4
Estonia	–	–	–	–	3.1	4.5	4.4	4.4	2.2	2.6	2.4	2.1
Latvia	7.5	9.4	9.4	8.8	–	–	–	–	7.1	11.1	9.6	13.3
Lithuania	4.7	4.7	4.9	4.0	5.5	7.4	7.2	7.5	–	–	–	–
EU15	54.0	55.0	51.9	61.8	44.0	56.6	52.7	63.6	36.4	38.0	35.1	49.9
of which:												
Finland	21.5	18.7	15.8	18.2	3.2	2.1	1.9	2.0	1.1	0.8	0.7	0.9
Germany	7.2	5.5	5.6	7.4	13.6	15.6	15.0	16.8	14.4	13.1	12.3	15.9
Sweden	10.9	16.7	16.6	19.4	9.3	10.3	9.6	11.1	2.5	2.6	2.2	4.0
Norway	1.9	2.1	1.9	2.2	1.7	n.a.	0.7	0.7	0.6	0.5	0.4	1.1
CIS	25.1	20.7	23.2	13.8	38.3	19.0	22.6	11.3	42.3	35.7	41.6	18.5
of which: Russia	17.7	13.4	15.0	9.0	25.3	12.1	15.3	6.9	20.4	16.5	20.4	6.9
Other	6.9	8.1	8.7	9.5	7.3	12.5	12.4	12.3	12.0	12.6	11.3	16.2
Imports												
World	100	100	100	100	100	100	100	100	100	100	100	100
Baltics	3.6	3.7	3.6	3.6	10.6	12.9	12.8	13.4	4.9	6.7	3.2	3.7
Estonia	–	–	–	–	5.1	6.3	6.5	6.4	1.8	2.7	1.4	1.5
Latvia	2.0	2.0	2.0	2.1	–	–	–	–	3.1	3.9	1.8	2.2
Lithuania	1.6	1.6	1.5	1.5	5.5	6.6	6.3	7.0	–	–	–	–
EU15	66.0	60.1	59.6	58.7	49.9	55.3	55.6	55.8	37.1	50.2	47.3	46.4
of which:												
Finland	32.6	22.6	22.0	22.9	10.4	9.5	9.3	9.5	3.3	4.2	4.1	4.4
Germany	9.6	10.8	10.9	9.3	15.4	16.8	17.1	15.7	14.3	20.0	18.6	16.8
Sweden	8.5	9.0	8.8	9.8	8.0	7.2	7.3	7.2	2.8	3.7	3.6	3.3
Norway	0.8	1.2	1.3	1.2	0.8	n.a.	1.3	1.7	0.9	0.9	0.9	0.7
CIS	18.8	14.2	14.4	16.4	28.2	16.0	15.9	14.1	42.0	24.7	26.4	24.5
of which: Russia	16.1	11.1	11.3	13.0	21.7	11.8	11.7	9.5	31.2	20.2	21.7	19.9
Other	10.8	20.9	21.0	20.0	10.5	15.8	15.7	15.0	16.0	16.4	23.1	25.4
Memorandum items:												
Exports total (mn local currency)	21 071	45 551	26 013	23 627	688	1 068	658	580	10 820	14 812	9 191	6 999
Imports total (mn local currency)	29 117	67 363	40 428	32 004	959	1 881	1 088	938	14 593	23 174	13 837	11 068
Exports total (mn US$)[1]	1 519	3 236	1 801	1 632	1 185	1 812	1 104	988	2 705	3 710	2 298	1 750
Imports total (mn US$)[1]	2 100	4 786	2 800	2 211	1 652	3 189	1 826	1 597	3 648	5 793	3 459	2 767

1. Converted at the annual average exchange rate.
Source: National Statistical Offices.

duties were designed to encourage domestic industries to consume local raw materials, and to prevent export of products considered to be in short supply. Rules of origin are identical to those applied by EU. In order to ensure proper implementation, the Agreement contains standard provisions on state aids, monopoly, dumping, competition, intellectual property rights and public procurement in line with WTO regulations. A Joint Committee supervises the implementation of the Agreement.

A second agreement was added to BAFTA relating to free trade in agricultural products, and came into force 1 January 1997. It is one of very few international agreements that stipulates tariff free movement of agricultural products. All customs duties, charges and quantitative restrictions on agricultural products were abolished. Taking into account the vulnerability of agricultural markets, the BAFTA includes provisions on dumping and export subsidies. As is the case with industrial products, the BAFTA also contains provisions regarding application of safeguard measures in some cases, notably the case of balance of payment problems.

Despite the radical nature of the BAFTA, the level of intra-Baltic trade has not much changed. In 1998, the highest share of exports to the Baltics was 14 per cent in Estonia and Lithuania and 12 per cent in Latvia (Table 32). There was a wider variation on the import side, around 13 per cent in Latvia, 7 per cent in Lithuania and only 4 per cent in Estonia. This outcome is largely a product of the Baltic countries sharing similar comparative advantages (see above). Nevertheless, the benefit of free trade lies also in giving successful companies the scope to generate economies of scale not available to them in their domestic market, and encouraging efficiency through greater competition. So far, chemicals, mineral products and machine tools have dominated intra-Baltic trade, but textile trade volumes have started to increase significantly during the last three years; trade in food products also increased after the BAFTA in agricultural goods came into force in 1997. Intra-Baltic trade accounted for 20 per cent of agri-food exports, and 18 per cent of imports, in Latvia. It is also seems likely that the BAFTA has stimulated investment, both from within the region and from outside, by offering investors a larger potential market.[171] However, given the different levels of agricultural support in the Baltics, operation of the BAFTA has highlighted the need for the countries to discuss agri-food policies in other to maximise the benefit from free-trade.

The existence of BAFTA has also provided a bulwark against pressure on government to protect particular sectors on political grounds. The Russian crisis was a particularly important test for free trade in agricultural goods. Intra-Baltic trade has recently experienced tensions in this sector (see Box 10). In addition to the BAFTA it is expected that other forms of Baltic co-operation will reduce existing barriers to intra-Baltic trade, such as delays in executing border controls.

Box 10. Cases of trade dispute resolution mechanisms within the Baltics

Trade tensions within the Baltics surfaced at the end of 1998 and beginning of 1999. Perhaps predictably, these tensions arose in agriculture, a particularly sensitive, and protected, sector in the Baltic economies as in many other countries. In Lithuania average external tariffs in this sector were around 17 per cent in 1997; in Latvia average production weighed tariffs were above 50 per cent. On the other hand, since 1995 Estonia has no agricultural tariffs. During the Baltic Joint Committee meeting in December 1998, Latvia raised a question on the increased imports of pork from Estonia (see Annex I). According to the Latvian representatives, rapid increases in pork imports from Estonia were damaging domestic producers. The Latvian Government approved a draft decree to establish several protection measures: tariff quotas were introduced not only on Estonian, but also Lithuanian pork. Lithuania reacted by indicating that the measures violated article 3 of the BAFTA in agricultural goods; the Estonian government also protested. As a result, the Latvian Government cancelled the draft decree. However, in May 1999 the Latvian Parliament passed a law introducing a 70 per cent tariff on pork imports irrespective of their source after the Latvian State Commission of Safeguards found evidence that increased pork imports were causing serious injury to the domestic industry. This took effect on 1 June 1999, as a WTO compatible safeguard measure to expire after 200 days. Estonia and Lithuania considered this measure a violation of the BAFTA on agricultural goods and called for a Joint Committee to evaluate the Latvian position. The issue remains on the agenda for future Joint Committee meetings.

On 1 January 1999 Latvian Customs authorities refused to recognise European (EUR) certificates of origin issued by Lithuanian customs since Lithuania had failed to ratify the EU rules of origin. Lithuania believed that Latvia had no legal justification to reject the certificates and entered a complaint under the BAFTA. During the Joint Committee meeting in February 1999 it was agreed that Latvia would recognise EUR certificates of origin.

During the Joint Committee meeting in March 1999, Latvia and Estonia raised the issue of a "customs valuation order" applied by Lithuania. They considered minimum prices used for customs valuation in Lithuania and a new mechanism for calculating reference prices introduced from 1 January 1999, to be in violation of the BAFTA and in conflict with WTO requirements. Latvia retaliated by introducing a reference price on Lithuanian imports in March 1999. Lithuania recognised that their existing customs valuation was not in compliance with WTO standards, and intend that WTO compatible measures will be applied from January 2000.

In this vein, an Agreement on the Baltic Common Transit Procedure entered into force on 1 June 1999. Extensions to BAFTA on trade in services and movement of labour are also under consideration. An agreement on abolition of non-trade barriers (NTBs) was signed in July 1998.

Integration in the Baltic Rim builds on historical ties

Regional economic development in the Baltic Rim has a long history. In the late middle age the Hanseatic League established a trade network of about 70 cities around the Baltic Sea. The economic, political and cultural ties with the Nordic countries have always been important for the Baltic countries. Co-operation amongst Baltic Sea States started from the beginning of transition with the development of technical assistance. Trade and foreign investment flows between the Nordic countries and Baltic countries also intensified. The institutionalised co-operation and assistance is channelled through the Nordic Council of Ministers (Box 11).

Box 11.   The institutional framework for co-operation with Nordic countries

Co-operation with the Nordic countries developed according to the "5+3" formula. The "5+3" meetings started in 1992 at Prime Ministerial level. Prime Ministers now meet annually to discuss common foreign policy and regional issues. Ministers for Foreign Affairs have met annually since 1993. Co-operation with the Nordic Countries is of particular relevance to regional integration. It is institutionalised through the co-operation of the Nordic Council of Ministers and the Baltic Council of Ministers. The Nordic Council of Ministers provides assistance to the Baltic States in the EU membership process. All Nordic countries have substantial bilateral programs to complement the EU PHARE program.

Intergovernmental regional Baltic co-operation is carried out via the *Council of the Baltic Sea States* (CBSS). The CBSS was established in March 1992 on a German-Danish initiative. Members include Denmark, Estonia, Finland, Germany, Iceland, Latvia, Lithuania, Norway, Poland, Russia, Sweden and the EU Commission. A permanent international CBSS Secretariat was established in Stockholm in October 1998.

The *Baltic Business Advisory Council* (BBAC) was established 1992 in the framework of the CBSS to provide advice to the relevant bodies of the CBSS and groups representatives of business organisations of the Baltic Sea Region. The BBAC is particularly focused on EU enlargement and the process of harmonising legislation and practices with those of the rest of the European Union as this of great importance to foreign investors.

The Baltics had concluded free trade agreements (FTAs) with Norway, Sweden and Finland in 1992 and 1993; agreements with Sweden and Finland continued in force after these countries joined the EU under the provisions of the Baltic-EU FTAs. These agreements have stimulated trade and investment with the Nordic States.

The Baltic states are in a stage of dynamic transition and were until recently amongst the fastest growing countries in Central and Eastern Europe. The region has strengths in some labour intensive sectors such as textiles, chemicals and wood processing. But there are also labour skills in (mainly military) electronics inherited from Soviet times, which could lay the foundation for developing some high-tech niches. Nordic partners have developed several strategies. One strategy was to first upgrade factories, transfer technology and train management and personnel in market economy and then integrate the companies into the parent group's international corporate structure. Another tendency has been to combine labour-intensive production of the low cost countries with the more advanced industries operating in the home country. The latter approach was notably developed in the textile industry.

Despite the fact that Nordic-Baltic trade grew quickly, it still accounts for a relatively small portion of exports and imports. As noted above, only Estonia has the Nordic countries among its largest trading partners (see Table 32). Imports from the Baltic States to Nordic countries consist mainly of timber, petroleum products and wearing apparel. But new more value-added products started to be produced with the involvement of Nordic capital. Exports by the Nordic states to the Baltics mainly consists of high-tech goods, transport equipment, electric machinery and textile fabrics.

Economic integration with the Nordic countries has taken place mainly through foreign direct investment (FDI). Scandinavian FDI is most visible in Estonia, and to a lesser extent in Latvia. Finland and Sweden dominate with respectively 30 and 36 per cent of total FDI stocks (Table 33). Finnish involvement is extensive with over 4 000 Finnish companies registered in Estonia in 1998. The

Table 33. **FDI stocks by country of origin, 1998**

	Estonia[1]	Latvia[2]	Lithuania[3]
Total stock (mln US$)	**1 810**	**1 558**	**1 625**
In per cent of total			
Norway	4	5	4
Sweden	37	8	18
Finland	30	5	10
Denmark	4	12	9
Germany	3	9	8
USA	4	13	15

1.   Per cent as of end Q1 1999.
2.   In company capital.
3.   1 July 1999.
Source: National Statistical Offices.

largest single investor in Latvia is a joint venture registered in Denmark related to the privatisation of Latvian Telecom (Denmark accounted for 15 per cent of FDI by March 1999), followed by USA, Russia, Germany, Sweden and the UK. By end-1998 Nordic countries accounted for 51 per cent of the total direct investment to Lithuania, with Sweden and Finland being the main investors (17 and 11 per cent, respectively). But the flows are not only in one direction: according to the Swedish Investment Agency, in 1998 the Baltic States have in turn started to invest in Sweden.

Relations with the EU

FTAs between the EU and the Baltic States came into force in January 1995. These agreements differ slightly between countries. Latvia had a 4-year transition period, and in Lithuania tariffs will be gradually abolished over six years. Estonia has no transitional period, and its agreement applies zero duties to all industrial goods. Latvia applied duties on some industrial products, which were eliminated by end-1998 and Lithuania by 2001. A separate regime is also applied to trade in "sensitive goods" such as agricultural products and textiles. Latvian and Lithuanian textile exports to the EU are free of duties and since January 1998 are no longer subject to annual quotas; all Baltic textile exports are under surveillance. It is likely that these restrictions may deter some of the export-related FDI in the textile sector. In the agricultural sector Estonia applied immediately a zero duties for all agricultural and fisheries goods. Lithuania and Latvia have applied some tariff restrictions to a list of agricultural products until 2000.[172] The EU applies reduced duties for some agricultural products and tariff quotas for some meat and fisheries products. Regular tariffs are applied to all other goods.

Existing Europe Agreements allow for rather limited free trade in services. The agreements anticipate negotiations on liberalisation of cross-border services to start eight years after the ratification of the agreements. The only exception is international maritime transport services, where there is open market access. Movement of labour is quite restricted and limited to temporary movement of professional service providers. National treatment, with some exemptions, is applied to capital movements (see below).

All three Baltic countries have formally applied for EU membership since 1995. On 30 March 1998, the accession process was formally launched. The examination on the implementation of the *acquis communautaire* ("the screening process") with all three Baltic States started a few days later on 3 April, with only Estonia included in the list of countries pursuing individual EU accession negotiations, or the so-called "first wave" of accession. In October 1999, the European Commission made a recommendation adopted at the European Council in Helsinki (December 1999) that the EU should begin accession negotiations with all applicant countries. According to this approach, negotiations take place country-by-country on a "differentiated" basis, with each country proceeding towards membership at its own pace.

The potential benefits of economic integration with the EU seem obvious. Cumulating the benefits from access to a large market, the differences in production structures and development levels create space for a wide range of trade complementarities, investments and technology transfers. However, the costs of membership, associated with fulfilling the requirements for EU accession, should not be underestimated. The mapping between the implementation of the *acquis communautaire* and the reform process is not always straightforward. Examples can be found in the area of trade liberalisation, where regional integration may have to be reconciled with pre-existing multilateral commitments. For example, all Baltic countries will have to raise the level of its agricultural protection in order to fit with common EU agricultural tariffs. The cost of protection may be a high burden for a small country. In order to achieve the highest possible rates of economic growth, it cannot afford to introduce large distortions in the process of resource allocation. Management of structural pre-accession funds (*e.g.* for regional policy) will also require adherence to best practice and regular evaluation if they are not to be wasted or even to have a disruptive effect at the local level. In face of this complex processes, including the changes that are taking place in the EU itself, the impact of integration could be manifold. Certainly, the most encouraging results have appeared at the level of the Baltic Sea region. Significant amounts of diversified foreign direct investment ranging from timber, to telecoms and banking brought new management and marketing skills and opened larger markets for trade.

Foreign investment liberalisation should be pursued further

Foreign investment in the Baltic countries, in particular FDI, has grown rapidly and, as discussed in this Survey, has played a key role in the restructuring of the enterprise and financial sectors. FDI has also been the main source of financing for the substantial current account deficits accumulated in recent years. Given these links, ensuring the right environment for attracting foreign investment is a key condition for success in other policy areas and the reform process, as a whole. The Baltic countries have embarked on a vast legislative programme aimed at encouraging FDI. There is a question of how important are remaining administrative barriers (see Box 12). Concerning direct barriers, the most important restriction relates to the availability of land. In principle, there are no restrictions in Estonia and Latvia, while in Lithuania foreigners can buy but not trade land. In practice, however, the market is still rather thin. Latvia has gone furthest in land reform, but still only 40 per cent of property is registered. Property can generally be leased, but this may undermine the predictability of future costs and creditors are unwilling to accept leases as mortgage guarantees.

Box 12. International investment: the OECD's rules of the game

The *acquis* of the OECD comprises four instruments:

i) The Capital Movements Code. In its original format (1961), it stipulated non-discrimination for certain portfolio capital movements and direct investment transfers; since 1984, the non-discriminatory right of establishment for foreign-controlled enterprises has been incorporated in the Code.

ii) Draft Convention on the Protection of Private Property (1967): it has never been ratified, but it has served as a model for many bilateral investment protection treaties, adopted since.

iii) The Declaration and Decisions on International Investment and Multinational Enterprises (1976-1991). Its main elements are: 1) the National Treatment Instrument, stipulating that foreign-owned enterprises will be accorded similar treatment as domestic ones in like circumstances ("National Treatment"); exceptions to National Treatment shall be notified to and examined by other OECD Members, who exert "peer pressure" to repeal exceptions; 2) The OECD Guidelines for Multinational Enterprises, promoting corporate responsibility and currently under review.

iv) Convention on Combating Bribery in International Business Transactions (1997), aimed against bribery of foreign civil servants.

The objective of these instruments is, put briefly, to remove impediments to foreign investment – in particular by removing discrimination between foreign and domestic investors – and to help ensure that foreign investment contributes to economic and social progress. These instruments are targeted at administrative barriers, and serve as a benchmark for activity in this area.

There are restrictions on foreign investment in specific sectors in the three Baltic States. For example, there are restrictions on foreign ownership of air transport (as is common throughout the OECD), partly motivated by security considerations. There are some other restrictions, such as those on the provision of medical and legal services by foreigners. Concern for financial stability considerations has led to restrictions on foreign investment in insurance in Latvia. Foreign insurers can set up a local legal entity, but may not operate representative offices. Cultural protection has been the reason for limitations on investment in the audio-visual media. Concern for depletable resources has led to restrictions on timber harvesting in Latvia.

A number of difficulties have been reported regarding more indirect barriers, such as the acquisition of visas, residence and work permits. Customs regulations have also been cited as impediments. It is important to deal with such problems, since the possibilities for trade are often a major reason for investing in the Baltic region. Tax issues and accounting standards have also been identified as impediments to foreign investment. VAT legislation is a case in point; the laws in this field have been frequently amended, and the accounting standards do not yet conform to the IAS (International Accounting Standards). But, this is likely to become less of an issue as Baltic countries adopt EU standards. Frequent changes in the law have also made it difficult for law enforcers to keep up with developments and to acquire the necessary skills. In consequence the implementation of laws has been unpredictable and not always uniform. There have been complaints about lengthy bureaucratic procedures and about a lack of accessibility to laws and court decisions. In all these areas further and continued progress would be desirable. In this regard, Latvia has established a Foreign Investors Council representing the largest foreign investors in Latvia and has begun semi-annual meetings with senior government representatives to discuss issues of concern to the foreign investment community. A World Bank report on administrative barriers to investment in Latvia has also been the catalyst for a structured discussion on identifying and reducing barriers.

Notes

1. See for example, Van Arkadie and Karlsson (1992), Ryder (1998).

2. Council for Mutual Economic Assistance.

3. Net material product in the Soviet national accounts system did not include services and administration. Other differences compared to GDP also prevent a precise comparison between the two aggregates.

4. The year 1989 has been chosen here for comparisons as it can be considered the last normal year during the Soviet period. After that, political confrontation with Russia in connection with the secession from the Soviet Union started to affect the Baltic economies.

5. The GDP data from the Soviet period has shortcomings due to the different statistical system applied at that time in the Soviet Union, but the data allows at least a rough comparisons between countries.

6. All-Union enterprises were directly controlled from ministries in Moscow, and they were often the sole producers of certain goods in the Soviet Union.

7. Co-operatives and individual enterprises.

8. The shale oil extracted from the deposits of tar sands is one of the most abundant primary energy sources at the world level but it also is one of the most polluting one. For example, the carbon content per unit of energy of the shale oil is 39 MT/TeraJoule, compared with (average) 24.7 for the coal, 19.5 for the oil and 13.5 for the gas.

9. Excluding branches and representatives offices of foreign banks (cf. Berengaut et al., 1998).

10. See for a example a discussion in Tornell (1999),"Privatizing the Privatized", NBER Working Paper No. 7206, July.

11. This is an estimate; the precise figures are not known. The State still has 3 large companies to be sold and kept a residual stake in around 100 companies.

12. See for example, OECD (1996, 1997, 1998b, 1999a) and Berg et al. (1999), "The evolution of Output in Transition Economies: Explaining the differences", IMF Working Paper 99/73, May.

13. Cf. OECD Economic Surveys of the Slovak Republic, Romania and Bulgaria.

14. By the national account identity $Q + M = D + X$, where Q, M, D and X represent respectively domestic output, imports, domestic demand and exports. The domestic demand to domestic producers is then by definition (D-M) and the external demand equal to X.

15. For each couple (Net debt/GDP, and current account/GDP) there is a line (in bold in the Figure) with slope equal to the growth rate of nominal GDP that ensures a stable debt ratio (all the variables are expressed in the same currency). For example, for a stable debt ratio at 30 per cent and nominal GDP growth at 10 per cent, the sustainable current account deficit is 3 per cent of GDP. Conversely, with a given growth rate of nominal GDP there is a maximum level of sustainable deficit that is compatible with a stable debt ratio. The deficits that are higher than the sustainable level increase, by definition, the debt to GDP ratio. Those deficits correspond to the region to the right of bolded lines in the Figure.

16. UN-ECE *Economic Survey of Europe*, 1999, No. 2, pp. 44-45, 49.

17. In Latvia, the registered insolvency cases peaked in 1997 at 433 then decreased to 408 in 1998. At September, 155 cases have been registered for 1999. In Estonia, the corresponding numbers are 30, 57 and 75 (January-October 1999).

18. See for a discussion Wirtschaftslage und Reformprozesse in Mittel-und Osteuropa, Bundesministerium für Wirtschaft und Tecnologie, Berlin, Sammelband 1999, nr. 459, in the corresponding chapters per country.

19. Previous plans had envisaged pegging to a 50:50 euro-dollar basket.

20. Two qualifications need to be attached to these data. First, as in other transition economies, such estimates of the extent of price liberalisation apparently refer to *unweighted* counts of the number of items in the consumer basket with market – determined prices. Given that important prices such as those of energy and housing are generally liberalised at a slower pace, estimates of price liberalisation based on expenditure weights would probably be lower. Second, some of the liberalisation measures introduced in Estonia in early-1992 were temporarily rolled-back in subsequent months as a result of food shortages and public discontent (World Bank 1993a).

21. Inflation in Russia in 1991 was around one-half that of the Baltic countries.

22. Data from Savalainen (1994). This author notes that the terms of trade shock in the Baltics was much more severe than in other central European economies, with the impact on Poland, Hungary and Czechoslovakia (as it was then) ranging from 3-5.5 per cent of GDP in 1991.

23. Lainela *et al.* (pp. 53-54) cite data indicating that, at end-1992, one-third to one-half of transactions were carried out in convertible currencies, and possibly 15 per cent in Russian roubles.

24. A more detailed account of this period can be found in Bank of Estonia (1998).

25. The net open position of Estonian banks to the deutschemark became negative for the first time in October.

26. Real rates are even lower using backward looking inflation outturns (*e.g.* over the previous year) or centred inflation (*e.g.* over the previous and next six months).

27. For example, the Bank of Lithuania intends to make greater use of open-market operations to smooth short-term interest rate fluctuations. In Estonia, the authorities are considering allowing banks' foreign asset holdings to be used as part of their reserve requirements, provided the Bank of Estonia is able to confirm the level of these foreign assets.

28. Baltic Business Weekly, March 15-21 1999. It is not clear what would be the views or policies of current euro area members regarding such a possibility.

29. It could be noted here that a certain consensus is emerging in the economic literature (*e.g.* Frankel, 1999) that exchange rate should either be firmly fixed (as in a currency union or board) or flexible and every compromise between these two options entails undesirable effects and risks. In other words, the choice between the *pros* and *cons* of each system should be clear-cut.

30. See Shteinbuka and Kazaks (1996) and Pautola (1997).

31. In 1989 net transfers to the Soviet budget were estimated at 14, 6 and 2 per cent of GDP respectively for Latvia, Lithuania and Estonia (see Pautola (1997)).

32. Tax revenues as a ratio to GDP reform can be expected to fall at the onset of reform, and then stabilise and recover as administrative reforms take hold and changes in tax policy become effective (see Ebrill and Havrylyshyn (1999)).

33. Dividends are paid by enterprises out of after-tax profits under an imputation system. In Estonia the imputed tax is equal to 26 per cent of the gross dividend. In Latvia, dividends are subject to tax if they are received from foreign companies or resident companies entitled to relief under the Law on Foreign Investment or in Special Economic Zones.

34. Latvia offers an 80 per cent tax credit on corporate income and property taxes to qualifying companies.

35. See EBRD (1994).

36. The size of government has not been stable during the period due to the immense structural changes taking place. In all three countries general government expenditure as a share of GDP increased between 1992 and 1998. Fluctuations are principally associated with varying rates of growth.

37. See "National Budget, 1999", Ministry of Finance, Republic of Latvia, Riga, 1999.

38. The government plans legislation to limit the creation of new agencies and set up clear operating rules for those already in existence. Any move to further financial delegation would create problems in the absence of rationalisati on and better financial control.

39. In accordance with SNA93, these figures treat proceeds from privatisation as a financing item rather than revenue, as in the official Estonian definition.

40. See Berengaut *et al.* (1998): 20.8 per cent were drawing old-age pensions, 3.6 per cent a disability pension, and 1.5 per cent a survivors or other pension

41. See also IMF (1998).

42. Although in some cases the authorities have indeed intervened to recapitalise failed banks or to bail out depositors, or have lowered reserve requirements to bolster liquidity.

43. The Baltic countries are gradually introducing three pillar funded pension schemes to replace pay-as-you-go systems.

44. These comprised regional branches of specialised banks such as Savings Bank, Industry Bank, Social Bank, Agricultural Bank and Vneshekonombank, and Gosbank.

45. For example, the minimum capital requirement for the establishment of a bank was RUB 5 million in Estonia (equivalent to USD 40 000) and its restrictive effect was eroded by the hyperinflation in 1991-92.

46. The average rate of recovery was below 50 per cent in Estonia and below 10 per cent in Latvia and 11 per cent in Lithuania.

47. For example in 1995 in Latvia total credit contracted by almost 50 per cent at the same time as growth was only −0.8 per cent. GDP growth was positive in 1996-1998 despite pre-crisis levels of credit to the private sector which were attained in 1998.

48. The only exceptions were two banks, whose problems were a result of Vnesheko-nombank of former Soviet Union freezing their accounts. These two banks were merged, restructured and recapitalised by the government, which also appointed new management. Frozen deposits with Vneshekonombank amounted to 56 per cent of combined assets of two banks in question.

49. Due to the loopholes in legal framework it was almost impossible to trace who were the owners of legal entities. It was usual that the content of the files in company register was outdated and incomplete. Moreover, there were no legal grounds to prohibit anybody to become a shareholder of a bank.

50. The total exposure amounted to about EEK 90 million that was more than 10 per cent of the equity capital of the whole banking system.

51. Bank Baltija had expanded its market share since the middle of 1993 by buying commercial branches of the Bank of Latvia and offering higher interest rates and requiring lower minimum amounts on deposits than other market participants. An aggressive strategy was likewise used in short-term high-risk lending operations. Almost all essential internal risk management policies and controls were underde-veloped or simply absent. As a result, the bank's negative net worth at the time of its closure amounted to almost 8 per cent of GDP. Lending to insiders, fraudulent and criminal activity were also uncovered during liquidation.

52. At the end of 1997 32 banks were operating in Latvia compared to 12 in both Estonia and Lithuania.

53. This change eliminated the major difference in the formula of the calculation of capital adequacy requirements in Lithuania compared to Basle standards, and made Lithuanian banks' financials comparable with those of their peers. Although the banks in Lithuania were required to meet a capital adequacy requirement of 13 per cent this was calculated according to Lithuanian accounting standards that did not require the deduction of loan losses from profits or writing them off against tier one capital.

54. Capital requirement for banks with the right to accept household deposits was LVL 2 million whereas the general requirement was LVL 1 million.

55. In Estonia bank intermediated capital flows increased from 0.7 per cent of GDP in 1995 to 4.1 per cent and 9.8 per cent of GDP in 1996 and 1997 respectively.

56. Estonian banks' loans in total assets had increased to 58 per cent at the end of 1998 at lending rates of 11-12 per cent (up from 44 per cent and down from 30 per cent in 1995 and 1994 respectively. For Latvia and Lithuania the share of loans in total bank assets was only 33 and 48 per cent in 1998.

57. In 1997, bank owned subsidiaries controlled 90 per cent of leasing market, banks' equities accounted for 60 per cent of Tallinn Stock Exchange capitalisation, banks were the main brokers on the securities market and bank controlled asset manage-ment companies managed more than 90 per cent of mutual funds.

58. In 1996, short term lending rates dropped by 10-11 percentage points and by another 8-9 percentage points in 1997 but still remained relatively high in real terms compared to Lithuania and Estonia.

59. According to the Bank of Latvia's regulation and consistent with Basle minimum standards, banks' claims on non-OECD central governments denominated in their domestic currency were assigned zero risk weighting in capital adequacy calculation. From 1999 domestic currency debt of non-OECD countries and some OECD countries (Mexico, Korea, Poland, Hungary and the Czech Republic) carries a 50 per cent risk weighting.

60. Its share in total financial assets increased from 1 per cent in 1996 to around 3.5 per cent in 1997.

61. This is explained by increased interest in financial assets of Baltic countries among institutional investors prevailing in 1996-1997 but also by intra-Baltic position taking, particularly by Estonian financial institutions.

62. These activities were, however, considerably downsized following the South East Asian turmoil.

63. As a result of the speculative pressure the EEK/DEM forward contracts increased by more than 4 billion EEK in last ten days of October 1997 and the net open position of Estonian banks in DEM became first time negative.

64. The fourth quarter accounted for more than 50 per cent of Bank of Latvia's total lending to banks in 1997.

65. One of the reasons for better performance of Latvian and Lithuanian banks was their smaller exposure to securities market compared to Estonian peers. Latvian banks' holdings in equities were 3 per cent in 1997 against 10 per cent in Estonia.

66. These two banks had direct exposure in Russia amounting to approximately 10 per cent of their combined assets.

67. Although Latvian banks used Russian banks to cover their ruble positions they remained unhedged against the counterparty risks.

68. During August-November 1998 non-resident liabilities of Latvian banks shrunk by about 14 per cent, whereas non-resident deposits declined by 15.7 per cent or LVL 73.3 million during 1998.

69. Together with Riga Komercbanka the consolidated loss exceeded LVL 80 million.

70. This trend is encouraged by regulations that mean banks are not allowed to acquire holding in a non-financial undertaking the value of which exceeds 15 per cent of their own funds. The total of qualified holdings (i.e., holding in an undertaking that represents 10 per cent or more of the share capital or of the voting rights) may not exceed 60 per cent of the own funds of a bank. These regulatory constraints are definitely limiting banks' involvement as a shareholder in the process of corporate restructuring or corporate governance.

71. The number of co-operatives in Estonia increased from 246 in January 1988, to 1 190 in January 1989, 4 086 in January 1990 and 4 797 in July 1990 (Goskomstat). Compared to other areas of the Soviet Union 'new co-operatives' also developed quite early and rapidly. In January 1990, there were more than 2 000 new co-operatives with about 7 per cent of employment (Van Arkadie et al, 1991). The number of co-operatives peaked in 1993. According to the Statistical Office of Estonia there were 2 943 co-operatives in August 1993. Since then many co-operatives have been transformed into other legal forms, and in July 1998 there were 2 124 co-operatives in the enterprise register though only 769 of them reported a profit (ESA 1998).

72.   In October 1990, the Latvian government made a decree to limit this type of privatisation when co-operatives leased assets from state owned enterprises (Frydman *et al.*, 1993).

73.   As they were not included in the list of official legal forms in the 1990 enterprise law, they were transformed into other legal forms such as partnerships and closed joint stock companies (Mygind, 1995).

74.   Shteinbuka (1996).

75.   Under Article 29.3 capital accumulated under the old leasing system could be transferred to the new contract which could be further arranged with an option to buy. If only some of the employees wanted to sign the new leasing contract, the capital was distributed between the lessee-employers and non-lessee-employees in proportion to their wage and time of service for the enterprise during the leasing period.

76.   According to Terk (1996, p. 199).

77.   By 1989 there were 461 small state-owned enterprises with nearly 6 000 employees and in July 1991 the Ministry of Economy had registered 705 of this type of semi-private enterprise.

78.   Frydman *et al.* (1993).

79.   Twelve large enterprises, with mainly Russian employees, were leased by the employees under Soviet law. The early reform programme also favoured so-called "peoples' enterprises" which also included forms of experimental leasing for insiders. But by 1991 only seven large enterprises had been taken over mainly by insiders, with five of these firms having full employee ownership. (Terk, 1996).

80.   Frydman *et al* (1993).

81.   Frydman *et. al.* (1993).

82.   Perju (1996).

83.   Between 1992 and 1994 76 per cent of small and medium and 75 per cent of large enterprises offered for sale in Lithuania had been sold. By the end of the LIPSP programme in 1995 99 per cent of all enterprises had been disposed of.

84.   Each person got one voucher for each year of residence in Latvia after the World War II. Pre-war citizens and their descendants received an additional 15 vouchers, while five vouchers were deducted from those people who had immigrated after the war. This deduction was justified as payment for "the use of Latvian infrastructure".

85.   EIU (2:93). By July 1995, 96.5 per cent of the population had received 104 million vouchers with a total nominal value of LVL 2.9 billion.

86.   People 35 years or older received a face value of 5 000 roubles. People younger than 18 years received 1 000 roubles, and those in between received a variable amount from 1 000 to 5 000 roubles. The nominal value of the vouchers was revalued several times to compen-sate for inflation and the revaluation of the assets to be privatised.

87.   According to the Estonian authorities, some EEK 8.3 billion capital vouchers and EEK 7.7 billion compensation vouchers were distributed.

88.   Emission of compensation vouchers will terminate in 2001, at the latest. In 1994, compensation and capital vouchers were merged into privatisation vouchers held in bank accounts (EVP accounts).

89.   Baltic Independent, 14 May 1993.

90.   In the first months prices were less than LVL 3 on a nominal value of LVL 28.

91. The voucher rights and all transactions were recorded in special accounts of the public Savings Bank. The account system was designed to limit voucher transferability. The vouchers could initially only be transferred to relatives, but it was later also possible to use vouchers to pay off outstanding loans in housing.

92. About 400 funds were established in relation to LIPSP privatisation. Some 300 funds were formed by insiders pooling their shares to acquire company control to purchase a single enterprises; 60-70 small funds had diversified ownership, and the remaining 30-40 had sizeable capital and up to 25 000 shareholders (Lee, 1996). They were actively involved in the privatisation of 1 092 enterprises and eventually acquired assets with a book value of LTL 737 million (21 per cent of the total), but worth an estimated LTL 1 586 million (Semeta, 1997).

93. Visokaviciene (1994).

94. The deadline was 1 July 1997, but many investment funds failed to meet the requirements.

95. Kein (1995).

96. Kein and Terk (1997).

97. The first two (the largest department store in Tallinn and the SAKU brewery) were sold by fixed price to around 50 000 buyers, using EEK 100 million in vouchers. Subsequent offerings were sold at auctions in which a much more limited number of bidders participated. In July 1997 a minority holding of shares in Eesti Gaas were sold for EEK 406 million worth of vouchers to 1 338 bidders.

98. The percentage of shares available to employees as pre-emption was increased from 10 per cent in 1991, to 30 per cent in 1992 and to 50 per cent after the labour party took office in early 1993.

99. Martinavicius (1996).

100. They were not terminated, but had still some limited use in acquiring plots of land and housing.

101. The government set a threshold book value below which enterprises were sold at auction for vouchers and cash. According to the Lithuanian Ministry of Economics, by August 1992 1 300 small enterprises had been privatised, by October 1994 this had increased to 2 498 (WB, 1993c), and by July 1995 to 2 727 – nearly half of all enterprises, though a rather smaller share of assets and employees.

102. Kein and Tali (1994).

103. Initial auctions by the EPA covered relatively small enterprises, often spin-offs from larger companies, though the average price per sale increased considerably partly due to the impact of high inflation. From June 1993 there were no formal ceiling on the value of enterprises which could be sold at auction.

104. Purju (1996).

105. Purchasers had to be Latvian citizens or have at least 16 years of residency.

106. Vojevoda and Rumpis (1993).

107. In 1992 only 8 per cent of small privatisation was sold at auction, though prices at auction were on average five times higher (and the average final price 3.7 times higher) than the initial price (Vojevoda and Rumpis, 1993).

108. Frydman et al. (1993).

109. Q1 1994 to Q1 1996.

110.   At the end of 1998 the EPA had sold 483 large enterprises by direct sale at a total price of around EEK 4.7 billion (USD 400 million).

111.   In Estonia foreigners were able to do both from the spring of 1996, two years later then domestic investors (Kein and Terk, 1997).

112.   Of these 147 were in fact intended to be leased with an option to buy (Jemeljanovs, 1996).

113.   In fact 234 firms. With a key role assigned to different ministries, insiders were able to make use of their existing networks (Shteinbuka, 1996).

114.   16 contracts were annulled.

115.   Usually employees could buy up to 20 per cent of the shares. By the end of 1998 shares of LVL 27 million (nominal value) had been sold for vouchers to 25 611 employees and pensioners, comprising in aggregate 13.56 per cent of the shares. Management took significant stakes in 24 enterprises: LVL 4.4 million of shares were sold for vouchers to 250 managers, comprising 13.6 per cent of the shares (LPA, 1998).

116.   These figures exclude the earliest insider take-overs which were formally outside the LIPSP programme.

117.   The initial offer was based on the book value revalued by some inflation parameter. If the bids did not come within 10 per cent of the book value, the value was adjusted and a new round of bids took place.

118.   5 714 enterprises with a capital of LTL 7 066 million had been sold (measured in 1995 indexed litas) by the end of the LIPSP programme in July 1995; of these 2 928 large enterprises with LTL 6 145 million of capital and 2 726 small enterprises with LTL 79 million of capital were sold mainly for vouchers. Holdings in 12 large strategic enterprises with capital of LTL 360 million were put on special tender where also vouchers could be used.

119.   Each with a capital of between LTL 15 and 580 million and between 300 and 2000 employees.

120.   In 1996 only 47 small blocks of residual shares were privatised for a total price of LTL 3.2 million. The process accelerated somewhat in 1997 to include 272 entities for LTL 81 million). In 1998, 344 entities were sold for litas 2329 million (SPF, 1999).

121.   In the "people's round" the price was based on the price at auction during a previous public offering.

122.   Each person with a voucher account could buy 100 shares for LVL 35 nominal voucher value per share. 18 204 persons obtained shares, though this still amounted to less than 1 per cent of the share capital.

123.   As a result of public offerings 110 659 Latvian individuals and firms have become shareholders. Of the 67 companies listed on the Riga Stock Exchange in 1998, 59 are privatised companies.

124.   On average, 60 per cent of the purchase price was met using vouchers.

125.   Kein and Terk (1997) and Purju (1998).

126.   ESA 1998.

127.   EPA (1996).

128. Privatisation of public utilities, communications and transport started with the sale, to a Danish company, of 66 per cent of the shares in Estonian Air in June 1996. In August part of Estonian Oil was sold to an American company. In 1997, a big shipping company was sold to a Norwegian investor and in 1998 parts of the energy sector were privatised. In February 1999 49 per cent of Eesti Telekom shares were sold through domestic and international stock exchanges.

129. At the end of 1995 a parliamentary committee agreed to give foreigners from states that had been OECD members in 1989 the right to buy land (*Baltic Independent*, 15 Dec. 1995).

130. The analysis carried out in this section is based on an enterprise level database for Estonia, Latvia and Lithuania. The coverage of the database varies across countries, but roughly it provides a comparable statistical basis. More details on the coverage and construction of this database can be found in Jones and Mygind (1998) and Mygind (1999).

131. See for example, "Corporate Governance: Effects on Firm Performance and Economic Growth", OECD DSTI/IND(99)13.

132. These loans initially had a fixed interest rate at 18 per cent and all applicants were subject to strict eligibility requirements.

133. Based on a survey on retail traders, small town shops on average were only two-thirds as productive as shops in Tallinn.

134. More precisely, Ventspils is a free port, Riga commercial port is a free economic zone, and Liepaja port is one part of the Liepaja special economic zone.

135. Comparisons between the three countries must be done with caution, because the cited household budget surveys use relatively small samples with significant non-response rates. However, the conclusion that fluctuations were greatest in Lithuania is also supported by wage statistics. Note, also, that the hardship associated with a high food share in consumption was exacerbated by a simultaneous increase in *housing* costs (corresponding to 10 percentage points in the case of Latvia, see Table A6).

136. Wages accounted for about two-thirds of disposable incomes in Estonia, but little more than half in the other two countries, according to household surveys in 1998. Pensions and other social transfers made up 24 per cent of the incomes in Estonia and Lithuania and 27 per cent in 1998 in Latvia. Incomes in-kind – especially farm produce – represented over 12 per cent of the total in Latvia and 17 per cent in Lithuania, but probably only 5 per cent in Estonia.

137. Lantz-de Bernardis, 1998. As an alternative method, the United Nations and the World Bank have used a poverty limit for Central and Eastern Europe corresponding to USD 4 per capita and per day by purchasing power parity, or about USD 2 per day by the Baltic countries' exchange rates (Cerniauskas, 1999, p. 6). This corresponds approximately to the lowest decile in Estonia's income distribution and the second to third-lowest deciles in the other countries.

138. *Estonian Statistics* (1999, No. 1, p. 35). The cited Gini coefficients refer to household consumption in Estonia, otherwise to household income.

139. The absolute decline in Latvia's service-sector employment started from relatively high level, as the sector was relatively more important in Latvia than in the other two countries under the previous regime.

140.   In Latvia, in particular, the intensity of the work performed on many farms may be relatively low. In spite of the still-high number of persons employed in farming, both the land area under cultivation and the output have declined substantially since 1990. Cf. *Statistical Yearbook of Latvia*, 1998, Tables 13-1 and 13-14.

141.   Estonia's labour force surveys (LFS) in 1995, 1997 and 1998 took a retrospective approach, asking sampled individuals about their labour market situation in each year since 1989. Emigrants were not included in the samples.

142.   The register-based unemployment rates, which are not internationally comparable, were about one-third higher in May 1999 than the respective averages for 1998, up from about 3 per cent to 4 per cent in Estonia, from 7.6 per cent to 10.7 per cent in Latvia and from 6 to 8 per cent in Lithuania. By contrast, LFS-unemployment has hardly changed in Latvia, while in Lithuania it has declined by over one percentage point since the second quarter 1998, with a larger decline in long-term unemployment and some increase in short-term unemployment.

143.   Unemployment rates for youths, especially teenagers, can be difficult to interpret if the group participating in the labour force is untypical of the age class as a whole. It is likely to include school dropouts and students looking for temporary work.

144.   A relatively small part of the part-time work is involuntary, resulting from production cuts in enterprises with excess capacity. After the Russian economic crisis in the autumn 1998, about 1 per cent of all Lithuanian workers were in such a situation.

145.   The LFS measures the proportions of part-time and temporary work as well as actual working time. In addition to the LFS, this sub-section relies on special surveys conducted in the autumn 1998 for the *Working Life Barometer in the Baltic States* (Antila and Ylöstalo, forthcoming in 1999). These generally confirm LFS results about working time.

146.   MOSSL, 1998. Cf. Statistics Lithuania: *Non-observed Economy: concepts, surveys and problems* (1998), which suggested on the basis of surveys that the "unofficial labour market" accounted for 14 per cent of employment and 6 per cent of GDP, while hidden incomes in enterprises represented another 9.6 per cent of GDP, not counting a further 7 per cent of GDP which could not be explained. A 1995 study by Lithuania's Labour and Social Research Institute (cited in UNDP, 1997b) indicated that 60 per cent of all private-sector workers did not declare their full incomes.

147.   Antila and Ylöstalo (1999), p. 23-25. The proportion of workers admitting that they earned "black" incomes was 19 per cent in Estonia, 16 per cent in Latvia and 7 per cent in Lithuania, of which in each country about half had such incomes every month. The authors considered these figures as underestimates. "Black" incomes were most common among workers with secondary jobs; *e.g.* in Estonia, the phenomenon concerned 18 per cent of the workers with one job and 29 per cent of those with two or more jobs.

148.   In Latvia in 1997, 29 per cent of the incomes reported for social security corresponded to the minimum wage; the same held for about 20 per cent of the wages reported by employers for statistical purposes. In Lithuania in 1995, a survey found that private enterprises reported on average only 63 per cent of their wage payments for social security purposes. But this underreporting was highly concentrated in a few sectors, especially construction and trade (MOSSL, 1998, p. 50).

149.   Latvia's Free Trade Union Federation claimed to have 252 000 members in March 1998, or just over 30 per cent of the dependent employees, of which 215 000 covered by collective agreements.

150. In Latvia, the amount of unpaid wages detected by the Labour Inspectorate increased significantly between 1993 and 1997 (MOW, 1998, p. 29).

151. Estonia's "social tax" amounts to 20 per cent of the wages for social insurance and 13 per cent for medical insurance.

152. Official wage statistics for Estonia in the fourth quarter 1998 reported over 50 per cent higher wages in foreign-owned compared with domestically-owned private companies (SOE, 1998b).

153. In Estonia in the fourth quarter 1998, the reported hourly gross wage was on average 23 per cent higher in state-owned than in Estonian-owned private companies. However, municipalities paid about the same wages as the latter (SOE, 1998b). It is not known to what extent these results are associated with different *occupational compositions* of the respective workforces.

154. In Latvia, for example, it appears unlikely that as many as 20 per cent of the private-sector full-time employees earn no more than the minimum wage, or less than one-third of the average wage, as was reported in November 1997 (*Statistical Yearbook of Latvia*, 1998, Table 6-6.). In the public sector, such very low wages were reported for 6 per cent of the workers. At the upper end of the wage scale, 13 per cent of Latvia's private-sector employees were reported to earn over 1.7 times the average, compared with 10.5 per cent in the public sector. This difference in the incidence of relatively high wages is moderate, but it includes a small number of predominantly private-sector employees with very high incomes (less than 1 per cent with over 6 times the average wage).

155. A person who collects unemployment benefits while working in a private farm is presumably counted as employed by the LFS. Such behaviour is not necessarily fraudulent if the income is low and the work covers few hours per week.

156. See, for example, OECD, 1994, Part II, Table 6.2.

157. In Latvia, the level of reported incomes affects individual pensions, sickness pay and unemployment benefits. But in Lithuania it only affects the pensions and sickness pay, and in Estonia only sickness pay. See the Box about pension reform and section below.

158. The cited number of uninsured employees was estimated in August 1998 (Rajevska, 1999, p. 17).

159. MOSSL, 1998, p. 65. Regarding non-agricultural self-employed persons, household income surveys have suggested that their actual incomes are on average over ten times the minimum wage.

160. UNDP (1998) reports results concerning the living conditions of pensioners in Estonia, suggesting that these are "forced to accept less substantial and less varied selection of food, to restrict expenditures on health and medicines, and to essentially give up all kinds of social expenditures".

161. Lithuania's "minimum subsistence level" (USD 31 in 1999), which determines the right to social assistance, was calculated to cover the cost of a basket of consumer goods in 1990, but its subsequent development has not kept pace with consumer prices (MOSSL (1998), p. 24).

162. Benefits are paid only to those who have worked and made social security contributions during two of the three years preceding registration as unemployed. The amount depends on the duration of previous employment and the reason for becoming unemployed

163. In Estonia, 30 000 persons received benefits in March 1999, roughly half of the unemployed according to the Labour Force Survey (ILO definition). The corresponding figure in Latvia in 1998 was about 26 000 or 15 per cent of the unemployed, while in Lithuania there were about 20 000 corresponding to only 8 of the unemployed. But the proportions receiving benefits among the LFS-unemployed are probably even lower than these figures suggest, because some benefit recipients may be employed or not in the labour force according to LFS definitions (*e.g.* some of those working part-time in small farms).

164. In Latvia, skills in the national language were until 1998 a condition for registration of job seekers. But this requirement has now been dropped insofar as it affects the right to unemployment benefits.

165. By western European standards, the staff resources of Lithuania's public employment service appear relatively good compared with the registered unemployment, which is currently a bit over 100 000 of which some 20 000 with benefits.

166. A tendency for such implicit or explicit "job guarantees" to trigger an excessive reliance on public works for the unemployed was documented in OECD reviews of the Public Employment Service in the Netherlands (1993), Denmark, Finland and Italy (1996) and Austria, Germany and Sweden (1996).

167. The Lithuanian Labour Market Training Authority, governed by a tripartite board under the Ministry of Social Security and Labour, runs 15 modern centres for labour-market training. They are largely concerned with training of employed workers, but the proportion of unemployed participants increased to almost half in 1998. The programme has benefited from several Phare programmes.

168. Latvia acceded to the WTO in February 1999, Estonia in November 1999 and Lithuania is in an advanced stage of negotiation.

169. The following simple indicator was used here (see OECD, 1996):

$$RCA_i = \left(\frac{X_i}{\Sigma X_i} - \frac{M_i}{\Sigma M_i} \right) \cdot 100$$

where X_i and M_i are respectively the exports and imports for a given sector i.

170. At present Lithuania applies export duties to a very limited number of goods such as raw hides and certain types of timber. Latvia also imposes duties on raw hides and skins, to be abolished by 2001, and to scrap metals, to be abolished January 2000.

171. Estonian investment accounted for 4.3 per cent of total FDI in Lithuania in January 1999 (Lithuanian Statistical Office); Estonia was also the tenth largest investor in Latvia in early 1999.

172. Note that except for the agricultural products listed in Protocole 2, Annex III of its Europe Agreement, Latvia applies a zero duty rate.

Bibliography

Antila, Juha and Ylöstalo, Pekka (1999),
Working Life Barometer in the Baltic Countries 1999, Finland's Ministry of Labour, Helsinki.

Bank of Estonia,
Bulletin (monthly, various issues), Tallinn.

Bank of Estonia (1998),
Monetary Developments and Policy Survey, Tallinn.

Bank of Latvia,
Monetary Review (quarterly, various issues), Riga.

Bank of Lithuania,
Quarterly Bulletin (various issues), Vilnius.

Berengaut, Julian, Augusto Lopez-Claros, Françoise Le Gall, Dennis Jones, Richard Stern, Ann-Margret Westin, Effie Psalida and Pietro Garibaldi (1998),
"The Baltic Countries: from economic stabilization to EU accession" in IMF Occasional Paper No. 173, Washington.

Blanchard, O. and M. Kremer (1997),
"Disorganization", Quarterly Journal of Economics, 112(4), November.

Bradshaw, Michael, Phillip Hanson and Denis Shaw (1994),
Economic Restructuring in The Baltic States: The National Self Determination of Estonia, Latvia and Lithuania, edited Graham Smith, pp. 158-180, New York, St. Martins Press.

Brock, G. (1998),
"Foreign Direct Investment in Russia's Regions 1993-95. Why so little and where has it gone?", The Economics of Transition, Vol. 6, No. 2, pp. 349-360.

Budina, Nina and Sweder van Wijnbergen (1997),
"Fiscal policies in Eastern Europe", Oxford Review of Economic Policy, Vol. 13.

Carlin W. and M. Landesmann (1997),
"From theory into practice? Restructuring and dynamics in transition economies" in Oxford Review of Economic Policy, Vol. 13, No. 2, pp 77-104.

Central Statistical bureau of Latvia (CSBL) (1998),
Labour Force in Latvia. Labour Force Survey Data. May 1998, Riga.

Cerniauskas, Gediminas (1999),
Monitoring Poverty, UNDP, Vilnius, Discussion Papers, No. 44.

DIW (1999),
Wirtschaftslage und Reformprozesse in Mittel- und Osteuropa", DIW/Berlin, HWWA/ Hambourg, IFO/Kiel, IFW/Halle and Oseuropa-Institut/Munchen), Berlin.

Eamets, Raul (1998),
"Gross flows in Estonian labour market and transition probabilities across labour market states", in OECD (1998).

Eamets, Raul (1999),
Estonian Labour Market and Labour Market Policy, Ministry of Social Affairs, Tallinn.

Earle, J.S., S. Estrin and L. Leshchenko (1995),
"Ownership Structures, Patterns of Control and Enterprise Behavior in Russia", mimeo, Central European University.

EBRD (1994), (1995), (1998),
Transition Report, London.

EBRD (1999),
Transition Report update, London.

Ebrill, L. and O. Havrylyshyn (1999),
"Reforms of tax policy and tax administration in the CIS countries and the Baltics, issues in transition" in IMF *Occasional Paper*, Washington.

EC (1998a),
"Agenda 2000: regular report 1998 from the Commission on Latvia's progress towards accession", *Bulletin of the European Union*, Sup. 9/98.

EC (1998b),
"Agenda 2000: regular report 1998 from the Commission on Estonia's progress towards accession", *Bulletin of the European Union*, Sup. 10/98.

EC (1998c),
"Agenda 2000: regular report 1998 from the Commission on Lithuania's progress towards accession", *Bulletin of the European Union*, Sup. 11/98.

Estonian Privatisation Agency (EPA) (1996),
Annual Report on Privatisation in Estonia, Tallinn.

Estrin, Saul (ed.) (1994),
Privatization in Central and Eastern Europe, Longmans.

Frankel, J (1999),
"No Single Currency Regime is Right for All Countries or At All Times", NBER Working Paper No. 7338.

Frydman *et al.* (1993a),
"The privatization process in Russia, Ukraine and the Baltic States" in CEU *Privatization Reports*, V. 2, Budapest/London/New York.

Frydman, R., C. Gray, M. Hessel and A. Rapaczynski (1997),
"Private ownership and corporate performance: some lessons from transition economies"in *Economic Research Reports*, C.V. Starr Center for Applied Economics.

Hansen, John and Piritta Sorsa (1994),
"Estonia: a shining star from the Baltics" in *Trade in the New Independent States*, Constantine Michalopoulos and David G. Tarr (eds), Studies of Economies in Transformation 13, The World Bank/UNDP, pp. 115-132.

Hanson, P. (1990),
The Baltic States, The EIU -Briefing, London.

IMF (1993),
IMF *Economic Reviews*, Estonia, Washington

IMF (1994),
    IMF *Economic Reviews*, Latvia, Washington

IMF (1994),
    IMF *Economic Reviews*, Lithuania, Washington.

IMF (1997),
    "Currency Board arrangements, issues and experience", IMF *Occasional Paper No. 151*, Washington.

IMF (1998),
    "The transition countries of Central and Eastern Europe: why EMU matters" in IMF *Working Paper*, Washington.

IMF (1998*a*),
    World Economic Outlook, May.

IMF (1998*b*) (1998*c*) (1998*d*) (1999*a*),
    "Selected Issues and Statistical Appendix" in *Country reports – Estonia, Latvia, Lithuania.*

IMF (1999*b*),
    Estonia: Staff Report for the 1999 Article IV Consultation, June.

IMF (1999*c*),
    Latvia: Staff Report for the 1999 Article IV Consultation, August.

IMF (1999*d*),
    Lithuania: Staff Report for the 1999 Article IV Consultation, August.

Jemeljanovs, O. (1996),
    "Employee ownership and the Political debate in Estonia 1987-1994" in N. Mygind (ed.) *Privatization and Financial Participation in the Baltic Countries* part I, CEES, Copenhagen Business School.

Jones, D., and N. Mygind (1998),
    "Ownership patterns and dynamics in privatized firms in transitions economies: evidence from the Baltics", CEES Working Paper Series No. 15, forthcoming in *Baltic Journal of Economics.*

Jones, D., and N. Mygind (1999*a*),
    "The nature and determinants of ownership changes after privatization: evidence from Estonia", CEES Working Paper Series No. 23, forthcoming in *Journal of Comparative Economics.*

Jones, D., and N. Mygind (1999*b*),
    "Ownership and productive efficiency: evidence from Estonia", CEES Working Paper Series No. 24.

Jones, D., and N. Mygind (1999*c*),
    "The effects of privatization on productive efficiency: evidence from the Baltic Republics", CEES Working Paper Series, No. 22.

Kein, A. (1995),
    Capital Market Institutions in Estonia, Estonian Academy of Sciences.

Kein, A., and V. Tali (1994),
    The Process of Ownership Reform and Privatization, paper from Institute of Economics, Estonian Academy of Sciences.

Kein and Terk (1997),
    Management-Buy-Out and Management-Buy-In in Estonia, Chapter 4.

Lainela, S., and P. Sutela (1994),
The Baltic Economies in Transition; Bank of Finland, Helsinki.

Lantz de Bernardis, Petra (1998),
Wealth and Poverty in Transition, UNDP, Tallinn.

Latvian Privatization Agency (LPA) (1995-1998),
Annual reports, Riga.

Lee, B. (1996),
Lithuania, in Between State and Market, Lieberman et al. (eds.), World Bank.

Lemaitre, Georges, and Reuterswärd, Anders (1998),
"Developing policy-relevant indicators", in OECD (1998).

Lithuanian Labour Exchange (LLE) (1998),
Activities of the Lithuanian Labour Exchange in 1998, Vilnius.

Liuhto, K. (1995),
"Foreign investment in Estonia: a statistical approach", Europe-Asia Studies, Vol. 47,
No. 3, pp. 507-525.

Lopez-Claros, A. (1999),
Lithuania: From Stabilisation to EU Accession, Lehman Brothers Economics.

Martinavicius, J. (1996),
"Privatization in Lithuania: the legislative and political environment and the results
achieved", in N. Mygind (ed.) Privatization and Financial Participation in the Baltic Countries
part I, CEES, Copenhagen Business School.

Ministry of Economic Affairs (1999),
Estonian Economy, A. Purju (ed.), 1998-99.

Ministry of Economy (1998),
Economic Development of Latvia, Riga.

Ministry of Social Security and Labour (MOSSL) (1998),
Social Report 1997, Vilnius.

Ministry of Welfare (MOW) (1998),
Social Report, Riga.

Mygind, N. (1994),
"The economic transition in the Baltic Countries – differences and similarities" in
The Politics of Transition in the Baltic States – Democratization and Economic Reform Policies,
J.Å. Dellenbrant and O. Nørgaard, Umeå University, Research Report No. 2,
pp. 197-234.

Mygind, N. (1995),
"Privatization and employee-ownership in the Baltic Countries – a comparative analy-
sis of conditions and development" in Privatization and Financial Participation in the Baltic
Countries – Midterm Results, Mygind (ed.), pp. 199-284, CBS.

Mygind, N. (1996),
Privatization and Financial Participation in the Baltic Countries, mimeo, CEES, Copenhagen
Business School.

Mygind, N. (1996b),
"The Baltic Countries in transition - a comparative analysis" in N. Mygind (ed.) Privatiza-
tion and Financial Participation in the Baltic Countries part I, CEES, Copenhagen Business
School.

Mygind, N. (1997),
"Different paths of transition in the Baltics", Copenhagen Business School, CEES Working Paper No. 5.

Mygind, N. (1997a),
"The economic performance of employee-owned enterprises in the Baltic Countries", CEES Working Paper Series, No. 6.

Mygind, N. (1997b),
"Employee ownership and participation in the Baltic Countries" in Uvalic and Vaughan-Whitehead (eds.) *Privatization Surprises in Transition Economies*, Elgar, Cheltenham, UK.

Mygind, N. (1998),
"The internationalization of the Baltic economies", University of Berkeley, California, BRIE Working Paper No. 130.

Mygind, N. (1999),
"Privatisation, Governance and Restructuring of Enterprises in the Baltics", *mimeo*, OECD.

Norgaard, Ole (1996),
The Baltic States after Independence, Edward Elgar.

OECD (1994),
The Jobs Study. Evidence and Explanations, Part II, Paris.

OECD (1996),
OECD *Economic Surveys: the Slovak Republic*, Paris.

OECD (1997),
OECD *Economic Surveys: Slovenia*, Paris.

OECD (1998a),
OECD *Workshop on the Use of Labour Force Surveys for Policy Making. Proceedings*, Tallinn 27-28 October 1997, Paris

OECD (1998c),
"The retirement decision" in OECD *Economic Outlook* No. 63, Paris.

OECD (1998b),
OECD *Economic Surveys: Romania*, Paris.

OECD (1999a),
OECD *Economic Surveys: the Slovak Republic*, Paris.

OECD (1999b),
OECD *Economic Surveys: Bulgaria*, Paris.

OECD (1999c),
Employment Outlook, Paris.

Pautola, N. (1997),
"Fiscal transition in the Baltics" in *Review of Economies in Transition* No. 2, [add].

Pautola, Niina and Peter Backé (1998),
"Currency boards in Central and Eastern Europe – experience and future perspectives" in *Focus on Transition* I/1998, Oesterreichische Nationalbank, Vienna.

Philips, Kaia (1999),
"Wage dynamics and labour mobility in Estonia" in Eamets (1999).

Psalida, E. (1998),
   in J. Berengaut *et al.* "The Baltic Countries: from economic stabilization to EU accession", IMF *Occasional Paper* No. 173, Washington.

Pohl G., R.E. Anderson, S. Claessens and S. Djankov (1997),
   "Privatization and restructuring in Central and Eastern Europe: evidence and policy options", World Bank Technical Paper No. 368, Washington D.C.

Purju, A. (1996),
   "The political economy of privatization in Estonia", Working Paper, Centre for Economic Reform and Transformation, Heriot-Watt University, Edinburgh.

Purju A. (1998),
   "Interrelationships between privatization methods, ownership structure and economic results: evidence from Estonia", Conference Paper, 1st INTER-conference, Copenhagen, CEES/CBS August.

Purju A. and J. Terk (1998),
   "Company adjustment and restructuring problems in Estonia between 1992-1995", Working Paper No. 11, March, Tallinn Technical University.

Rainys, Gediminas (1998),
   "Industrial restructuring in Lithuania: analysis by branch and case studies" in *New Neighbours in Eastern Europe: Economic and Industrial Reform in Lithuania, Latvia and Estonia,* Christian von Hirschhausen (ed.), Les Presses de l'École des Mines, pp. 112-127.

Rajasalu, T. (1994),
   "Estonian economy: Summer 1994", Report No. 2, Institute of Economics.

Rajevska, Feliciana *et al.* (1999),
   Monitoring the Development of Social Protection Reform in the CEECs, 1: *Pension system, Health Care, Unemployment Protection,* National Survey: Latvia, Phare Consensus II Programme, University of York.

Reardon, Jack (1996),
   "An assessment of the transition to a market economy in the Baltic Republics" *Journal of Economic Issues,* Vol. 30, No. 2, June, pp. 629-638.

Roland, G. and T. Verdier,
   "Transition and the output fall", *Economics of transition,* 7(1), pp. 1-28.

Ryder, Andrew (1998),
   Regional Problems and Policies in the Baltics and Kalinningrad, OECD/TDS report prepared for the Working Party on Regional Development Policies.

Saavalainen, Tapio (1994),
   "Stabilization in the Baltic Countries: a comparative analysis". IMF *Working Paper,* Washington.

Semeta, A. (1997),
   "Economic transition in Lithuania – 1996", mimeo, Vilnius.

Sorsa, Piritta (1994*a*),
   "Latvia: trade issues in transition" in *Trade in the New Independent States,* Constantine Michalopoulos and David G. Tarr (eds), Studies of Economies in Transformation, 13, The World Bank/UNDP, pp. 141-155.

Sorsa, Piritta (1994*b*),
   "Lithuania: trade issues in transition" in *Trade in the New Independent States,* Constantine Michalopoulos and David G. Tarr (eds), Studies of Economies in Transformation, 13, The World Bank/UNDP, pp.157-170.

Statistical Office of Estonia (SOE),
  Estonian Statistics, various editions.

Statistical Office of Estonia (SOE) (1997),
  Household's Income and Expenditure, Tallinn.

Statistical Office of Estonia (SOE) (1998a),
  Labour Force, Tallinn.

Statistical Office of Estonia (SOE) (1998b),
  Wages and Salaries, Tallinn.

Statistics Lithuania (LS),
  Economic and Social Development in Lithuania, various editions, Vilnius.

Statistics Lithuania (LS) (1998),
  Labour Force, Employment and Unemployment. May 1998 (Labour Force Survey Results), Vilnius.

Statistics Lithuania (LS) (1999),
  Household Budget Survey Results, 1 quarter, Vilnius.

Steinbuka, I. (1996),
  "Privatization in Latvia and the role of employee ownership", in N. Mygind (ed.) *Privatization and Financial Participation in the Baltic Countries* part I, CEES, Copenhagen Business School.

Steinbuka, I. and M. Kazaks (1996),
  "Fiscal adjustment in Latvia under transition", Heriot-Watt Discussion Paper 96/1, Edinburgh.

Steinbuka, I. and I. Kodolina (1998),
  Enu ekonomika un neiekasetie nodokli Latvija (The Shadow Economy and Tax Evasion in Latvia), Ministry of Finance, Riga.

Sutela, P. (1994),
  "Privatization, employment and inflation in the Baltic Countries" in *Communist Economies and Economic Transformation*, Vol. 6, No. 2.

Terk, E. (1996),
  "Employee ownership and the Political debate in Estonia 1987-1994" in N. Mygind (ed.) *Privatization and Financial Participation in the Baltic Countries* part I, CEES, Copenhagen Business School.

Tornell, A. (1999),
  "Privatizing the Privatized", NBER Working Paper No. 7206, July.

UNICEF (1998),
  Education for All? The MONEE Project: Regional Monitoring Report No. 5, CEE/CIS/Baltics, Florence.

United Nations Development Program (UNDP) (1996) (1997a) (1998b),
  Lithuanian Human Development Report, Vilnius.

United Nations Development Program (UNDP) (1997a),
  Latvia Human Development Report, Riga.

United Nations Development Program (UNDP) (1998a),
  Estonian Human Development Report 1998, Tallinn.

United Nations Development Program (UNDP) (1999),
  Socio-economic trends in Lithuania, the UNDP home page, Vilnius.

Uvalic, Milica and Daniel Vaughan-Whitehead (1997),
Privatization Surprises in Transition Economies, Elgar, Cheltenham, UK.

Van Arkadie, Brian *et. al.* (1991),
Economic Survey of the Baltic Republics, Stockholm.

Van Arkadie, Brian and Mats Karlsson (1992),
Economic Survey of the Baltic States, Pinter Publishers.

Venesaar U. and J. Hackey (1995),
Economic and social changes in the Baltic States in 1992-1994. Estonian Academy of Sciences, Tallinn.

Vojevoda, L. and L. Rumpis (1993),
"Small privatization in Latvia", mimeo, Institute of Economics, Latvian Academy of Sciences.

World Bank (1993),
Latvia: The Transition to a Market Economy.

World Bank (1993*a*),
Estonia: The Transition to a Market Economy, A World Bank Country Study, Washington.

World Bank (1993*b*),
Latvia: The Transition to a Market Economy, A World Bank Country Study, Washington.

World Bank (1993*c*),
Lithuania: The Transition to a Market Economy, A World Bank Country Study, Washington.

World Bank (1993*d*),
Statistical Handbook 1993, *States of the Former* USSR, Studies of Economies in Transformation 8.

World Bank (1995),
World Tables 1995.

World Bank (1996),
World Development Report: From Plan to Market, Oxford Press, New York

World Bank (1998),
Lithuania: An Opportunity for Economic Success, A World Bank Country Study, Washington.

Annex I

Agriculture in Estonia, Latvia and Lithuania: developments and policies

In the latter half of 1998 and the beginning of 1999, as growth in Estonia, Latvia and Lithuania slowed sharply, the agricultural sector suffered a serious setback. Against a background of depressed commodity markets, exports of agricultural products and farm incomes fell sharply. Moreover, the prospects for any improvement in the short term are rather poor; the medium term outlook will depend on a recovery in demand, as well as the supply response in OECD countries. The general policy response in the Baltic countries has been to raise budgetary expenditures on agricultural support and raise import tariffs on selected agricultural products, as well as to reorient trade to the EU, the CEECs and other OECD countries. Implementation of the Baltic Free Trade Area (BAFTA) continued in 1998-1999, and this has led to some increase in agricultural trade flows between the three countries, which in turn has contributed to further convergence in farmgate and retail prices for the main agricultural and food products across the region.

While agricultural exports fell sharply in the latter quarter of 1998 and in 1999, especially exports to Russia and the CIS, imports have also contracted resulting in a narrowing of the agro-food trade deficit. In all three Baltic countries agricultural producers have experienced sharply falling incomes due to a decline in output, lower farm gate prices and rising input prices. To some extent the fall in farm incomes has been offset by higher budgetary expenditures in the form of direct payments and input subsidies. During 1998-99, the Baltic countries made significant progress in harmonising their veterinary and phytosanitary measures and in aligning their agricultural policy framework and instruments with those of the EU. Moreover, Latvia and Estonia have acceded to the WTO, while Lithuania is at an advanced stage in the negotiations. The Baltic countries are therefore subject to the commitments under the Uruguay Round Agreement on agriculture based on the three pillars; market access, domestic policy measures and export subsidies.

In the short-medium term there are several important challenges facing the agro-food sector in the Baltic region. These include the need to deepen the implementation of the BAFTA, to strengthen co-operation in the harmonisation of policies for in the agro-food sector and border measures, as well as to develop alternative export markets for agricultural products. A major further challenge relates to the implementation of policies that will facilitate further restructuring and the development of off-farm employment opportunities for those leaving agriculture. Additional improvements are also needed in developing appropriate institutions for the operation of a market based agro-food sector, particularly in relation to market information systems, rural development and environmental measures. The long-term challenge facing the agro-food sector is accession to the EU and the adoption of the CAP framework for agricultural policies. At the same time, there is the need to improve efficiency and to develop a more sustainable agro-food sector that is competitive on both the domestic and foreign markets. Problems encountered in overcoming technical barriers to trade, sanitary and phytosanitary measures are particularly challenging to the Baltic countries as well as raising quality standards to internationally accepted levels.

Agricultural output and employment

Agriculture continues to be an important sector in the Baltic region and represents a significant, albeit declining share of economic output in the three countries. During the 1990s the relative importance of agriculture has fallen sharply, especially in Estonia and Latvia, and to a lesser extent in Lithuania, due to the contraction of the sector, as well as the more rapid development of non-agricultural activities. Preliminary estimates indicate that in 1998 agriculture's share of GDP fell to about 4 per cent in Estonia, 5 per cent in Latvia and 10 per cent in Lithuania (Figure A1). However, when primary agriculture is combined with food and beverages, the agro-food sector accounts for a much larger share of GDP, ranging from 10 per cent in Estonia, to 11 per cent in Latvia and 14 per cent in Lithuania.

As regards employment in the sector, agriculture has played an important buffer role to rising levels of unemployment during the transition process, especially in rural areas. Although starting at a similar position in 1990, the trend in agriculture's share of total employment differs across the Baltic countries, showing a gradual fall in Estonia, remaining relatively stable in Latvia, while increasing in Lithuania (Figure A2). In 1998 the share of total employment engaged in agriculture ranged from 7 per cent in Estonia, to 17 per cent

Figure A1.   **Share of agriculture in GDP**

Per cent

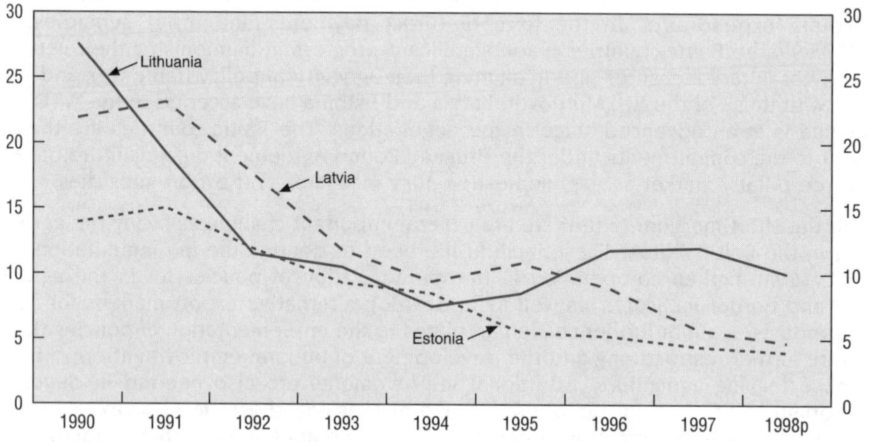

p: preliminary.
Source: OECD.

Figure A2.   **Share of agriculture in employment**
Per cent

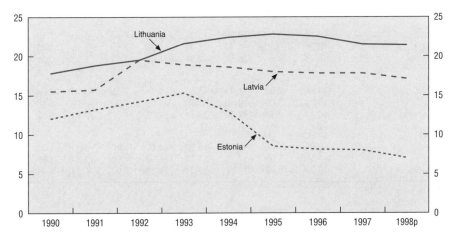

p: preliminary.
Note: For Latvia, agriculture also includes forestry, fishing and hunting.
Source: OECD.

in Latvia and 22 per cent in Lithuania. The high proportion of labour employed in agriculture relative to its share of GDP reflects a rather low level of labour productivity in the sector. Part of the increase in employment in the sector has been due to the nature of land reform, with land privatisation taking place largely via the restitution process, in addition to the lack of off-farm employment opportunities in the region.

Agricultural output fell by over 50 per cent in the three Baltic countries between 1990 and 1995, however, in 1996 and 1997 the rate of decline in gross agricultural output (GAO) slowed in Estonia and Latvia, while in Lithuania output increased. As regards the composition of agricultural output, livestock production continues to be the dominant component, although it has steadily declined during the 1990s. Both livestock and crop production have contracted sharply during the 1990s due to the uncertainties associated with the transition process, deterioration in the terms of trade for agricultural products, as well as greater competition on the domestic and export markets. In 1998 agricultural output continued to fall in the three Baltic countries, albeit to a lesser extent in Estonia, where livestock production even showed some increase (Table A1). One of the important consequences of the sharp decline in agricultural production has been the increase in excess capacity in the food processing sector across the region.

After the initial price-cost squeeze on agricultural producers in the early 1990s, the income situation of producers improved during mid 1990s due to the introduction of support policies, better market opportunities, as well as stronger international commodity markets. However, a renewed price-cost squeeze has emerged over the last two years arising from depressed commodity markets, exacerbated by the spillover effects of the

Table A1.   **Gross agricultural output, total, crops and livestock**

Per cent change from previous year

	1990	1991	1992	1993	1994	1995	1996	1997	1998p
Total									
Estonia	−13.10	−5.80	−19.50	−12.20	−12.90	−0.90	−6.30	−1.50	−0.50
Latvia	−10.20	9.80	8.30	−11.00	−16.30	−1.60	−3.40	4.70	−5.00
Lithuania	−6.50	−4.86	−26.80	−2.01	−16.95	7.67	8.50	5.80	−2.52
Crops									
Estonia	−24.80	−2.00	−11.90	−3.80	−15.20	7.80	−4.30	−2.00	−1.50
Latvia	−19.30	5.00	−10.50	−1.10	−23.70	−7.00	−6.10	−3.30	−8.00
Lithuania	−8.13	2.29	−33.39	29.11	−27.02	14.77	22.10	5.62	−3.83
Livestock									
Estonia	−8.00	−10.60	−19.60	−18.10	−11.00	−5.90	−8.20	−1.00	1.00
Latvia	−5.50	−8.00	−17.40	−34.20	−18.00	−4.90	−12.80	−5.70	−2.00
Lithuania	−5.22	−10.28	−21.11	−29.73	−4.35	0.90	−6.27	6.09	−0.68

p: Preliminary.
Source: OECD Secretariat.

Russian financial crisis and the collapse of the Russian market for agricultural products. For example, in Estonia the farm gate price of milk fell by 40 per cent in the fourth quarter of 1998 compared with the same period the previous year. In 1998 the average rural family income in Estonia fell to 75 per cent of the average urban family income.

While inflows of foreign direct investment into the Baltic region have risen sharply during the 1990s, a small, but increasing share of these inflows has been to the agro-food sector. Most of the investment in the agro-food sector has been into the higher value added products such as confectionery, tobacco and beverages, with investment in primary agriculture almost negligible. In 1998, inflows of foreign investment into the agro-food sector were estimated at US$26 million in Estonia, US$60 million in Latvia, and over US$100 million in Lithuania.

Agricultural trade

Trade policies

Since independence Estonia has maintained a completely open trade regime for agricultural and food products, while Latvia and Lithuania took a more cautious approach to liberalisation and implemented internal market border protection measures. However, since 1993 the current system of tariffs has been in place. It consists of three broad types; conventional or MFN tariffs, preferential or tariffs under free trade agreements, and autonomous or sanctional tariffs. Latvia continues to maintain a rather liberal approach to agricultural trade policy, gradually lowering the average import tariff rates. Agricultural trade policies in Lithuania have been quite inconsistent during the 1990s. For example, Lithuania has used both export subsidies on meat and milk products and at other times applied quantitative restrictions in the form of quotas on grains. Latvia has also applied export subsidies on dairy products. And automatic licensing for grain exports in order to maintain grain balances. While import tariffs in Latvia and Lithuania are still used to regulate food imports, they are mainly applied on an *ad valorem* basis.

Unlike many of the transition economies, the three Baltic countries have not resorted to import surcharges on agricultural and food imports, while other non-tariff barriers in the form of automatic licensing have been used only by Latvia. As regards quantitative restrictions on agricultural imports, both Latvia and Lithuania have applied such measures on an *ad hoc* basis. One area of concern in all three Baltic countries is the rapidly appreciating real exchange rates which have eroded the competitiveness of exports and have contributed to the growth in food imports (see Chapters I and II).

During 1998 and early 1999, the Baltic countries have implemented several measures to regulate imports. In 1998 Estonia introduced a licensing system for imports of all agricultural and food products. The main objective of this measure is to ensure the proper handling of food products in response to consumer concerns over food safety. In May 1999 the Estonian government initiated a draft law which would permit the introduction of custom tariffs in 2000 towards third countries. This therefore excludes most Estonian trade partners such as the EU, Latvia and Lithuania. The introduction of custom tariffs is part of the process of aligning Estonian border measures with those of the EU in preparation for full accession.

In Latvia, agricultural and food imports are subject to tariffs which range from 0 per cent for wheat to 60 per cent for refined sugar. At the beginning of 1999 Latvia imposed a unilateral ban on imports of minced poultry meat from Estonia due to sanitary concerns. With the collapse in farmgate prices for pigs, which fell by more than 50 per cent in 1998-99, the Latvian government, in June 1999, (as a safeguard measure) introduced a 70 per cent duty on imported pigmeat for a specified period of two hundred days. This measure is a direct response to the acceleration in pigmeat imports, which has caused major disruption of the domestic market. In December 1999 the Latvian parliament passed legislation extending domestic pork market protection measures to the end of 2001.

In 1998 Lithuania increased tariffs on imports of agricultural and food products from the EU in response to the financial crisis in Russia. In January 1999 the Lithuanian government also introduced a new reference price calculation mechanism as the basis for calculating custom duties on a range of food imports, in particular meats, dairy products and eggs, from all countries, including Estonia and Latvia. However, following strong protests from Latvia and Estonia, imports of food products from these countries were exempted from the new calculation mechanism. In response to the worsening international prices for meat and dairy products, the Lithuanian government increased export subsidies by over 50 per cent in 1998. However, this development has caused serious difficulties in Lithuania's on-going negotiations for WTO membership. The WTO approved Latvian and Estonian applications for membership in October 1998 and April 1999 respectively.

Trade flows

The share of agriculture and food products in total exports has fluctuated widely for the three Baltic countries during the 1990s, though it has more recently stabilised somewhat at a lower, but similar level in all three countries (Table A2). On the other hand, the share of food in total imports has increased in all three countries. During the early 1990s the three Baltic countries were net exporters of agricultural products, but since 1995 agriculture and food imports have been rising faster than exports. Since 1996 all three countries have been net food importers. The growing imbalance in the agro-food trade is a

Table A2.   **Share of agriculture and food products in total trade**

Per cent

	1992	1993	1994	1995	1996	1997	1998p
Exports							
Estonia	15.7	23.5	22.0	16.4	15.8	16.5	15.9
Latvia	10.6	14.9	12.8	16.4	16.9	14.5	10.8
Lithuania	n.a.	n.a.	24.1	18.3	17.1	16.0	14.1
Imports							
Estonia	9.0	14.7	15.9	14.2	15.5	16.4	16.9
Latvia	7.5	6.4	10.7	10.9	13.4	13.9	13.3
Lithuania	n.a.	n.a.	10.0	13.4	13.1	11.1	11.2

p: Preliminary.
n.a. Not available.
Source: OECD Secretariat.

cause of particular concern in the region. In 1998 the agro-food trade deficit deteriorated further, largely due to the collapse of the Russian market and low commodity prices.

The product composition of exports and imports is similar for the three Baltic countries, with dairy products, livestock, fish and beverages accounting for the bulk of food and beverage exports, while imports consist largely of high-value added food products, tobacco, beverages, feed grains, fruits and vegetables. In recent years, imports of beef, poultry and pigmeat have increased especially in Estonia and Latvia. In the case of Lithuania a substantial proportion of food and beverage exports is attributed to re-exports.

As regards the pattern of trade, Russia and the CIS have been the most important export markets and accounted for over three-fifths of agricultural and food exports from the Baltic region up to 1997, but fell sharply in 1998 (Table A3). The share of exports destined for the EU continues to increase, aided by the implementation of the Europe Agreements and the desire for greater integration with western Europe. Trade in agricultural and food products between the Baltic countries has also increased significantly in recent years, albeit from a rather low base, driven by the implementation of the BAFTA. The EU is the main source of food imports and accounts for over 50 per cent of all food imports into the Baltic region in recent years (Table A4). Imports from other CEECs have also increased steadily, helped by the implementation of various bilateral agreements, while imports from Russia and the CIS have fallen sharply since 1996.

Estonia, Latvia and Lithuania have recorded substantial deficits on their agro-food trade balances with the EU, in particular, and the deficit has increased significantly since 1996. On the other hand, the three Baltic countries have maintained a significant surplus on their trade balance with the CIS, in particular Russia, Ukraine and Belarus.

Impact of the Russian crisis on agricultural trade

Since Russia has been the major export destination for agricultural and food products from the Baltic region, the financial crisis has severely disrupted trade flows between the two regions. The spillover effects of the Russian economic crisis, and in particular the redirection of third country agricultural exports from the Russian market to the Baltics has resulted in a collapse in prices across the region. This in turn has resulted in steadily

Table A3. **Agricultural and food exports by destination, 1993-98**

Per cent

	EU	Other OECD	CEECs[1]	NIS	Other	Total
1993						
Estonia	18	0	21	45	17	100
Latvia	10	5	20	66	1	100
Lithuania	16	4	12	66	2	100
1994						
Estonia	15	8	20	55	2	100
Latvia	8	4	13	74	1	100
Lithuania	20	2	13	63	2	100
1995						
Estonia	29	1	15	53	2	100
Latvia	11	2	9	76	2	100
Lithuania	26	0	14	59	1	100
1996						
Estonia	20	3	15	59	2	100
Latvia	15	1	11	73	1	100
Lithuania	17	5	12	63	3	100
1997						
Estonia	16	3	16	64	2	100
Latvia	11	0	16	68	4	100
Lithuania	20	7	12	59	3	100
1998						
Estonia	16	4	19	61	1	100
Latvia	20	1	22	47	9	100
Lithuania	24	11	17	46	2	100

p   Preliminary.
1.   Figures for Poland, Hungary and the Czech Republic are included in the CEECs from 1996 to ensure consistency, although they are members of OECD.
Source: OECD Secretariat.

growing pressure in the Baltic region for increased protection of the domestic market for selected products, and the reintroduction (Latvia), or increase in export subsidies (Lithuania) for the main agricultural products.

Estimates indicate that agricultural and food exports from the Baltic region fell by at least 30 per cent in the last quarter of 1998 compared to the same period in 1997. In overall terms, however, the decline was less dramatic with agricultural exports for 1998 declining by about 18 per cent in Latvia and Lithuania, but increasing in Estonia. In the first half of 1999, exports of agricultural and food products have continued to fall with some estimates indicating that exports fell by a further 20 per cent compared to the same period in 1998. Agricultural exports to Russia and the CIS are likely to remain far below their past levels for the foreseeable future, and developing new export markets is a high priority for the three Baltic countries.

Table A4. **Agricultural and food imports by source, 1993-98**

Per cent

	EU	Other OECD	CEECs[1]	NIS	Other	Total
1993						
Estonia	50	0	5	9	36	100
Latvia	36	11	17	25	10	100
Lithuania	n.a.	n.a.	n.a.	n.a.	n.a.	n.a.
1994						
Estonia	41	36	6	9	8	100
Latvia	38	13	20	11	18	100
Lithuania	40	24	18	14	4	100
1995						
Estonia	66	12	11	10	1	100
Latvia	50	14	14	12	10	100
Lithuania	42	12	15	21	10	100
1996						
Estonia	64	8	12	10	6	100
Latvia	51	6	18	12	12	100
Lithuania	45	13	17	21	3	100
1997						
Estonia	47	20	8	4	21	100
Latvia	53	11	25	4	7	100
Lithuania	51	14	22	10	3	100
1998						
Estonia	49	23	10	5	13	100
Latvia	51	8	29	4	8	100
Lithuania	53	12	25	8	2	100

p   Preliminary.
n.a.   Not available.
1.   Figures for Poland, Hungary and the Czech Republic are included in the CEECs from 1996 to ensure consistency, although they are Members of OECD.
Source: OECD Secretariat.

Of the three Baltic countries, Lithuania continues to be the most vulnerable to economic developments in Russia. The sharp fall in demand in Russia and the CIS has resulted in severe financial losses for the Lithuanian agro-food sector. At the same time as exports of high value added processed food products fell, exports of unprocessed agricultural products increased. As regards the geographic structure of the agricultural and food trade flows, the share of Lithuania's food exports to the CIS and EU declined by 33 per cent and 2 per cent respectively. This fall was partly offset by a rise in agro-food exports to the Czech Republic, Hungary and Poland (by 78 per cent), albeit from a low base. Trade in agricultural products with Estonia and Latvia also increased substantially, with exports rising by about 14 per cent and imports by 9 per cent in 1998. On the other hand, food imports from the CEECs and the EU increased by 30 per cent and 7 per cent respectively, but fell by almost 19 per cent for the CIS. In overall terms, agricultural and food imports into Lithuania decreased by 1.7 per cent in 1998 compared with 1997.

Despite the economic crisis in Russia, overall agro-food exports from Estonia rose by 6 per cent, largely due to increased demand from Latvia, Lithuania and Ukraine. One of the major export destinations for Estonian food products was Latvia, which accounted for 21 per cent of exports; of which, 67 per cent consisted of meat products. Food exports to the European Union experienced a slight increase of about 2 per cent. In 1998, agricultural and food imports to Estonia increased by almost 10 per cent. For Latvia, shrinking demand in 1998 from the CIS was partly offset by a sharp increase in exports to the European Union and the CEECs, which increased by about 41 per cent and 14 per cent respectively. Agro-food imports increased by about 12 per cent in 1998 mainly from the EU and the CEECs.

The dairy industry in the Baltic region was particularly affected by the collapse in demand in Russia, with a significant fall in exports of dairy products in the last quarter of 1998. This resulted in Baltic dairies slashing prices to producers and/or temporarily closing their processing facilities. For example, some farmers have not been paid for up to 6 months for milk delivered to the dairies. Exports of dairy products from Estonia fell by about 29 per cent in 1998 compared to the same period in 1997, while exports of milk powder fell by almost 50 per cent.

On the other hand, exports of fresh and frozen fish rose by 45 per cent and processed fish and meat products by 6 per cent. As regards the composition of agricultural imports, dairy products account for almost 9 per cent, meat products about 7 per cent and beverages 12 per cent of total Estonian agro-food imports.

In Latvia, the composition of agro-food exports and imports remained relatively stable in 1998, except for exports of fish products, which fell by about 36 per cent. The composition of Latvian exports shows a clear trend toward more processed food products. In spite of the tightening of EU standards for health and hygiene regulations after 1997 towards the CEEC, the EU market has continued to play an important role in the export structure of Latvian dairy products. At this juncture, nine Latvian dairies are EU approved to export milk and milk products to the European Community. The EU ban on imports of Estonian dairy products was lifted at the beginning of 1999, following improvements in the implementation of the sanitary regulations.

Policy developments

Structural policies and privatisation

Privatisation and restructuring of the agricultural sector has led to fundamental changes in ownership and land use patterns across the Baltic region. Prior to independence, state and collective farms accounted for almost all of the agricultural land. However, by mid-1999, land privatisation had been completed in Latvia and was well advanced in Lithuania and Estonia. Most of the agricultural land has been privatised via the restitution process (in-kind or through privatisation vouchers) in the Baltic region, in particular, in Latvia and Lithuania, with private family farms becoming the dominant ownership structure, although a small but significant amount of land is owned by corporate entities, to a lesser extent in Latvia.

Farm structures continue to evolve across the region, with small and medium sized family farms dominant in Latvia and Lithuania while large farm size is dominant in Estonia. Despite the fact that land restitution has been ongoing for several years, almost 70 per cent of agricultural land in Estonia remains under state control. In this country most of this land is leased on the basis of 1-3 year contracts. An amendment to the Land Reform Law was approved in March 1999, and is aimed at accelerating the development of a functioning land market by simplifying procedures for land privatisation and long-term leasing of agricultural land. In principle, this development should help encourage greater interest in private land ownership and provide greater stability in the sector. In Latvia, after decollectivisation and land privatisation the on-going restructuring has resulted in an increase in the average family farm size to about 14 ha of agricultural land. In Lithuania, the number of family farms continue to increase while household plots and agricultural partnerships are declining. A small scale farming structure is emerging in Lithuania, since almost three-fifths of farms have less than 10 ha, while a further one-quarter have between 10-20 ha. Most of these small scale farms are non-viable as full-time units, and further restructuring is likely in the medium term. Nevertheless, the development of a functioning land market should help to resolve many of the current structural problems in the sector, and should lead to a more efficient and viable farming structure in the region.

While the three Baltic countries have implemented legislation which permits the functioning of a land market, demand for agricultural land is low due to the lack of profitability in the sector, the high degree of economic uncertainty, and low employment opportunities in rural areas outside agriculture. Most of the demand for agricultural land comes from outside the agricultural sector, mainly entrepreneurs who purchase land for non-agricultural use. However, an active land leasing market has developed in all three Baltic countries with much of the land leased through various types of informal leasing arrangements. Only Latvia, however, allows foreigners to purchase agricultural land. Most of the land in State ownership in Latvia (less then 0.4 per cent of total) and Lithuania is comprised of experimental and training farms and land managed by local authorities.

The downstream industries

The upstream and downstream industries are completely privatised in Latvia and Estonia, and nearing completion in Lithuania. In all three Baltic countries privatisation of the high value added industries such as bakeries and confectionery took place relatively rapidly. However, the privatisation of meat processing enterprises, and to some extent dairies, have proven to be more difficult. In particular, the heavy debt overhang, low level of efficiency and poor management have impeded the privatisation of these enterprises. In Estonia, there is substantial foreign involvement in the privatised industries, whereas in Latvia a large number of processing enterprises have been taken over by producers' associations or processing co-operatives which in the short run may mean there is little pressure for further restructuring of these entities. In Lithuania, also special share preferences were given to agricultural producers in the privatisation process in an attempt to increase the degree of vertical integration in the agro-food sector. However, this approach, while well intentioned, in many cases has led to the crowding out of much needed investment in the sector. In 1998 the Lithuanian government abolished the system of allocating shares on preferential terms to agricultural producers.

In 1998 the sugar processing industry in Lithuania was privatised with government shares sold to a Danish company. The lowest level of privatisation is in the canned fruit and vegetable industry in Lithuania. With the implementation of stricter bankruptcy procedures, several of these enterprises were liquidated in 1998. This should help to speed up the restructuring of the industry.

While there has been a relatively rapid change in the ownership of food processing enterprises, the restructuring of their management and the modernisation of their plant and equipment have progressed more slowly, mainly due to the lack of investment in the sector. Another development in the downstream sector in recent years has been the establishment of many small meat processing plants, especially in rural areas. While these new plants have increased competition and lower consumer prices in the short-run, they are unlikely to survive in the longer term because of their small size and their inability to neither exploit economies of scale, nor to produce high value differentiated products. The economic performance of the food processing sector deteriorated in 1998 and the first part of 1999 due to the continued overcapacity in the sector in addition to the collapse of the Russian market and the slowdown in economic activity in western Europe. The continued fall in GAO, and in particular livestock production has exacerbated the problem of excess capacity in the meat processing sector, and the general lack of management and marketing expertise will continue to inhibit the development of a more efficient and market oriented agro-food processing sector.

Further rationalisation and restructuring of the food processing sector is required if a competitive Baltic food sector is to be established. Given the relatively small consumer base in the Baltic region, it is likely that this will lead to the development of pan-Baltic processing enterprises in the region. One of the major problems is the need to improve hygiene and quality standards, although significant progress has been made in implementing EU sanitary and phytosanitary regulations.

Support to the agricultural sector

The medium-long-term policy goal for the Baltic countries is membership in the European Union. In this context, the three Baltic countries have started to harmonise their agricultural policies with those of the EU and are in the process of implementing the EU veterinary and phytosanitary measures as well as support policies similar to those of the CAP. A high priority has been given, especially in Lithuania to the introduction of direct payments, price regulation, intervention measures and customs tariffs. Estonia was the only Baltic country selected for the "first wave" of EU membership negotiations, though at its summit in December 1999 the EU opened membership negotiations with all the remaining candidate countries.

Agricultural support policies

The level of support to agriculture in the three Baltic countries as measured by the percentage PSE (total support as a share of the value of production) has been relatively low (even negative) during the early transition years (Table A5). However, support started to increase in 1993, but remained negative until 1995. These negative estimates between 1992 and 1994 represent an implicit taxation of the sector. Support continued to increase through to 1998. The main element of support is market price support (MPS) which reflects the various border measures that have been in operation in Latvia and Lithuania. In Estonia, which until recently had no border tariffs, support in the form of credit subsidies and general services have played a more important role in total support. The introduction of direct payments in Latvia and Lithuania in 1996 contributed to the more rapid increase in the PSEs in these countries. In 1998, the large increase in the PSEs for the three countries reflects an increase in MPS, due to the more rapid fall in world commodity prices relative to domestic producer prices. The slower fall in producer prices tends to suggest a relatively poor transmission of world prices, due to the apparent time-lags involved in reflecting such changes at farm level.

Table A5. **Estimates of support to agriculture by country, 1986-98**

	Units	1986	1987	1988	1989	1990	1991	1992	1993	1994	1995	1996	1997p	1998e
Estonia														
Total PSE	mn US$	2 472	2 592	2 764	2 704	3 060	1 708	-274	-113	-42	-1	41	28	86
	mn ECU	2 519	2 248	2 339	2 456	2 410	1 382	-212	-97	-35	0	32	25	77
General Support Estimate	mn US$	25	21	21	28	30	34	6	9	10	17	13	10	13
Total Support Estimate	mn US$	3 490	3 692	3 850	3 812	4 289	1 791	-264	-104	-32	16	54	39	99
	% GDP	n.c.	n.c.	n.c.	n.c.	n.c.	n.c.	-25.4	-6.2	-1.4	0.5	1.2	0.8	1.9
Percentage PSE	**%**	**76**	**75**	**79**	**74**	**71**	**59**	**-97**	**-32**	**-10**	**0**	**7**	**5**	**16**
Latvia														
Total PSE	mn US$	4 380	4 449	5 678	5 437	5 547	13 653	-485	-222	43	35	22	35	65
	mn ECU	4 463	3 859	4 805	4 938	4 369	11 045	-375	-189	37	27	17	31	58
General Support Estimate	mn US$	120	133	119	132	150	1 301	13	18	8	13	8	8	11
Total Support Estimate	mn US$	5 669	5 878	7 002	6 946	7 865	15 613	-479	-217	51	49	30	43	76
	% GDP	n.c.	n.c.	n.c.	n.c.	n.c.	n.c.	n.c.	-10.0	1.4	1.1	0.6	0.8	1.2
Percentage PSE	**%**	**83**	**82**	**83**	**78**	**76**	**83**	**-101**	**-39**	**7**	**4**	**3**	**4**	**10**
Lithuania														
Total PSE	mn US$	5 205	5 511	7 401	6 610	7 670	-915	-733	-298	-137	5	74	132	231
	mn ECU	5 304	4 780	6 262	6 004	6 041	-740	-566	-254	-116	4	59	116	207
General Support Estimate	mn US$	1 010	266	504	498	119	10	13	18	40	43	52	60	55
Total Support Estimate	mn US$	7 970	7 693	9 829	9 129	9 556	-905	-720	-279	-97	48	126	192	286
	% GDP	n.c.	n.c.	n.c.	n.c.	n.c.	n.c.	-37.4	-10.4	-2.3	0.8	1.6	2.0	2.9
Percentage PSE	**%**	**79**	**77**	**80**	**75**	**72**	**-262**	**-124**	**-37**	**-15**	**0**	**5**	**7**	**14**
Czech Republic														
Total PSE	mn US$	5 104	4 525	4 184	5 258	5 306	4 449	1 689	1 329	869	610	636	409	731
	mn ECU	5 201	3 925	3 541	4 775	4 179	3 600	1 305	1 134	733	467	501	361	654
General Support Estimate	mn US$	19	20	20	56	26	35	25	22	62	119	124	110	99
Total Support Estimate	mn US$	5 939	5 366	4 986	6 741	6 067	4 484	1 714	1 350	931	728	760	519	831
	% GDP	n.c.	n.c.	n.c.	n.c.	n.c.	8.8	4.3	3.5	2.3	1.4	1.3	1.0	1.5
Percentage PSE	**%**	**66**	**59**	**53**	**55**	**54**	**52**	**31**	**27**	**21**	**13**	**13**	**10**	**17**
Hungary														
Total PSE	mn US$	3 393	3 047	2 707	2 132	1 914	793	905	1 005	1 357	840	680	433	642
	mn ECU	3 458	2 643	2 290	1 936	1 507	641	699	858	1 144	642	536	382	574
General Support Estimate	mn US$	86	83	78	81	75	73	84	87	90	95	122	92	126
Total Support Estimate	mn US$	3 879	3 512	2 901	2 308	2 053	913	989	1 092	1 446	935	802	525	768
	% GDP	n.c.	n.c.	n.c.	n.c.	n.c.	2.7	2.7	2.8	3.5	2.1	1.8	1.2	1.6
Percentage PSE	**%**	**45**	**40**	**35**	**27**	**24**	**13**	**17**	**20**	**25**	**14**	**10**	**8**	**12**

Table A5. **Estimates of support to agriculture by country, 1986-98** (cont.)

	Units	1986	1987	1988	1989	1990	1991	1992	1993	1994	1995	1996	1997p	1998e
Poland														
Total PSE	mn US$	6 161	3 688	3 157	869	-1 159	-49	2 598	2 134	2 556	3 190	4 599	3 404	3 746
	mn ECU	6 278	3 199	2 672	789	-913	-39	2 008	1 821	2 155	2 440	3 623	3 003	3 350
General Support Estimate	mn US$	294	303	276	212	224	481	376	323	421	450	526	465	474
Total Support Estimate	mn US$	8 114	5 067	6 481	3 008	-773	436	2 977	2 458	2 979	3 643	5 129	3 873	4 225
	% GDP	n.c.	n.c.	n.c.	n.c.	-1.3	0.6	3.5	2.9	3.2	3.1	3.8	2.9	2.8
Percentage PSE	**%**	**40**	**25**	**30**	**9**	**-18**	**0**	**20**	**15**	**19**	**17**	**24**	**21**	**25**
Slovakia														
Total PSE	mn US$	1 786	1 723	1 664	2 346	2 069	986	596	481	442	403	249	299	464
	mn ECU	1 820	1 494	1 408	2 131	1 630	798	461	410	372	308	196	264	415
General Support Estimate	mn US$	112	128	145	143	139	122	79	52	59	64	59	51	48
Total Support Estimate	mn US$	2 159	2 129	2 091	3 040	2 474	1 107	676	533	501	466	307	350	512
	% GDP	n.c.	n.c.	n.c.	n.c.	n.c.	n.c.	n.c.	4.1	3.6	2.7	1.6	1.8	2.5
Percentage PSE	**%**	**57**	**51**	**46**	**51**	**51**	**35**	**29**	**27**	**24**	**19**	**11**	**14**	**23**
Russia														
Total PSE	mn US$	157 947	162 935	183 996	189 116	148 181	86 172	-13 751	-5 092	-2 766	7 043	12 426	14 476	5 130
	mn ECU	160 948	141 330	155 697	171 755	116 722	69 713	-10 624	-4 347	-2 332	5 388	9 790	12 768	4 627
General Support Estimate	mn US$	6 475	7 326	8 266	8 509	7 452	4 768	362	591	1 002	787	758	2 973	349
Total Support Estimate	mn US$	213 522	220 485	265 276	275 174	224 379	122 960	-13 004	-4 085	-1 566	7 830	13 185	17 449	5 480
	% GDP	n.c.	n.c.	n.c.	n.c.	n.c.	n.c.	-13.2	-2.2	-0.6	2.2	3.1	3.9	2.0
Percentage PSE	**%**	**81**	**80**	**80**	**76**	**69**	**59**	**-86**	**-22**	**-11**	**18**	**26**	**32**	**19**
EU[1]														
Total PSE	mn US$	93 084	106 646	99 054	77 372	125 068	138 549	132 712	121 934	121 146	131 826	109 361	109 670	129 808
	mn ECU	94 853	92 505	83 819	70 269	98 516	112 086	102 533	104 095	102 138	100 847	86 155	96 729	116 075
General Support Estimate	mn US$	8 685	8 794	11 571	8 494	12 988	17 416	14 518	14 626	8 029	7 683	9 519	9 585	8 407
Total Support Estimate	mn US$	104 515	118 955	114 461	89 726	142 695	160 949	152 939	142 385	133 957	144 333	122 585	123 030	142 201
	% GDP	3.1	2.1	1.7	1.5	1.5	1.6	1.3	1.6	1.4	1.0	0.9	1.2	1.4
Percentage PSE	**%**	**48**	**48**	**41**	**36**	**44**	**49**	**46**	**45**	**42**	**40**	**34**	**38**	**45**
OECD[2]														
Total PSE	mn US$	214 259	233 319	214 314	185 521	247 820	263 476	261 167	248 030	249 683	249 148	224 683	215 541	251 155
	mn ECU	218 330	202 380	181 353	168 490	195 208	213 152	201 777	211 743	210 508	190 598	177 006	190 107	224 582
General Support Estimate	mn US$	62 974	57 650	54 655	52 312	53 983	69 784	68 351	77 953	67 522	68 610	62 043	60 760	58 394
Total Support Estimate	mn US$	291 751	303 895	283 351	252 483	320 325	354 157	351 969	349 515	338 535	341 097	307 046	298 887	334 554
	% GDP	2.7	2.1	1.7	1.6	1.6	1.7	1.5	1.6	1.5	1.2	1.1	1.2	1.4
Percentage PSE	**%**	**43**	**43**	**37**	**32**	**38**	**40**	**39**	**38**	**36**	**34**	**31**	**32**	**38**

p: provisional; e: estimate; n.c.: not calculated.
1. EU-12 for 1986-1994, EU-15 from 1995; as from 1990, includes ex-GDR.
2. OECD does not include Czech Republic, Hungary, Poland, Mexico and Korea.
Source: OECD, PSE/CSE database.

The PSE estimates for Estonia are similar to those for Lithuania in 1998, and above the estimates for Latvia in that year. They are also similar to some other central European countries such as the Czech Republic (17 %) and Hungary (12 %), and significantly below the estimates for the EU (45 %) and OECD (38 %) averages. As already noted, while the aggregate level of support to agriculture is relatively low, support varies substantially between crops and livestock. More specifically, since 1996 support to crops has been substantially higher than for livestock. In 1998, the highest figures were for poultry, milk, sugar and coarse grains, while the least supported product was beef.

In Estonia and Latvia the share of the state budget allocated to the agro food sector is relatively low, at less than 5 per cent, but for Lithuania it accounted for some 7 per cent of the state budget. In Lithuania, most of this support is for the implementation of the minimum marginal purchase prices for the major commodities, input subsidies, research and education as well as for supporting exports of selected commodities. In 1998 the Agricultural Loan Guarantee Fund was expanded and provides guarantees for long-term loans for the purchase of machinery and equipment. Also in 1998 an Agricultural and Food Products Market Regulation Agency was established to implement the market regulations, as well as for export promotion.

The Latvian government introduced an intervention scheme for the major grains in 1998 in an attempt to provide a floor price in the face of falling prices. Also there was an increase in direct payments to livestock producers, in particular pig producers, in response to the difficult market conditions. However, the central intention of the Latvian government's agriculture support policies remains to increase farming competitiveness through support to land improvement and investment in the sector. In Estonia, direct payments to crop and livestock producers were introduced in 1998. These payments were mainly aimed at the more efficient farmers as they were based on the criteria of efficiency and size. The Estonian government is also in the process of establishing a new crop insurance programme with the aim of reducing market risks to producers. Part of the premium for the early years is paid by the government, but once established it is envisaged that this programme will be self financing.

Credit and investment policies

The shortage of credit continues to hinder the development of the agricultural sector in the three Baltic countries. Much of the credit available to agriculture is channelled through the state credit institutions – "Maapank" in Estonia, the "Laukkredits" in Latvia and the Agricultural Bank in Lithuania. In 1998 "Maapank" was declared bankrupt, while in Latvia after the successful operation the "Laukkredits" was merged with the state owned commercial bank – Land and Mortgage Bank. In an attempt to overcome the lack of credit in rural areas, several credit and savings co-operatives have been established with the assistance of the EU. However, the amount of finance available from these co-operatives is rather limited.

In Estonia there are two programmes that channel credit to the agricultural sector. The government allocates about EEK 100 million through the Rural Life Credit Fund to commercial banks for agricultural and rural credits, of which, 70 per cent is allocated to agriculture in the form of credit subsidies and investment grants. The other programme is the Rural Life Credit Guarantee Fund (RLCGF), under which the government acts as a guarantor for part of the loans provided by commercial banks to farmers provided they meet certain criteria. In 1998, EEK 47 million of guarantees were issued under this programme. In addition, the investment support scheme was expanded in 1998 with about EEK 52 million allocated for investment in farm buildings and machinery.

In 1998 the Latvian government increased investment support to agriculture in the form of co-financing and credit guarantees. A new World Bank Rural Development project which started in 1998 followed the earlier Agriculture Development project (now implemented), and provides loans for the development of small businesses in rural areas. To encourage investment in the agricultural sector a new programme which provides a subsidy on capital investment in agriculture has been introduced. The cofinancing rate can vary depending on farm location, and whether or not the appliant belongs to the "young farmer" group. To increase the availability of credit, the activities of the Credit Guarantee Fund are being expanded.

In Lithuania, part of the Rural Support Fund is used to subsidise working capital loans to agricultural producers. Individual farmers as well as agricultural partnerships are eligible to participate in this programme. The credit subsidy amounts to about 60 per cent of the market interest rate on one-year loans which bank and credit unions have extended to farmers for the purchase of fuel, fertilisers and chemicals. Farmers, farmer co-operatives and farmer partnerships who take out long-term bank loans are partially compensated on the interest component of the loans. In the case where a farmer raises a loan to buy new agricultural machinery and equipment, the amount of compensation covers 50 per cent of the loan interest; if the loan is utilised for other investment projects, 30 per cent of the loan interest is covered. In addition to loan interest compensation, those who purchase equipment or carry out investment projects are also compensated for part of the capital costs. There are over 23 credit unions in Lithuania, of which, about 12 concentrate on providing loans to the agricultural sector. The Agricultural Loan Guarantee Fund has become more active in the agricultural credit market in recent years. The Fund provides collateral on loans to farmers by sharing the loan risks with the lending bank, and in the event of default, guarantees to repay 80 per cent of the loan to the lending institution.

Rural development policies

Policies aimed at developing rural areas are becoming increasingly important in the Baltic region, in light of the growing regional disparities such as the high and growing level of unemployment in rural areas, the increase in poverty and the need to improve rural infrastructure. In Estonia the development of rural areas has centred around two programmes; the Village Movement Programme and the Programme for Peripheral Regions. The core of the former programme relates to the development of general infrastructure, while the latter programme focuses on providing support to small cottage enterprises, rural tourism and the development of the agro-food sector. In 1998, about EEK 13 million was allocated to these programmes and this was substantially increased in 1999.

While there are no real rural development programmes in operation in Latvia *per se*, a range of programmes are implemented in the rural areas, including the developing of different farming employment opportunities, alternative agricultural businesses, SMEs, etc. However, further elaboration of a more complex rural development programme is envisaged

In 1998 the Lithuanian government increased financial support to the development of rural areas with the launching of a new programme which is aimed at developing alternative sources of incomes for rural inhabitants. The new programme is financed from the Rural Support Fund. About 15 per cent of the Rural Support Fund is devoted to the improvement of infrastructure in rural areas. In seeking to achieve a more sustainable development of the regions, financial support is increased for holdings situated in less favoured areas.

Emerging issues, concerns and challenges

Many of the emerging issues and policy challenges facing the agro-food sector in the Baltic region are similar to those in OECD countries. These include the need to reform domestic support and trade policies, to establish conditions conducive to a competitive and sustainable agro-food industry, and to adopt effective policies to address identified concerns in rural areas and in the area of environmental sustainability. While domestic support to agriculture is currently low compared to the OECD average, there are growing pressures to increase budgetary and market support to the sector. The policy response to such demands should be effectively targeted to overcome the structural weaknesses in the sector, and should not create new economic distortions and inefficiencies that could impede further restructuring of the sector. A key challenge to the Baltic countries is to develop and implement policies that are decoupled from production.

There is a growing awareness that policies should be designed to treat agriculture as an integral part of the broader agro-food chain, and of the overall economy. In this context, the key role of government is to provide the legal and macroeconomic framework to facilitate the mobility of the key factors of production, with important implications for farm incomes. The sector will need to continue to shed labour, as farm size increases and the sector becomes more capital intensive, productive and profitable. Over the long term, policies should target a globally competitive agriculture and agro-food sector.

Transparent, efficient and well functioning input and output markets are crucial for the further development of the farm sector, in the Baltics as elsewhere. The pace of restructuring and developing a competitive industry could be speeded up across the region if liquidation and bankruptcy laws were more rigorously enforced. While substantial progress has been made in land reform, additional efforts are needed to complete the privatisation of unclaimed state owned land and to streamline land legislation in Estonia. An important element in land reform is the need to develop well functioning land markets, which is particularly difficult given the low current profitability levels in agriculture and rural businesses.

The low level of price transmission and lack of transparency remain serious impediments to improving efficiency in the agro-food sector. Foreign investment in the sector is low, but increasing, while trade in agricultural and food products continues to be very important for the Baltic countries. Since the implementation of the BAFTA in 1997, trade in agricultural and food products between the Baltic countries had increased significantly, albeit from a low base. Further deepening of co-operation under the BAFTA is likely to speed up the restructuring and rationalisation in the food processing sector, and may lead to the emergence of several pan-Baltic food processing companies in the medium term. In addition, the Agreement will lead to greater harmonisation of agricultural policies in the three countries, as well as common external tariffs and thus should facilitate integration into the EU. Otherwise the positive impacts from the greater trade openness may be offset by the discrepancies in support policies. Consistent macro-economic policies and a stable price environment with low inflation are crucial to encourage investment and to develop a modern competitive agro-food sector.

In addition, the three Baltic countries face some formidable challenges not faced by most OECD member countries. Foremost amongst them is the need to harmonise national legislation with that of the EU, as harmonisation is a precondition for accession. Of particular concern is the need to ensure internal and external veterinary and phytosanitary control and the development of appropriate institutions at national and regional level. The Baltic countries also face an enormous challenge in developing the administrative and institutional capacities to implement the various elements of the *acquis communautaire*, to gain access to pre-accession funding and to cope with the post-accession responsibilities embodied in the *acquis*. Other important areas which also need to be addressed include the adoption and implementation of the policy instruments of the CAP, rural development measures, taxation, competition policy, as well as relevant environmental and consumer concerns.

Annex II
Statistical Annex

Table A6. **Indicators of living standards**

	1990	1991	1992	1993	1994	1995	1996	1997	1998	1999[1]
A. Real wage indices[1]										
Estonia	100	61	34	36	45	45	47	52	53	
Latvia	100	68	47	49	55	55	51	58	61	
Lithuania	100	71	44	27	31	32	33	37	43	46
B. Main components of household consumption (per cent of expenditure)										
Estonia										
Food	29	36	43	43	41	40	44	39	n.a.	n.a.
Housing, energy	n.a.	n.a.	13	17	17	21	18	18	n.a.	n.a.
Clothing and footwear	18	15	10	8	8	8	7	7	n.a.	n.a.
Other	n.a.	n.a.	35	33	34	30	35	35	n.a.	n.a.
Latvia										
Food	38	n.a.	n.a.	48	46	44	51	47	41	n.a.
Housing, energy	4	n.a.	n.a.	15	14	14	14	15	17	n.a.
Clothing and footwear	19	n.a.	n.a.	8	8	8	6	6	7	n.a.
Other	39	n.a.	n.a.	29	33	34	29	32	35	n.a.
Lithuania[2]										
Food	34	38	60	62	57	57	55	52	48	46
Housing, energy	n.a.	n.a.	n.a.	n.a.	13	15	12	12	12	17
Clothing and footwear	n.a.	n.a.	n.a.	n.a.	10	8	8	8	8	6
Other	n.a.	n.a.	n.a.	n.a.	20	20	25	28	32	31

C. Key consumption items	Kg per year per capita:									
Latvia										
Meat	83	74	63	61	51	52	57	56	60	
Dairy products	454	420	370	355	344	348	311	291	284	
Potatoes	125	115	116	119	108	105	152	144	135	
Vegetables	69	69	75	71	58	61	97	103	93	
Fruits and berries	33	37	34	50	33	37	44	53	44	
Lithuania										
Meat[3]	89	66	65	56	50	52	51	49	53	
Dairy products	476	315	334	319	291	238	213	208	187	
Potatoes	146	128	95	122	99	127	133	124	131	
Vegetables	79	83	65	69	65	65	71	70	78	
Fruits and berries	33	51	30	50	45	48	52	60	60	

	Per 1 000 inhabitants:									
Telephone lines										
Estonia	231	233	247	268	n.a.	276	297	321		
Latvia[4]	247	254	263	269	277	289	302	314	336	
Lithuania	209	217	223	231	241	254	268	283		300
Registered cars										
Estonia	153	n.a.	181	208	223	257	275	293		
Latvia[2]	106	124	134	143	99	133	153	176	198	
Lithuania	132	142	151	160	175	193	212	238		265

Table A6. **Indicators of living standards** *(cont.)*

	1990	1991	1992	1993	1994	1995	1996	1997	1998	1999[1]
D. Health indicators										
Male life expectancy at birth, years										
Estonia	65	64	63	62	61	62	64	65		
Latvia	64	64	63	62	61	61	64	64	64	
Lithuania	67	65	65	63	63	64	65	66		67
Female life expectancy at birth, years										
Estonia	70	70	69	68	67	68	70	70		
Latvia	75	75	75	74	73	73	76	76	76	
Lithuania	76	76	76	75	75	75	76	77		77
Infant mortality[5]										
Estonia	12	13	16	16	15	15	10	10		
Latvia	14	16	17	16	16	19	16	15	15	
Lithuania	10	14	16	16	14	12	10	10		9

1. Indices of after-tax wages divided by the consumer price index. For Estonia, the fourth quarter each year.
2. In 1990-1995 percentage in monetary expenditures; 1996-1999 percentage in total (monetary + in-kind expenditure).
3. Lithuania: meat and meat products, including offals and category II sub-products.
4. Introd. of a new car register in 1994 led to the de-registration of many cars.
5. Deaths before the age of 1 year per 1 000 live births.
Source: *Statistical yearbooks;* data submitted by the Central Statistical Bureau of Latvia; MOSSL, 1998; LS, 1999.

Table A7. Employment by main sector

A. Per cent distribution

	Estonia					Latvia					Lithuania				
	Agriculture[1]	Industry	Construction	Services	Total	Agriculture[1]	Industry	Construction	Services	Total	Agriculture[1]	Industry	Construction	Services	Total
1989	21	29	8	42	100						18	30	12	40	100
1990	21	29	8	42	100	17	28	10	45	100	21	30	11	38	100
1991	20	28	8	43	100	18	27	9	46	100	18	30	10	43	100
1992	19	28	8	46	100	20	25	7	48	100	20	29	9	43	100
1993	17	26	7	50	100	20	23	5	52	100	23	26	7	45	100
1994	15	25	7	53	100	19	21	6	54	100	23	22	7	48	100
1995	11	29	5	55	100	18	20	5	56	100	24	21	7	48	100
1996	10	28	6	57	100	18	20	6	56	100	24	20	7	49	100
1997	9	26	7	57	100	19	20	6	55	100					
1998	10	26	8	57	100	18	18	6	58	100	22	20	7	61	100

B. Employment index: 1990 = 100

	Estonia					Latvia					Lithuania				
	Agriculture[1]	Industry	Construction	Services	Total	Agriculture[1]	Industry	Construction	Services	Total	Agriculture[1]	Industry	Construction	Services	Total
1989	102	104	98	100	101						86	105	108	109	103
1990	100	100	100	100	100	100	100	100	100	100	100	100	100	100	100
1991	95	96	99	100	98	101	95	96	102	99	85	104	87	115	102
1992	84	88	91	100	93	110	87	65	102	95	92	98	81	112	100
1993	68	76	79	103	86	99	73	50	102	88	101	84	61	113	96
1994	58	73	75	106	84	85	58	44	92	77	99	69	53	113	90
1995	40	79	54	104	79	79	55	41	92	74	99	64	55	112	89
1996	37	75	56	105	78	76	52	43	90	72	101	61	57	114	90
1997	35	71	72	106	78	79	53	44	90	74	92	61	57	121	90
1998	35	69	73	106	78	75	49	46	92	74	90	61	57	121	89

1. Including forestry, hunting and fishing.
Source: Estimations based on official statistics.

Table A8. **Employment in industry by sector**

Thousands

Type of industry	Estonia			Latvia			Lithuania[1]		
	1990	1996	1998	1990	1996	1997	1992	1995	1997
Consumer-oriented industry	*76*	*89*	*89*	*123*	*94*	*106*	*134.5*	*129*	*134.4*
Food, tobacco	32	31	28	43	41	46	65	61	58.6
Clothing, shoes	20	20	20	31	16	18	35	33	32.7
Wood products	6	19	22	16	21	28	12	18	22.3
Other manufacturing	18	19	19	28	8	8	19	12	12.9
Publishing	n.a.	n.a.	n.a.	6	7	7	4	6	7.9
Producers of industrial inputs	*88*	*51*	*41*	*97*	*39*	*38*	*114*	*76*	*67.7*
Mining	12	9	7	4	3	2	5	3	3.7
Metallurgy	8	6	6	3	3	3	3	1	1.8
Textiles	23	12	9	40	14	15	52	34	28.7
Pulp, paper	9	6	5	4	2	2	7	5	4.1
Fuels, chemicals	16	8	8	17	9	9	15	11	11.8
Rubber, plastics	5	3	2	3	2	2	4	4	3.9
Non-metallic minerals	15	8	4	26	6	5	29	18	13.7
Engineering industry	*56*	*25*	*18*	*154*	*46*	*41*	*127*	*70*	*55.4*
Machinery, metal products	31	10	8	70	19	19	55	32	24.3
Electrical machinery	19	8	7	57	13	10	59	29	22.3
Transport equipment	6	8	4	27	14	12	13	9	8.7
Energy and water	*19*	*16*	*17*	*14*	*19*	*20*	*30*	*35*	*36.2*
Total	**238**	**181**	**165**	**388**	**202**	**209**	**405**	**310**	**293.7**

1. Dependent employees.
Source: Statistical yearbooks, various editions.

Table A9. **Labour force developments in Estonia, 1989-98**

Age	Labour force participation Per cent of age-group population			Employment Per cent of age-group population			Unemployment Per cent of the labour force		
	1989	1995	1998	1989	1995	1998	1989	1995	1998
Women									
15-19	32	21	14	31	17	11	2	21	20
20-24	66	58	63	65	50	57	1	14	10
25-49	90	86	83	90	79	75	–	8	10
50-54	90	84	87	90	77	82	–	8	5
55-59	54	44	57	54	42	55	–	5	4
60-64	46	23	25	46	22	24	–	2	4
65-69	35	11	9	35	10	8	1	9	3
15-64	74	66	66	74	61	61	1	9	9
15-	62	53	53	62	49	48	–	9	9
Men									
15-19	25	23	20	24	16	14	1	32	33
20-24	83	88	78	81	81	68	–	8	12
25-49	98	94	93	98	84	84	–	11	10
50-54	94	86	87	93	80	80	–	8	8
55-59	85	78	78	85	71	70	–	9	10
60-64	63	39	47	63	36	47	–	6	2
65-69	51	17	17	50	17	17	–	5	1
15-64	84	79	78	83	71	70	–	11	11
15-	78	71	70	77	64	62	–	11	10

Note: Persons who left Estonia in the period are not included. Small values may not be statistically significant.
Source: Labour Force Surveys, 1995 and second quarter 1998.

Table A10. **Labour force participation, employment and unemployment**

Age	Labour force participation Per cent of age-group population			Employment Per cent of age-group population			Unemployment Per cent of the labour force		
	Total	Urban	Rural	Total	Urban	Rural	Total	Urban	Rural
Estonia									
15-24	43	46	37	37	40	31	15	14	16
25-49	88	90	84	79	81	75	10	10	11
50-74	44	47	36	41	44	34	6	5	7
15-74	65	67	59	58	61	53	10	9	10
Latvia									
15-24	37	38	36	26	25	29	30	35	19
25-49	88	89	86	76	75	80	13	15	8
50-64	58	57	62	51	48	59	12	15	5
65-	10	6	17	9	5	17	8	18[1]	2
15-64	70	70	69	60	58	63	15	18	8
15-	59	59	59	51	49	54	15	17	8
Lithuania									
14-24	42	36	54	32	26	43	24	28	20
25-49	92	93	90	80	79	80	14	14	12
50-64	57	60	51	52	54	48	9	10	7
65-	6	5	7	6	5	7	1	1	–
14-64	72	72	70	62	61	63	14	15	12
14-	62	64	58	53	54	51	14	15	12

Note. The age groupings differ between countries.
1. Age for urban unemployment: 64-
Source: Labour Force Surveys, second quarter 1998.

Table A11. **Employment and educational attainment**

Level of education attained	Estonia		Latvia		Lithuania	
	Labour force participation	Unemployment	Labour force participation	Unemployment	Labour force participation	Unemployment
A. Age from about 15[1]						
Primary or less	14	15	16	23	12	15
Lower secondary	38	16	35	20	51	19
Upper secondary	74	11	71	15	76	18
Tertiary	81	5	79	7	82	9
Average	*65*	*10*	*59*	*15*	*62*	*14*
B. Age 25-64						
Less than upper-secondary	57	15	60	13	61	11
Upper secondary	83	10	79	9	79	7
Tertiary	87	5	88	6	87	4

Note: Labour force participation as per cent of the adult population. Unemployment as per cent of the labour force.
1. Age 15-74 in Estonia, 15 or more in Latvia, 14 or more in Lithuania.
Source: Labour Force Surveys, second quarter 1998. For OECD countries, 1996 data from *Employment Outlook*, 1999, Table D.

Table A12. **Wage characteristics**

Per cent of the workers concerned

	Fixed pay	Only performance pay[1]	Combinations	Other, don't know	Delays in wage payment[1]		
					No delay	Up to one month	Over one month
Estonia	46	22	25	7	81	15	4
Latvia	60	21	14	5	84	12	4
Lithuania	55	22	17	6	75	16	9

1.   Proportion having experienced a delay during the past year.
Source: Antila and Ylöstalo, 1999. The figures represent replies by workers interviewed in surveys.

Table A13. **Relative wages by sector**

Wages before tax as per cent of the national average

	Estonia			Latvia			Lithuania[1]	
	1992	1994	1998	1990[2]	1993[2]	1998	1994	1998
Finance	196	206	224	145	190	233[3]	232	177
Energy and water	152	143	135[3]	101	128	145[3]	164	129
Public administration	97	130	127	125	105	126	140	145
Transports and communication	158	134	125	118	173	139	141	115
Mining and quarrying	134	141	117[3]	98	96	105	120	120
Real-estate management	89	104	111	101	77	105[3]	91	112
Construction	118	116	100	132	97	99	163	102
Manufacturing	98	101	97	106	90	101	108	98
Education	84	78	87	67	76	81	70	89
Health and social care	76	77	94	70	77	78	69	79
Other services	80	80	81[3]	83	77	84[3]	65	82
Trade	94	85	84	97	88	72	98	89
Hotels and restaurants	73	66	61[3]	74	89	64[3]	80	66
Agriculture and forestry	73	53	57[3]	97	77	70	66	59
Total	100	100	100	100	100	100	100	100

Note: Sectors were ranked according to unweighted averages of their relative wages in the three countries in 1998.
1.   September. Sole proprietorships are excluded.
2.   Public sector only.
3.   Sectors accounting for 1 to 5 % of employment in 1998.
Sources: Statistical yearbooks. 1998 data quoted from *Estonian Statistics* (1998) and No. 2 (86), 1999; *Monthly Bulletin of Latvian Statistics*, No. 3 (58), 1999 and *Economic and Social Development in Lithuania*, October 1998.

Table A14. **Consumption expenditure in rural versus urban households**

Per cent

Type of expenditure	Distribution by type of expenditure		Ratio of rural to urban per-capita consumption[1]
	Rural households	Urban households	
		Estonia	
Monetary	81	93	67
In kind	19	7	216
Total	100	100	78
		Latvia	
Monetary	73	92	59
In kind	27	8	241
Total	100	100	74
		Lithuania	
Monetary	68	89	56
In kind	32	11	208
Total	100	100	73

1.   Rural household consumption per capita as per cent of urban household consumption per capita.
Source: SOE, 1997; LS, 1998; data submitted by the Central Statistical Bureau of Latvia.

Table A15. **Regional disparities**
Estonia

District	Employment/population ratio Per cent of the working-age population				Unemployment rate (LFS) Per cent of the labour force	Wages National	Population (1 000)
	1989	1992	1995	1998	1998	Q4 1998	1998
Harju (Tallinn)	78	73	66	63	9	122	538
West							
Lääne	73	69	61	59	6	86	32
Hiiu	85	78	69	66	3	71	12
Saare	77	68	62	57	7	85	40
North East							
Ida-Viru	78	69	59	54	14	79	198
Lääne-Viru	76	71	61	57	7	83	76
Järva	76	72	67	57	11	79	43
Rapla	76	68	59	56	10	83	40
South-Centre							
Pärnu	75	67	60	62	6	79	100
Viljandi	75	68	60	56	8	83	63
Jõgeva	75	68	56	52	14	79	42
South East							
Tartu	71	68	62	55	9	88	151
Pölva	74	59	52	50	13	88	36
Valga	71	63	53	55	11	75	39
Võru	75	61	55	50	11	73	43
Total	*76*	*70*	*62*	*58*	*10*	*100*	*1 454*

Source: Labour Force Surveys. For 1989-1995, age 15-69; for 1998, age 15-74. Wage data from SOE, 1998.

Table A15. **Regional disparities** *(cont.)*
Latvia

District	Unemployment rate			Wages (National average = 100)		Population (1 000)
	1995	1997	1997	1995	1997	1998
	Registers	Registers	LFS			
Riga city	3	4	11	112	115	806
Riga district	4	5	13	101	100	145
Centre						
Jelgava city	5	9	16	83	83	71
Jelgava district	6	10	18	71	70	35
Jurmala city	5	6	15	97	99	59
Ogre	3	4	12	86	87	64
Bauska	5	7	14	78	78	52
South East						
Daugavpils city	8	9	16	93	83	117
Daugavpils district	15	15	23	72	68	44
Kraslava	24	26	31	71	68	38
Aizkraukle	11	11	19	79	81	43
Jekabpils	18	17	23	74	74	57
East						
Rezekne city	13	13	20	84	82	41
Rezekne district	26	30	36	61	62	42
Aluksne	10	13	19	69	71	27
Gulbene	8	11	18	76	70	29
Balvi	21	23	29	72	68	32
Ludza	14	17	25	64	65	39
Madona	14	14	21	72	69	48
Preili	23	23	29	64	67	42
West						
Liepaja city	9	8	15	97	97	96
Liepaja district	11	11	18	71	71	50
Ventspils city	2	3	11	184	780	47
Ventspils district	5	8	15	79	73	14
Saldus	2	5	13	76	73	39
Talsi	6	5	13	84	86	49
Tukums	4	5	13	80	76	55
Dobele	8	11	18	79	78	41
Kuldiga	7	7	15	78	82	38
North						
Cesis	5	8	15	74	81	62
Valka	5	7	15	81	80	35
Valmiera	6	10	17	86	83	61
Limbazi	5	6	14	90	101	41
Total	*6*	*8*	*15*	*100*	*100*	*2 458*

Source: Statistical yearbooks, Labour Force Survey.

Table A15. **Regional disparities** *(cont.)*
Lithuania

Province	Employment/population ratio Per cent of the working-age population (14 years and older)	Unemployment rate Per cent of the labour force				Population (1 000)
	1998	1992	1995	1998	1998	1996[1]
	LFS	Registers	Registers	Registers	LFS	
Vilnius	53	1.5	5	6	15	898
Kaunas	54	0.8	5	5	12	756
Klaipéda	55	0.9	7	5	13	416
Alytus	52	1.2	9	9	17	203
Marijampolé	55	1.2	6	8	12	199
Panevézys	50	1.4	6	8	17	324
Siauliai	54	1.3	7	9	15	402
Tauragé	46	2.9	13	9	15	130
Telsiai	50	0.9	7	6	12	183
Utena	54	2.1	6	7	16	203
Total	*53*	*1.3*	*6*	*6*	*14*	*3 712*

1. 1st January.
Source: Statistical yearbooks and Labour Force Survey, May 1998.

Table A16. **Internal and external mobility**

Persons moving per year as per cent of the population

	Internal migration[1]	*Of which:* between districts	Emigration (abroad)	Immigration (from abroad)	Total	Net emigration
Estonia						
1995	2.0	n.a.	0.7	0.1	2.8	0.6
1996	2.3	1.0	0.5	0.1	2.9	0.4
1997	2.2	0.9	0.3	0.1	2.6	0.2
Latvia						
1995	1.6	n.a.	0.5	0.1	2.2	0.4
1996	1.6	1.3	0.4	0.1	2.1	0.3
1997	1.6	1.3	0.4	0.1	2.1	0.3
1998	1.5	1.3	0.3	0.1	1.9	0.2
Lithuania						
1995	2.3[2]	n.a.	0.10	0.05	2.4	−0.05
1996	2.2	n.a.	0.11	0.1	2.3	−0.02
1997	2.1	n.a.	0.1	0.1	2.2	0.00
1998	1.7	n.a.	0.1	0.1	1.8	−0.01

1. Includes mobility between small territorial units within districts.
2. Demographic Yearbook 1998.
Source: Statistical yearbooks.

Table A17. **Balance of payments**
Estonia

Millions of US$

	1992	1993	1994	1995	1996	1997	1998
Trade balance	−90.4	−144.8	−355.3	−664.2	−1 021.1	−1 127.7	−1 116.8
Exports of goods	460.7	811.7	1 218.4	1 694.6	1 814.3	2 295.9	2 684.6
Imports of goods	551.1	956.5	1 573.7	2 358.8	2 835.4	3 423.6	3 801.4
Service balance	42.7	75.2	104.9	377.7	519.0	593.0	571.9
Service exports	203.1	334.5	512.4	874.2	1 109.6	1 323.1	1 478.1
Service imports	160.4	259.3	407.5	496.5	590.6	730.1	906.2
Net income	−13.2	−13.9	−29.6	2.8	2.3	−146.1	−81.0
Income receipts	0.5	26.9	37.3	63.6	112.4	115.3	133.5
Income payments	13.6	40.8	66.9	60.9	110.1	261.4	214.5
Net current transfers	97.1	105.2	114.8	126.3	100.7	116.7	148.4
Current account balance	36.2	21.6	−165.2	−157.9	−399.4	−562.8	−479.7
Net capital account	27.4	0.0	−0.6	−0.8	−0.6	−0.3	1.7
Foreign direct investment, net	80.4	156.0	212.2	199.0	110.6	129.9	574.6
Portfolio investment	0.0	−0.2	−14.1	−22.1	145.4	262.4	−9.7
Other net investment	−81.7	63.0	−30.7	69.1	274.3	391.9	−76.7
Net errors and omissions	−4.4	−45.8	30.5	18.1	−30.8	−24.0	−0.7
Reserves and related items	−57.9	−194.7	−30.7	−105.5	−101.0	−196.5	−11.1
Gross international reserves	197.5	389.2	446.4	583.0	639.8	760.0	743.2
Long-term debt	47.8	96.1	117.0	164.9	220.3	296.5	
Share of GDP (%)							
Trade balance	−8.3	−8.9	−15.6	−18.7	−23.4	−24.3	−21.5
Exports of goods	42.2	49.7	53.5	47.7	41.6	49.5	51.6
Imports of goods	50.5	58.5	69.1	66.4	65.1	73.9	73.1
Current account balance	3.3	1.3	−7.3	−4.4	−9.2	−12.1	−9.2
Foreign direct investment, net	7.4	9.5	9.3	5.6	2.5	2.8	11.0
Gross international reserves	18.1	23.8	19.6	16.4	14.7	16.4	14.3
Long-term debt	18.1	23.8	19.6	16.4	14.7	16.4	
Memo item:							
GDP at market price	1 091.7	1 634.2	2 278.5	3 550.4	4 358.1	4 633.6	5 201.7

Source: National Bank of Estonia.

Table A18. **Balance of payments**
Latvia

Millions of US$

	1992	1993	1994	1995	1996	1997	Prelim. 1998
Trade balance	−40.3	3.1	−300.6	−579.6	−798.3	−847.9	−1 130.4
Exports of goods	799.9	1 054.4	1 021.7	1 367.6	1 487.6	1 838.1	2 011.1
Imports of goods	840.2	1 051.3	1 322.3	1 947.2	2 285.9	2 686.0	3 141.5
Service balance	134.1	328.6	360.5	474.1	383.8	370.6	279.8
Service exports	290.5	533.4	657.1	720.1	1 125.5	1 033.0	1 040.2
Service imports	156.4	204.8	296.7	246.0	741.7	662.4	760.4
Net income	1.5	7.2	8.6	18.6	41.2	54.9	53.7
Income receipts	2.5	17.3	50.8	71.1	140.5	177.0	207.6
Income payments	1.0	10.0	42.2	52.5	99.3	122.1	153.9
Net current transfers	96.1	77.9	132.8	70.8	93.5	77.4	84.3
Current account balance	191.4	416.8	201.2	−16.2	−279.8	−345.0	−712.7
Net capital account	0.0	0.0	0.0	0.0	0.0	13.7	11.0
Foreign direct investment, net	27.3	49.6	279.1	244.6	378.7	515.0	302.5
Portfolio investment	0.0	0.0	−22.0	−37.0	−141.0	−571.0	−6.6
Other net investment	−137.4	17.4	106.3	428.0	299.4	403.0	304.5
Net errors and omissions	−43.8	−186.2	−508.0	−652.6	−46.3	86.5	163.9
Reserves and related items	−37.5	−297.6	−56.5	33.2	−211.1	−102.2	−62.6
Gross international reserves	n.a.	526.4	640.7	602.1	746.1	776.3	789.0
Long-term debt	30.0	123.6	207.5	271.1	300.6	352.3	
Share of GDP (%)							
Trade balance	−2.7	0.1	−8.2	−13.0	−15.5	−15.0	−17.7
Exports of goods	54.5	48.5	28.0	30.7	29.0	32.6	31.4
Imports of goods	57.2	48.3	36.2	43.7	44.5	47.6	49.1
Current account balance	13.0	19.2	5.5	−0.4	−5.4	−6.1	−11.1
Foreign direct investment, net	1.9	2.3	7.6	5.5	7.4	9.1	4.7
Gross international reserves	n.a.	24.2	17.6	13.5	14.5	13.8	12.3
Long-term debt	2.0	5.7	5.7	6.1	5.9	6.2	
Memo item:							
GDP at market price	1 468.7	2 175.3	3 650.1	4 452.6	5 136.3	5 639.6	6 397.8

Source: National Bank of Latvia.

Table A19. **Balance of payments
Lithuania**

Millions of US$

	1993	1994	1995	1996	1997	1998
Trade balance	−154.8	−204.9	−698.0	−896.2	−1 147.5	−1 518.4
Exports of goods	2 025.8	2 029.2	2 706.1	3 413.1	4 192.4	3 961.6
Imports of goods	2 180.5	2 234.1	3 404.1	4 309.3	5 339.9	5 480.0
Service balance	−55.1	−54.5	−12.9	120.9	134.5	240.7
Service exports	197.8	322.0	485.3	797.6	1 031.9	1 109.1
Service imports	252.9	376.5	498.2	676.7	897.4	868.5
Net income	8.3	8.6	−12.9	−91.0	−198.4	−255.5
Income receipts	12.5	21.4	50.9	51.9	80.1	124.6
Income payments	4.3	12.8	63.8	142.9	278.5	380.0
Net current transfers	115.9	156.8	109.3	143.8	230.0	235.0
Current account balance	−85.7	−94.0	−614.4	−722.6	−981.4	−1 298.1
Net capital account	..	12.9	2.7	5.5	4.5	0.9
Foreign direct investment, net	30.2	31.3	71.6	152.3	327.5	921.4
Portfolio investment	−0.3	4.4	76.2	187.7	188.2	−52.8
Other net investment	271.8	272.6	449.7	337.9	501.6	545.4
Net errors and omissions	68.4	−43.4	287.7	54.5	197.7	285.0
Reserves and related items	−284.2	−183.8	−231.8	−15.3	−237.8	−399.0
Total international reserves	412.3	587.2	819.0	834.3	1 062.7	1 460.0
Long-term debt	200.2	268.3	452.5	796.8	1 107.0	
Share of GDP (%)						
Trade balance	−5.8	−4.8	−11.6	−11.4	−12.0	−14.2
Exports of goods	75.8	52.6	56.5	54.6	55.7	51.3
Imports of goods	81.6	47.8	56.5	43.2	43.7	37.1
Current account balance	−3.2	−2.2	−10.2	−9.2	−10.3	−12.1
Foreign direct investment, net	1.1	0.7	1.2	1.9	3.4	8.6
Gross international reserves	15.4	13.8	13.6	10.6	11.1	13.7
Long-term debt	7.5	6.3	7.5	10.1		
Memo item:						
GDP at market price	2 670.7	4 247.2	6 025.8	7 892.3	9 585.3	10 692.0

Source: National Bank of Lithuania.

Table A20. **GDP by expenditure**
Estonia

Million EEK

	1993	1994	1995	1996	1997	1998
Current prices						
GDP	21 610	29 600	40 705	52 446	64 324	73 213
Final consumption	17 185	25 038	34 309	44 477	52 210	60 191
Private	12 711	18 248	23 959	31 845	37 990	43 656
Public	4 474	6 790	10 350	12 632	14 219	16 534
Gross capital formation	5 821	8 184	10 881	14 579	20 385	21 481
Gross fixed capital formation	5 280	8 004	10 576	14 015	17 962	21 311
Change in stocks	541	181	305	564	2 423	170
Trade balance	−928	−3 253	−3 285	−6 043	−7 423	−7 070
Exports of goods and services	15 197	22 486	29 451	35 186	50 238	58 394
Imports of goods and services	16 125	25 739	32 736	41 229	57 661	65 464
Statistical discrepancy	−469	−369	−1 200	−567	−848	−1 387
Constant prices of 1995						
GDP	39 827	39 031	40 705	42 297	46 789	48 682
Final consumption	31 074	31 451	34 309	36 215	38 641	40 996
Private	22 552	22 742	23 959	25 950	28 247	29 833
Public	8 522	8 709	10 350	10 265	10 394	11 163
Gross capital formation	10 343	10 382	10 881	12 245	15 796	15 107
Gross fixed capital formation	9 569	10 166	10 576	11 777	13 836	14 960
Change in stocks	774	216	305	468	1 960	147
Trade balance	−714	−3 139	−3 285	−5 091	−6 432	−6 758
Exports of goods and services	26 887	27 914	29 451	30 099	39 244	44 005
Imports of goods and services	27 601	31 053	32 736	35 190	45 676	50 763
Statistical discrepancy	−875	337	−1 200	−1 072	−1 216	−663

Source: Statistical Office of Estonia.

Table A21. **GDP by expenditure**
Latvia
Million lats

	1990	1991	1992	1993	1994	1995	1996	1997	1998
Current prices									
GDP	62	143	1 005	1 467	2 043	2 349	2 829	3 276	3 773
Final consumption	38	81	521	1 094	1 610	1 992	2 525	2 807	3 404
Private	33	66	396	770	1 199	1 471	1 913	2 181	2 412
Public	5	15	125	324	411	522	612	626	992
Gross capital formation	25	48	414	135	391	414	533	746	868
Gross fixed capital formation	14	9	112	202	304	355	513	614	757
Change in stocks	11	40	302	-67	87	59	20	133	111
Trade balance	-1	14	69	239	42	-57	-229	-278	-499
Exports of goods and services	30	51	803	1 074	949	1 101	1 440	1 669	1 801
Imports of goods and services	31	37	734	836	907	1 158	1 669	1 947	2 300
Constant prices of 1995									
GDP	4 737	4 243	2 764	2 353	2 368	2 349	2 428	2 637	2 731
Final consumption	4 241	3 252	2 088	1 971	2 011	1 992	2 153	2 236	2 363
Private	3 742	2 769	1 566	1 450	1 496	1 471	1 622	1 704	1 802
Public	499	483	522	521	515	522	531	533	561
Gross capital formation	1 741	1 466	1 100	379	443	414	438	492	629
Gross fixed capital formation	1 497	540	385	324	327	355	434	524	582
Change in stocks	244	926	715	55	116	59	4	-32	47
Trade balance	-1 246	-474	-424	4	-86	-57	-164	-91	-261
Exports of goods and services	1 907	1 294	1 486	1 153	1 056	1 101	1 324	1 498	1 596
Imports of goods and services	3 153	1 768	1 909	1 149	1 142	1 158	1 488	1 589	1 858

Source: Statistical Office of Latvia.

Table A22. **GDP by expenditure**
Lithuania
Million litas

	1990	1991	1992	1993	1994	1995	1996	1997	1998
Current prices									
GDP	134	415	3 406	11 590	16 904	24 103	31 569	38 340	42 768
Final consumption	102	278	2 753	10 274	14 808	20 987	26 939	32 216	35 792
Private	76	233	2 308	8 474	11 489	16 240	20 973	24 939	27 500
Public	26	45	445	1 800	3 319	4 747	5 966	7 277	8 292
Gross capital formation	44	101	536	2 222	3 113	5 959	7 731	10 176	12 087
Gross fixed capital formation	37	93	783	2 677	3 905	5 554	7 269	9 337	11 020
Change in stocks	7	8	–247	–455	–792	405	462	840	1 067
Trade balance	–11	36	116	–905	–1 017	–2 844	–3 101	–4 052	–5 110
Exports of goods and services	70	123	795	9 567	9 361	12 765	16 843	20 897	20 283
Imports of goods and services	81	87	679	10 472	10 378	15 609	19 944	24 949	25 393
Constant prices of 1995									
GDP						24 103	25 238	27 075	28 469
Final consumption						20 987	21 526	23 575	
Private						16 240	17 603	18 940	
Public						4 747	4 557	4 635	
Gross capital formation						5 959	6 452	8 315	
Gross fixed capital formation						5 554	6 160	7 610	
Change in stocks						405	392	705	
Trade balance						–2 844	–2 740	–4 815	
Exports of goods and services						12 765	14 216	18 894	
Imports of goods and services						15 609	16 956	23 709	
Statistical discrepancy						0	634	0	

Source: Statistical Office of Lithuania.

Table A23. **Employment, output and productivity growth, 1994-97**
Estonia

NACE	Title	Change in employment	Growth rate in % — Employment	Growth rate in % — Output	Growth rate in % — Productivity	Structure of employment in % — 1994	Structure of employment in % — 1997
20	Manufacture of wood	3 865	37.0	131.9	123.9	6.7	9.7
28	Manufacture of fabricated metal products	1 625	27.2	67.9	57.5	3.8	5.2
32	Manufacture of radio, television and communication equipment and apparatus	1 432	106.5	15.0	-27.2	0.9	1.9
18	Manufacture of wearing apparel	1 288	10.1	-2.2	-12.8	8.2	9.5
22	Publishing, printing and reproduction of recorded media	1 131	24.8	-10.2	-9.9	2.9	3.9
36	Manufacture of furniture and other manufactured goods	707	6.1	60.2	71.3	7.4	8.3
25	Manufacture of rubber and plastic products	637	41.3	103.1	77.7	1.0	1.5
21	Manufacture of paper and paper products	523	63.3	130.3	33.5	0.5	0.9
10+14	Mining of coal and lignite and other	312	3.0	9.2	22.1	6.6	7.2
23	Manufacture of coke, refined petroleum products	-29	-17.4	-17.0	18.4	0.1	0.1
37	Recycling	-68	-36.6	-42.4	-0.9	0.1	0.1
27	Manufacture of basic metals	-106	-28.0	-33.3	-35.3	0.2	0.2
16	Manufacture of tobacco products[1]	-270	..	..	..	0.2	0.0
33	Manufacture of medical, precision and optical instruments, watches and clocks	-291	-10.1	8.5	82.6	1.8	1.7
35	Manufacture of other transport equipment	-365	-10.5	-5.1	2.3	2.2	2.1
30	Manufacture of office machinery and computers	-379	-74.2	102.2	3.2	0.3	0.1
34	Manufacture of motor vehicles	-791	-30.4	-4.3	27.8	1.7	1.2
24	Manufacture of chemicals and chemical products	-982	-12.7	5.9	41.8	5.0	4.6
31	Manufacture of electrical machinery and apparatus	-1 128	-25.0	5.0	39.7	2.9	2.3
19	Tanning and dressing of leather and manufacture of footwear	-1 700	-38.0	1.2	36.4	2.9	1.9
26	Manufacture of other non-metallic mineral products	-2 059	-29.2	17.7	30.5	4.5	3.4
15	Manufacture of food products, beverages	-2 387	-8.5	5.3	15.8	17.9	17.3
40	Energy supply	-2 713	-19.7	20.7	32.9	8.8	7.5
29	Manufacture of machinery and equipment	-2 890	-35.1	8.3	71.8	5.3	3.6
17	Manufacture of textiles	-3 941	-31.1	106.6	202.3	8.1	5.9
	Total industry	-8 579	-5.5	20.7	32.9	100.0	100.0

1. One enterprise only which closed after 1994.
Source: Annual Industry Survey, Statistical office of Estonia.

Table A24. **Employment, output and productivity growth, 1995-98**
Latvia

NACE	Title	Change in employment	Growth rate in %			Structure of employment in %	
			Employment	Output	Productivity	1995	1998
20	Manufacture of wood and of products of wood and cork	7 932	50.2	104.6	36.2	8.5	14.2
18	Manufacture of wearing apparel	3 660	37.8	33.0	-3.5	5.2	8.0
22	Publishing, printing and reproduction of recorded media	1 444	21.2	64.1	35.3	3.7	4.9
28	Manufacture of fabricated metal products, except machinery and equipment	1 087	24.2	164.0	112.6	2.4	3.3
40	Electricity, gas, steam and hot water supply	759	4.1	-0.5	-4.4	10.0	11.5
15	Manufacture of food products and beverages	134	0.4	23.4	22.9	19.3	21.5
27	Manufacture of basic metals	93	3.5			1.4	1.6
30	Manufacture of office machinery and computers	78	106.8			0.0	0.1
25	Manufacture of rubber and plastic products	26	1.4	87.3	84.6	1.0	1.1
33	Manufacture of medical, precision and optical instruments	24	2.8			0.5	0.5
37	Recycling	19	3.9	19.7	15.2	0.3	0.3
23	Manufacture of coke, refined petroleum products	-19	-18.1			0.1	0.1
16	Manufacture of tobacco products	-42	-12.4			0.2	0.2
14	Other mining and quarrying	-48	-10.6	40.3	56.9	0.2	0.2
41	Collection, purification and distribution of water	-69	-7.3	-10.8	-3.7	0.5	0.5
10	Mining of coal and lignite; extraction of peat	-315	-22.9	4.0	34.9	0.7	0.6
21	Manufacture of pulp, paper and paper products	-462	-25.5	165.1	255.9	1.0	0.8
19	Tanning and dressing of leather	-2 288	-50.8	-40.1	21.7	2.4	1.3
24	Manufacture of chemicals and chemical products	-2 435	-27.6	-5.6	30.4	4.8	3.8
31	Manufacture of electrical machinery and apparatus n.e.c.	-2 445	-39.9	25.6	109.1	3.3	2.2
34	Manufacture of motor vehicles, trailers and semi-trailers	-2 525	-78.7	-76.1	12.5	1.7	0.4
26	Manufacture of other non-metallic mineral products	-2 543	-39.3	47.2	142.4	3.5	2.3
36	Manufacture of furniture; manufacturing n.e.c.	-2 740	-31.2	16.8	69.7	4.7	3.6
35	Manufacture of other transport equipment	-3 712	-33.3	-32.7	0.9	6.0	4.4
17	Manufacture of textiles	-3 792	-27.0	64.7	125.8	7.5	6.1
29	Manufacture of machinery and equipment n.e.c.	-4 657	-37.2	-41.7	-7.2	6.7	4.7
32	Manufacture of radio, television and communication equipment and apparatus	-5 646	-69.7	-3.4	218.7	4.4	1.5
	Total industry	-18 482	-9.9	23.8	37.5	100.0	100.0

Source: Statistical Office of Latvia.

Table A25. **Employment, output and productivity growth, 1995-97**
Lithuania

NACE	Title	Change in employment	Growth rate in %			Structure of employment in %	
			Employment	Output	Productivity	1995	1997
18	Manufacture of wearing apparel, dressing and dyeing of fur	2 960	13.9	55.5	36.5	8.9	11.3
20	Manufacture of wood and wood products	945	7.0	18.9	11.1	5.6	6.7
23	Manufacture of refined petroleum products	417	13.1	39.7	23.5	1.3	1.7
10	Extraction and agglomeration of peat	267	22.7	12.5	-8.3	0.5	0.7
22	Publishing, printing and reproduction of recorded media	239	3.9	19.4	15.0	2.6	3.0
25	Manufacture of rubber and plastic products	192	6.2	16.2	9.5	1.3	1.5
16	Manufacture of tobacco products	82	26.6	..	..	0.1	0.2
33	Manufacture of medical, precision and optical instruments	-33	-1.0	-49.0	-48.4	1.3	1.5
27	Manufacture of basic metals	-64	-3.9	-19.0	-15.8	0.7	0.7
11	Extraction crude of petroleum	-69	-16.3	..	..	0.2	0.2
37	Recycling of metal waste and scrap	-113	-23.6	-6.0	:	0.2	0.2
36	Manufacture of furniture, manufacture of n.e.c	-173	-1.5	-1.1	0.4	4.8	5.2
35	Manufacture of other transport equipment	-219	-3.2	-7.7	-4.6	2.8	3.1
14	Quarrying of stone, clay and sand	-351	-22.2	24.1	59.5	0.7	0.6
24	Manufacture of chemicals and chemical products	-435	-5.4	11.5	17.8	3.4	3.5
30	Manufacture of office machinery and computers	-545	-35.9	-16.6	30.2	0.6	0.5
31	Manufacture of electrical equipment and apparatus	-736	-11.1	73.6	95.3	2.8	2.7
21	Manufacture of pulp, paper and paper products	-830	-17.7	-13.1	5.6	1.9	1.8
28	Manufacture of fabricated metal products, except machinery and equipment	-841	-12.4	22.4	39.8	2.8	2.8
15	Manufacture of food products and beverages	-885	-1.9	-3.8	-2.0	19.8	21.7
34	Manufacture of motor vehicles, trailers and semi-trailers	-1 002	-41.7	-1.7	68.6	1.0	0.7
19	Manufacture of leather and leather products	-1 758	-25.4	-2.2	31.2	2.9	2.4
26	Manufacture of other non-metallic mineral products	-3 455	-22.7	-2.0	26.8	6.3	5.5
32	Manufacture of radio, television and communication equipment and apparatus	-4 263	-31.4	8.4	58.2	5.6	4.3
17	Manufacture of textiles	-5 807	-19.0	1.8	25.6	12.7	11.6
29	Manufacture of machinery and equipment	-6 014	-27.3	-27.5	-0.2	9.2	7.5
	Total industry	-25 519	-10.6	8.5	21.4	100.0	100.0

Source: Statistical Office of Lithuania.

Table A26. Trade structure
Estonia

SITC code	Main comparative advantages	RCA 1994	RCA 1996	RCA 1998	Export share 1998	Cumulative share of exports 1998
24	Cork and wood	6.8	6.8	8.6	9.16	9.16
76	Telecommunication and sound reproducing apparatus	-2.1	-1.8	6.2	12.18	21.34
84	Articles of apparel and clothing accessories	5.4	4.8	4.1	6.47	27.81
82	Furniture and parts; bedding and similar stuffed furnit.	2.3	3.0	2.6	3.64	31.45
63	Cork and wood manufactures	2.0	3.1	2.4	3.50	34.95
03	Fish, crustaceans, molluscs, aquatic invertebrates	6.6	4.2	2.1	3.12	38.07
28	Metalliferous ores and metal scrap	1.8	1.4	1.8	2.84	40.90
02	Dairy products and birds' eggs	3.6	3.2	1.1	2.44	43.34
65	Textile yarn, fabrics, made-up articles, n.e.s.	-0.6	1.5	1.1	5.20	48.55
52	Inorganic chemicals	1.3	1.1	0.8	1.50	50.05
32	Coal, cokes and briquettes	0.6	0.9	0.7	0.73	50.77
07	Coffee, tea, cocoa, spices, and manufactures thereof	-0.2	-0.7	0.6	4.38	55.15
56	Fertilisers	0.6	0.5	0.6	1.87	57.03
35	Electric current	1.7	1.3	0.5	0.46	57.49
51	Organic chemicals	0.3	0.9	0.4	0.90	58.39
81	Prefab buildings, sanitary, light fittings	0.1	0.2	0.3	1.19	59.58
87	Professional, scientific, control instruments n.e.s.	-0.6	-0.4	0.3	1.41	60.98
61	Leather, leather manufactures, dres. Furskins	0.0	0.2	0.2	0.50	61.48
22	Oil seeds and oleaginous fruits	-0.1	0.0	0.1	0.36	61.85
85	Footwear	-0.1	0.3	0.1	1.15	62.99

SITC code	Main comparative disadvantages	RCA 1994	RCA 1996	RCA 1998	Import share 1998	Cumulative share of imports 1998
77	Electrical machinery, apparatus and appliances, n.e.s.	-2.85	-2.70	-6.36	9.64	9.64
78	Road vehicles (including air-cushion vehicles)	-0.89	-1.41	-4.10	8.20	17.84
74	General industrial machinery and equipment, n.e.s.	-1.98	-2.02	-2.16	3.54	21.38
67	Iron and steel	-0.91	-2.43	-2.14	4.47	25.85
33	Petroleum, petroleum products and related material	-5.91	-3.37	-2.00	4.52	30.38
72	Machinery specialised for particular industries	-2.00	-1.35	-1.89	3.26	33.64
75	Office machines and automatic data processing mach.	-1.73	-0.88	-1.53	2.42	36.06
89	Miscellaneous manufactured articles, n.e.s.	-0.30	-1.05	-1.17	3.36	39.42
26	Textile fibres and their wastes	-1.38	-1.44	-1.13	1.19	40.61
55	Essential oils, perfume mater; toilet; cleans. Prep.	-0.85	-1.10	-1.12	1.39	42.00
34	Gas, natural and manufactured	-2.83	-1.82	-1.09	1.09	43.09
54	Medicinal and pharmaceutical products	-0.85	-0.56	-1.01	1.76	44.85
05	Vegetables and fruits	-0.46	-0.90	-0.98	1.46	46.31
01	Meat and meat preparations	-0.02	-0.80	-0.81	2.97	49.28
04	Cereals and cereal preparations	-0.77	-1.57	-0.79	1.07	50.35
58	Plastics in non-primary form	-0.86	-0.78	-0.79	1.03	51.38
62	Rubber manufactures, n.e.s.	-0.43	-0.62	-0.56	0.93	52.31
12	Tobacco and tobacco manufactures	-0.04	-0.50	-0.54	0.74	53.05
09	Miscellaneous edible products and preparations	-0.75	-0.57	-0.48	0.91	53.96
11	Beverages	-0.67	-0.62	-0.46	1.31	55.27

Note: RCA: Revealed Comparative Advantage indicator (see main text).
Source: Statistical office of Estonia.

Table A27. **Trade structure**
Latvia

SITC code	Main comparative advantages	RCA 1994	RCA 1996	RCA 1998	Export share 1998	Cumulative share of exports 1998
24	Cork and wood	16.2	18.5	26.0	26.4	26.4
63	Cork and wood manufactures, excluding furniture	3.7	5.4	6.7	7.1	33.5
84	Articles of apparel and clothing accessories	2.9	5.7	6.5	9.5	43.0
65	Textile yarn, fabrics, made-up art., related products	5.1	5.0	3.7	7.6	50.6
82	Furniture and parts thereof	2.6	2.3	2.9	4.0	54.6
67	Iron and steel	5.0	0.7	1.7	5.7	60.2
03	Fish, crustaceans, molluscs, preparations thereof	4.5	7.9	1.7	2.5	62.8
02	Dairy products and birds' eggs	0.9	1.7	1.5	1.9	64.7
28	Metalliferous ores and metal scrap	0.2	0.3	1.1	1.7	66.4
..	Unspecified tender	0.1	0.0	0.7	0.7	67.1
21	Hides, skins and furskins, raw	0.2	0.2	0.3	0.4	67.4
32	Coal, coke and briquettes	-0.3	-0.1	0.3	0.5	67.9
61	Leather, leather manuf. n.e.s. and dressed furskins	1.2	0.9	0.2	0.4	68.2
68	Non-ferrous metals	-0.3	-0.3	0.2	0.7	69.0
25	Pulp and waste paper	0.0	0.1	0.1	0.1	69.0
97	Coin (other than gold), not being legal tender	0.0	0.0	0.0	0.0	69.0
23	Crude rubber (including synthetic and reclaimed)	0.0	-0.1	0.0	0.0	69.0
73	Metalworking machinery	-0.2	0.2	0.0	0.3	69.3
41	Animal oils and fats	0.0	0.0	0.0	0.0	69.3
00	Live animals chiefly for food	-0.6	0.0	-0.1	0.0	69.4

SITC code	Main comparative disadvantages	RCA 1994	RCA 1996	RCA 1998	Import share 1998	Cumulative share of imports 1998
78	Road vehicles incl. air cushion vehicles	0.2	-2.8	-7.8	8.9	8.9
33	Petroleum, petroleum products and related materials	-17.7	-12.5	-4.7	5.9	14.8
72	Machinery specialised for particular industries	-2.9	-2.2	-3.5	4.3	19.1
34	Gas, natural and manufactured	-6.9	-3.8	-3.4	3.4	22.5
76	Telecommunications, sound recording apparatus	-0.7	-1.7	-3.3	3.9	26.3
75	Office machines, automatic data-processing equip.	-1.9	-2.0	-2.5	3.2	29.5
74	General industrial machinery and equipment and parts	-0.7	-1.9	-2.4	4.0	33.5
64	Paper, paperboard, paper articles, paper-pulp/board	-1.7	-2.5	-2.3	3.5	37.0
69	Manufactures of metal n.e.s.	-0.9	-1.0	-1.9	3.2	40.2
77	Electrical machinery, apparatus and appliances n.e.s.	0.1	0.8	-1.7	4.8	44.9
54	Medicinal and pharmaceutical products	-1.3	-0.6	-1.4	4.0	48.9
66	Non-metallic mineral manufactures n.e.s.	-0.4	-0.6	-1.3	2.4	51.3
55	Essential oils, perfume materials, toilet-cleansing mat.	1.1	-1.2	-1.2	1.8	53.1
87	Professional, scientific and controlling instruments	-1.4	-1.3	-1.1	1.5	54.7
51	Organic chemicals	-1.7	-1.2	-1.1	1.5	56.2
07	Coffee, tea, cocoa, spices, manuf. thereof	0.4	-0.3	-1.0	1.6	57.8
58	Plastics in non-primary forms	-0.4	-0.7	-1.0	1.1	59.0
26	Textile fibres (except wool tops) and their wastes	-0.1	-0.8	-0.9	1.1	60.0
12	Tobacco and tobacco manufactures	0.3	-0.2	-0.9	1.0	61.0
62	Rubber manufactures n.e.s.	-0.7	-0.7	-0.9	1.0	62.1

Note: RCA: Revealed Comparative Advantage indicator (see main text).
Source: Statistical Office of Latvia.

Table A28. **Trade structure**
Lithuania

SITC code	Main comparative advantages	RCA 1994	RCA 1996	RCA 1998	Export share 1998	Cumulative share of exports 1998
84	Articles of apparel and clothing accessories	4.3	8.0	9.9	11.2	11.2
56	Fertilisers	3.9	4.2	4.4	4.8	16.1
33	Petroleum, petroleum products and related materials	-7.1	-1.7	3.7	14.5	30.6
35	Electric current	-0.5	2.5	2.9	3.0	33.6
24	Cork and wood	2.5	4.1	2.7	3.2	36.7
82	Furniture and parts; bedding and similar stuffed furniture	1.2	1.1	1.5	2.1	38.8
28	Metalliferous ores and metal scrap	1.6	1.4	1.2	1.4	40.3
77	Electrical machinery, apparatus and appliances, n.e.s.	1.8	1.5	1.1	6.1	46.4
63	Cork and wood manufactures	0.9	1.1	0.9	1.6	47.9
65	Textile, yarn, fabrics, made-up articles, n.e.s.	1.6	1.0	0.5	6.8	54.7
79	Other transport Equipment	0.0	0.3	0.4	1.3	56.0
61	Leather, leather manufactures, n.e.s., dres. furskins	0.7	0.5	0.3	0.7	56.7
83	Travel goods, handbags and similar containers	0.0	0.0	0.2	0.3	57.0
32	Coal, cokes and briquettes	1.0	-0.2	0.1	0.4	57.3
51	Organic chemicals	1.8	0.6	0.1	0.5	57.9
22	Oil seeds and oleaginous fruits	-0.9	0.1	0.0	0.6	58.4
21	Hides, skins and furskin, raw	0.1	-0.2	0.0	0.3	58.7
71	Power generating machinery and equipment	0.2	0.1	0.0	0.7	59.4
23	Crude rubber (incl. synthetic and reclaimed)	0.0	0.2	0.0	0.1	59.5
25	Pulp and waste paper	0.0	0.0	0.0	0.2	59.7

SITC code	Main comparative disadvantages	RCA 1994	RCA 1996	RCA 1998	Import share 1998	Cumulative share of imports 1998
78	Road vehicles (including air-cushion vehicles)	-2.1	-2.8	-4.2	10.8	10.8
72	Machinery specialised for particular industries	-3.9	-2.1	-2.9	3.7	14.5
34	Gas, natural and manufactured	-5.5	-3.7	-2.6	3.0	17.5
74	General industrial machinery and equipment, n.e.s.	-1.2	-1.4	-2.4	4.1	21.6
67	Iron and steel	-1.1	-2.0	-2.0	2.9	24.5
76	Telecommunications and sound reproducing apparatus	-1.9	-1.1	-1.7	3.3	27.8
54	Medicinal and pharmaceutical products	-1.5	-1.4	-1.6	3.1	30.9
89	Miscellaneous manufactured articles, n.e.s.	-0.5	-1.2	-1.6	3.2	34.1
75	Office machines and automatic data processing machines	-1.8	-1.3	-1.5	2.0	36.1
64	Paper, paperboard, articles of paper pulp, paper, etc.	-0.7	-1.2	-1.3	2.4	38.5
69	Manufactures of metals	-0.5	-1.2	-1.2	2.4	40.9
27	Crude fertilisers and crude minerals	-0.8	-1.1	-1.1	1.2	42.1
53	Dyeing, tanning and colouring materials	-0.8	-0.9	-1.0	1.4	43.5
26	Textiles fibres and their wastes	-0.5	-0.9	-1.0	1.4	44.9
57	Plastics in primary form	-0.4	-0.8	-0.9	1.5	46.4
93	Special transactions and commodities not classified	0.0	-1.1	-0.8	0.8	47.3
55	Essential oils, perfume mater; toilet, cleans. Prep	-0.6	-0.8	-0.8	1.9	49.2
62	Rubber manufactures, n.e.s.	-0.4	-0.6	-0.7	1.0	50.2
87	Professional, scientif., control. Instruments, n.e.s.	-0.4	-0.5	-0.7	1.6	51.8
58	Plastics in non-primary form	-0.5	-0.6	-0.7	1.4	53.2

Note: RCA: Revealed Comparative Advantage indicator (see main text).
Source: Statistical Office of Lithuania.

Table A29.   **Consolidated general government operations, 1994-99**
Estonia

Per cent GDP

	1994	1995	1996	1997	1998	1999p
Total revenue	**41.3**	**40.5**	**39.0**	**39.6**	**39.5**	**38.2**
Tax revenues	38.8	38.4	37.0	37.4	37.1	36.2
Direct taxes	24.6	24.2	22.6	22.5	23.7	22.6
Corporate tax	3.4	2.6	1.7	1.9	2.6	1.9
Income tax	7.9	8.8	8.3	8.1	8.5	8.6
Social security tax	12.8	12.4	12.2	12.0	12.1	11.7
Property taxes	0.4	0.4	0.4	0.4	0.4	0.4
Indirect taxes	13.6	13.0	13.3	14.1	12.6	12.7
VAT	11.0	10.1	10.0	10.4	8.8	8.6
Excise	2.0	2.8	3.3	3.7	3.8	4.1
Other	0.6	0.2	0.0	0.0	0.0	0.0
Other	0.6	1.2	1.0	0.8	0.8	1.0
Non-tax revenue	2.5	2.1	2.0	2.2	2.4	2.0
Total expenditures	**38.5**	**41.4**	**40.4**	**37.7**	**39.7**	**41.7**
Current expenditures	34.3	36.7	35.5	33.9	35.4	37.8
Wages and salaries	10.6	10.4	9.4	8.3	9.3	10.5
Goods and services	11.4	14.3	14.3	14.6	15.1	14.9
Subsidies	0.9	0.5	0.4	0.3	0.4	0.5
Transfers to households	10.4	11.0	11.1	10.4	10.3	11.5
of which: Pensions	6.5	7.1	7.6	7.2	7.1	8.2
Other taxes	1.1	0.5	0.3	0.4	0.3	0.3
Capital expenditures	4.1	4.7	4.9	3.9	4.2	4.0
Discrepancy	0.1	0.0	0.0	0.0	0.0	0.0
Overall balance excluding net lending	**2.8**	**−0.9**	**−1.5**	**1.9**	**−0.2**	**−3.5**
Net lending (−)	−1.6	−0.4	−0.1	0.1	−0.2	−0.1
Overall balance	**1.3**	**−1.3**	**−1.5**	**2.0**	**−0.3**	**−3.6**
Borrowing requirement	−1.3	1.3	1.5	−2.0	0.3	3.6
Domestic financing (net)	−2.7	−0.4	0.6	−1.9	0.0	3.2
Privatisation receipts	..	..	..	..	..	..
Foreign financing (net)	1.5	1.6	1.0	−0.1	0.3	0.4

p   Projections
Source: IMF.

Table A30. **Consolidated general government operations, 1994-99**
Latvia

Per cent GDP

	1994	1995	1996	1997	1998	1999p
Total revenue	**36.1**	**37.2**	**37.4**	**41.3**	**40.6**	**40.4**
Tax revenues	31.7	32.9	32.9	34.3	34.3	33.8
Direct taxes	20.6	20.9	19.5	21.1	20.9	21.3
Corporate tax	3.6	2.0	2.0	2.4	2.4	2.3
Income tax	4.4	5.4	5.6	6.0	5.8	6.2
Social security tax	11.6	11.9	13.4	13.1	13.4	11.6
Property taxes	1.1	1.1	1.1	1.1	1.3	1.1
Indirect taxes	11.1	11.9	13.4	13.1	13.4	12.6
VAT	8.5	9.4	9.5	8.8	8.4	7.9
Excise	1.4	1.8	3.3	3.7	4.5	4.3
Other	1.1	0.8	0.7	0.7	0.5	0.4
Other	0.0	0.0	0.0	0.0	0.0	0.0
Non-tax revenue	4.4	4.4	4.4	7.0	6.3	6.6
Total expenditures	**38.2**	**40.5**	**39.0**	**40.7**	**41.3**	**43.6**
Current expenditures	37.4	40.0	36.9	38.3	37.4	39.5
Wages and salaries	6.6	8.9	9.4	9.1	9.4	9.9
Goods and services	7.4	9.1	9.5	9.7	8.1	7.9
Subsidies	0.0	0.0	0.8	5.2	4.5	5.3
Transfers to households	16.6	17.4	15.8	13.3	14.2	15.7
of which: Pensions	. .	9.6	10.2	10.4	10.6	11.8
Other taxes	6.7	4.6	1.4	1.0	1.1	0.8
Capital expenditures	1.1	0.9	2.1	2.4	3.9	4.1
Discrepancy	−0.2	−0.4	0.0	0.0	0.0	0.0
Overall balance excluding net lending	**−2.1**	**−3.3**	**−1.7**	**0.6**	**−0.7**	**−3.2**
Net lending (−)	−2.3	−0.6	−0.2	−0.3	−0.1	−0.4
Overall balance	**−4.4**	**−3.9**	**−1.8**	**0.3**	**−0.8**	**−3.6**
Borrowing requirement	4.4	3.9	1.8	−0.3	0.8	3.6
Domestic financing (net)	2.3	2.2	1.1	−1.7	−0.6	−0.5
Privatisation receipts	0.3	0.4	0.3	1.3	1.0	0.5
Foreign financing (net)	1.7	1.4	0.4	0.2	0.3	3.7

p Projections
Source: IMF and National Authorities.

Table A31. **Consolidated general government operations, 1994-99**
Lithuania

Per cent GDP

	1994	1995	1996	1997	1998	1999p
Total revenue	**32.5**	**32.3**	**29.6**	**32.6**	**34.1**	**33.7**
Tax revenues	31.4	31.6	28.8	32.0	33.5	32.9
Direct taxes	19.2	18.4	17.3	18.7	20.5	20.0
Corporate tax	3.3	2.3	1.9	1.6	1.4	1.0
Income tax	7.0	7.0	6.6	5.1	5.7	5.9
Social security tax	8.7	8.4	8.3	11.5	12.9	12.5
Property taxes	0.2	0.7	0.6	0.6	0.5	0.6
Indirect taxes	11.0	12.3	10.5	12.5	12.2	11.6
VAT	6.8	8.2	7.2	8.7	8.4	8.5
Excise	1.7	2.5	2.6	3.0	3.1	3.2
Other	2.5	1.6	0.7	0.7	0.6	0.5
Other	1.1	0.9	1.0	0.7	0.8	0.8
Non-tax revenue	1.2	0.7	0.8	0.7	0.7	0.8
Total expenditures	**33.8**	**34.9**	**32.1**	**34.1**	**38.5**	**39.0**
Current expenditures	31.0	29.9	29.4	30.6	34.1	35.0
Wages and salaries	8.7	9.2	9.6	8.7	10.0	10.6
Goods and services	9.7	9.2	7.7	9.7	11.7	10.2
Subsidies	1.7	1.1	1.3	0.9	0.7	0.7
Transfers to households	10.8	9.9	10.0	10.5	10.5	12.0
of which: Pensions	6.3	6.2	6.1	6.4	7.0	7.6
Other taxes	0.1	0.4	0.9	0.8	1.2	1.5
Capital expenditures	3.9	3.8	2.7	2.7	2.7	1.7
Savings restitution	0.0	0.0	0.0	0.0	1.0	2.2
Discrepancy	−1.2	1.2	−0.1	0.8	0.6	0.0
Overall balance excluding net lending	**−1.3**	**−2.6**	**−2.5**	**−1.5**	**−4.3**	**−5.3**
Net lending (−)	−3.6	−1.9	−2.0	−0.3	−1.5	−2.6
of which: Mazeikiu Nafta						−1.9
Overall balance	**−4.9**	**−4.5**	**−4.5**	**−1.8**	**−5.8**	**−7.8**
Borrowing requirement	4.9	4.5	4.5	1.8	5.8	7.8
Domestic financing (net)	1.6	0.7	1.1	0.0	−0.7	0.2
Privatisation receipts	0.4	0.2	0.1	0.3	5.3	1.3
Foreign financing (net)	2.9	3.6	3.3	1.6	1.3	6.4

p   Projections.
Source: IMF.

Table A32. **Composition of consolidated bank balance sheets: assets**

Per cent

	December 1993	December 1994	December 1995	December 1996	December 1997	December 1998	June 1999
				Estonia			
Cash	9	6	5	4	3	3	3
Claims on the central bank	17	8	5	5	7	9	7
Claims on government	7	4	3	2	1	1	1
Claims on non-residents	18	23	19	12	11	10	14
Claims on residents	38	41	48	52	48	53	49
Other assets	12	18	20	24	29	25	25
Total assets	**100**	**100**	**100**	**100**	**100**	**100**	**100**
Total assets (EEK million)	*6 391.1*	*10 222.2*	*15 022.5*	*22 140.9*	*39 185.6*	*41 945.9*	*45 126.5*
				Latvia			
Cash	5	2	2	2	1	2	2
Claims on the central bank	8	3	6	5	4	5	4
Claims on government	−1	13	19	15	8	6	7
Claims on non-residents	25	33	39	50	57	45	46
Claims on residents	56	36	24	20	23	33	33
Other assets	6	13	11	9	6	9	7
Total assets	**100**	**100**	**100**	**100**	**100**	**100**	**100**
Total assets (LVL million)	*545.2*	*1 103.0*	*835.1*	*1 137.4*	*1 847.9*	*1 800.5*	*1 825.4*
				Lithuania			
Cash			1	1	2	2	2
Claims on the central bank			7	7	6	10	7
Claims on government			11	14	21	20	22
Claims on non-residents			7	16	15	10	9
Claims on residents			55	48	44	45	48
Other assets			19	14	13	13	12
Total assets			**100**	**100**	**100**	**100**	**100**
Total assets (LTL million)			*6 728.5*	*7 346.9*	*9 838.9*	*11 865.7*	*12 423.0*

Source: National authorities and OECD.

Table A33.   **Composition of consolidated bank balance sheets: liabilities**

Per cent

	December 1993	December 1994	December 1995	December 1996	December 1997	December 1998	June 1999
				Estonia			
Total deposits	75	68	64	63	54	51	54
Demand deposits	57	46	42	42	34	28	33
Time and savings deposits	4	−1	−2	0	0	5	3
Foreign exchange deposits	5	11	11	13	14	13	15
Other government deposits	8	12	13	8	6	5	4
Foreign liabilities[1]	3	8	9	16	30	28	27
Other liabilities	15	24	25	26	34	30	28
Provisions	0	2	1	1	1	2	2
Equity	11	6	9	10	10	16	15
Total liabilities	**100**	**100**	**100**	**100**	**100**	**100**	**100**
				Latvia			
Total deposits	57	45	45	35	33	36	36
Demand deposits	32	13	17	14	13	14	15
Time and savings deposits	25	14	3	2	2	5	4
Foreign exchange deposits	0	17	20	18	15	15	15
Other government deposits	0	1	4	1	3	2	1
Foreign liabilities[2]	10	19	26	39	43	41	42
Other liabilities	20	17	10	9	9	9	9
Provisions	0	0	0	0	3	3	5
Equity	14	18	19	18	12	11	7
Total liabilities	**100**	**100**	**100**	**100**	**100**	**100**	**100**
				Lithuania			
Total deposits			64	58	58	53	54
Demand deposits			23	23	26	23	20
Time and savings deposits			10	7	6	6	8
Foreign exchange deposits			21	18	16	17	19
Other government deposits			10	11	10	7	7
Foreign liabilities			5	11	12	15	13
Other liabilities			15	12	10	9	9
Provisions			0	0	0	0	0
Equity			15	20	21	23	23
Total liabilities			**100**	**100**	**100**	**100**	**100**

1.   Included in total "Other Liabilities".
2.   Foreign equity has been included under Equity rather than Foreign Liabilities.
Source: National authorities and OECD.

Table A34. Monetary survey of Estonia
End of period, millions of EEK

	1993	1994	1995	1996	Q1 1997	Q2	Q3	Q4	Q1 1998	Q2	Q3	Q4	Q1 1999	Q2	Q3
Assets															
Foreign assets (net)	5 691	7 114	7 544	7 171	7 929	8 544	8 737	5 535	6 568	7 267	5 531	5 514	7 037	8 878	8 596
Foreign assets	7 642	9 402	10 785	12 809	14 017	15 628	17 110	19 879	20 175	21 067	18 646	18 266	21 392	21 811	21 982
Bank of Estonia (BoE)	6 211	6 382	7 480	8 788	9 055	9 567	10 742	11 801	10 705	12 732	11 396	11 785	11 249	12 035	12 796
Other depository corporations[1] (ODC)	1 431	3 021	3 305	4 021	4 962	6 061	6 368	8 078	9 469	8 335	7 250	6 481	10 144	9 776	9 186
Foreign liabilities	-1 950	-2 288	-3 241	-5 638	-6 089	-7 084	-8 373	-14 344	-13 607	-13 800	-13 115	-12 752	-14 355	-12 933	-13 385
Bank of Estonia	-1 751	-1 644	-1 547	-1 434	-1 419	-1 389	-1 319	-1 253	-1 224	-1 377	-1 006	-890	-1 638	-950	-1 336
Other depository corporations	-199	-644	-1 694	-4 204	-4 670	-5 695	-7 054	-13 090	-12 383	-12 423	-12 109	-11 862	-12 717	-11 983	-12 049
Domestic credit	2 206	3 139	4 425	10 301	12 178	14 057	16 510	19 184	20 754	21 789	22 285	23 622	22 308	22 905	23 624
Claims on general government[2] (net)	-698	-1 418	-2 341	-1 712	-1 541	-2 119	-3 186	-2 762	-2 347	-2 552	-2 851	-1 469	-1 999	-1 258	-1 079
BoE claims on general government	45	0	3	3	3	4	3	4	4	3	3	3	3	3	3
General government deposits in BoE	-6	-1	0	-1	-4	-4	-5	-356	-5	-116	-129	-6	-5	-26	-6
ODC claims on general government	295	405	129	821	1 149	1 078	1 059	1 087	978	995	856	946	860	1 014	1 049
General government deposits in ODC	-1 031	-1 823	-2 473	-2 535	-2 689	-3 196	-4 244	-3 497	-3 323	-3 434	-3 581	-2 412	-2 857	-2 249	-2 125
Claims on non bank financial institutions	9	12	596	2 026	2 499	3 499	4 434	4 980	4 860	5 600	5 767	6 326	5 943	5 435	5 573
Claims on non financial public enterprises	480	361	318	417	433	443	308	320	240	107	107	226	267	256	346
Claims on private sector	2 414	4 184	5 852	9 569	10 786	12 234	14 954	16 646	18 001	18 634	19 262	18 540	18 097	18 473	18 785
Liabilities															
Money	5 228	6 320	8 203	10 757	11 160	12 643	13 557	13 223	13 305	13 808	12 856	12 750	13 268	15 388	15 728
Currency in circulation	2 381	3 071	3 804	4 268	4 293	4 611	4 662	4 588	4 478	4 865	4 568	4 539	4 495	4 902	5 084
Demand deposits	2 848	3 249	4 400	6 488	6 867	8 032	8 895	8 635	8 826	8 943	8 288	8 212	8 772	10 487	10 644
Quasi-money	852	1 609	2 142	3 367	4 094	4 399	4 908	6 286	7 088	7 338	7 893	8 047	8 258	8 648	8 664
Time and saving deposits	572	684	1 015	1 836	2 146	2 417	2 720	3 160	4 239	4 169	4 640	4 701	4 526	4 701	5 020
Foreign currency deposits	280	925	1 127	1 530	1 948	1 982	2 188	3 126	2 849	3 170	3 253	3 346	3 732	3 948	3 644
Bonds	0	40	14	68	879	1 607	2 308	369	733	655	271	201	311	309	372
Government lending funds	152	487	819	915	966	850	702	672	783	686	707	555	564	552	543
Other items (net)	1 665	1 797	1 964	2 714	3 008	3 102	3 771	4 170	5 414	6 568	6 090	7 582	6 946	6 887	6 913

1. Other depository corporations cover credit institutions and saving and loan assosiations licenced by the Bank of Estonia. Starting from 1 July 1999 savings and loan co-operatives are not included any more in banking survey.
2. General government includes central government, extra-budgetary funds and local governments.
Source: National Bank of Estonia.

Table A35. **Monetary survey of Latvia**

End of period, millions of LVL

	1993	1994	1995	1996	Q1 1997	Q2	Q3	Q4	Q1 1998	Q2	Q3	Q4	Q1 1999	Q2	Q3
Net foreign assets	313	371	306	452	462	533	614	602	608	677	488	416	417	497	418
Domestic credit	268	444	332	351	376	395	436	489	488	530	575	639	669	614	677
Credits to government (net)	-1	79	127	140	150	136	130	115	54	27	8	70	79	15	60
Credit to private persons	17	32	28	21	23	25	32	37	44	52	59	65	70	79	
Claims on private enterprises	0	294	152	173	187	214	253	309	367	430	486	481	494	490	617[1]
Claims on public enterprises	252	40	25	17	17	21	22	29	23	21	23	24	26	29	
Other items (net)	-119	-134	-114	-175	-183	-204	-244	-220	-217	-233	-142	-133	-165	-139	-137
Broad money (M2)	462	682	524	628	654	725	806	871	879	975	921	923	921	971	948
Money (M1)	208	337	334	405	407	453	496	550	549	620	588	580	585	624	581
Currency outside banks	153	213	210	264	274	286	304	333	332	352	344	340	358	372	352
Demand deposits in lats	55	124	124	141	133	167	192	217	217	268	244	240	227	252	229
Quasi-money	255	344	190	223	248	272	310	322	330	355	334	343	336	348	367
Time deposits	129	154	24	28	35	38	38	43	56	53	63	77	76	75	72
Deposits in foreign currency	126	190	166	196	213	234	272	279	274	302	271	266	261	273	295

1. Includes credit to private persons, claims on private enterprises and claims on public enterprises.
Source: National Bank of Latvia.

Table A36. **Monetary survey of Lithuania**

End of period, millions of LTL

	1995	1996	1997 Q1	Q2	Q3	Q4	1998 Q1	Q2	Q3	Q4	1999 Q1	Q2	Q3
Net foreign assets	2 377	2 639	2 724	3 208	3 763	3 483	3 296	3 283	4 452	4 292	4 144	3 747	3 260
Foreign assets	3 778	4 520	4 318	5 018	5 626	5 741	5 570	5 762	7 004	7 056	6 813	6 349	6 130
Foreign liabilities	1 401	1 880	1 594	1 810	1 863	2 258	2 273	2 479	2 552	2 764	2 669	2 602	2 870
Domestic credit	3 211	3 268	3 324	3 275	3 255	4 498	4 525	5 230	4 223	5 253	5 716	6 567	7 083
Claims on central government (net)	–751	–458	–550	–608	–711	–43	–358	15	–1 350	–566	–506	–22	274
Claims on local government	8	37	20	28	34	52	40	104	105	124	126	140	174
Claims on non-financial public enterprises	238	134	242	123	101	149	152	84	230	352	400	440	554
Claims on private sector	3 667	3 506	3 546	3 670	3 744	4 170	4 475	4 717	4 794	4 874	5 238	5 544	5 601
Claims on non-monetary financial institutions	50	48	65	63	88	170	216	312	443	470	458	465	480
Other items (net)	–31	483	493	349	255	709	681	935	979	1 218	1 717	1 488	1 530
Broad money (M2)	5 618	5 424	5 554	6 135	6 763	7 272	7 141	7 578	7 695	8 327	8 143	8 827	8 813
Money	3 488	3 611	3 598	3 951	4 450	5 110	4 860	5 161	5 146	5 571	5 205	5 470	5 214
Currency in circulation	1 907	1 899	1 973	2 162	2 255	2 536	2 490	2 726	2 554	2 800	2 663	2 942	2 737
Demand deposits	1 581	1 712	1 625	1 789	2 196	2 574	2 370	2 434	2 592	2 770	2 542	2 528	2 477
Quasi-Money	2 130	1 813	1 957	2 184	2 313	2 162	2 281	2 418	2 550	2 756	2 939	3 357	3 599
Time and savings deposits	667	488	533	574	683	623	647	685	699	750	915	1 052	1 035
Foreign currency deposits	1 463	1 326	1 423	1 610	1 630	1 539	1 634	1 733	1 850	2 007	2 023	2 305	2 565

Source: Bank of Lithuania.

BASIC STATISTICS

BASIC STATISTICS:

INTERNATIONAL COMPARISONS

	Units	Reference period [1]	Australia	Austria
Population				
Total	Thousands	1997	18 532	8 072
Inhabitants per sq. km	Number	1997	2	96
Net average annual increase over previous 10 years	%	1997	1.3	0.6
Employment				
Total civilian employment (TCE)[2]	Thousands	1997	8 430	3 685
of which:				
Agriculture	% of TCE	1997	5.2	6.8
Industry	% of TCE	1997	22.1	30.3
Services	% of TCE	1997	72.7	63.8
Gross domestic product (GDP)				
At current prices and current exchange rates	Bill. US$	1997	392.9	206.2
Per capita	US$	1997	21 202	25 549
At current prices using current PPPs[3]	Bill. US$	1997	406.8	186.3
Per capita	US$	1997	21 949	23 077
Average annual volume growth over previous 5 years	%	1997	4.1	1.9
Gross fixed capital formation (GFCF)	% of GDP	1997	21.5	24.1
of which:				
Machinery and equipment	% of GDP	1997	10.3 (96)	8.8 (96)
Residential construction	% of GDP	1997	4.4 (96)	6.2 (96)
Average annual volume growth over previous 5 years	%	1997	7.3	2.8
Gross saving ratio[4]	% of GDP	1997	18.4	23
General government				
Current expenditure on goods and services	% of GDP	1997	16.7	19.4
Current disbursements[5]	% of GDP	1996	34.8	48
Current receipts	% of GDP	1996	35.4	47.9
Net official development assistance	% of GNP	1996	0.28	0.24
Indicators of living standards				
Private consumption per capita using current PPP's[3]	US$	1997	13 585	12 951
Passenger cars, per 1 000 inhabitants	Number	1995	477	447
Telephones, per 1 000 inhabitants	Number	1995	510	465
Television sets, per 1 000 inhabitants	Number	1994	489	480
Doctors, per 1 000 inhabitants	Number	1996	2.5	2.8
Infant mortality per 1 000 live births	Number	1996	5.8	5.1
Wages and prices (average annual increase over previous 5 years)				
Wages (earnings or rates according to availability)	%	1998	1.5	5.2
Consumer prices	%	1998	2.0	1.8
Foreign trade				
Exports of goods, fob*	Mill. US$	1998	55 882	61 754
As % of GDP	%	1997	15.6	28.4
Average annual increase over previous 5 years	%	1998	5.6	9
Imports of goods, cif*	Mill. US$	1998	60 821	68 014
As % of GDP	%	1997	15.3	31.4
Average annual increase over previous 5 years	%	1998	7.5	7
Total official reserves[6]	Mill. SDR's	1998	10 942	14 628 (97)
As ratio of average monthly imports of goods	Ratio	1998	2.2	2.7 (97)

* At current prices and exchange rates.
1. Unless otherwise stated.
2. According to the definitions used in OECD Labour Force Statistics.
3. PPPs = Purchasing Power Parities.
4. Gross saving = Gross national disposable income minus private and government consumption.

EMPLOYMENT OPPORTUNITIES

Economics Department, OECD

The Economics Department of the OECD offers challenging and rewarding opportunities to economists interested in applied policy analysis in an international environment. The Department's concerns extend across the entire field of economic policy analysis, both macro-economic and microeconomic. Its main task is to provide, for discussion by committees of senior officials from Member countries, documents and papers dealing with current policy concerns. Within this programme of work, three major responsibilities are:

- to prepare regular surveys of the economies of individual Member countries;
- to issue full twice-yearly reviews of the economic situation and prospects of the OECD countries in the context of world economic trends;
- to analyse specific policy issues in a medium-term context for the OECD as a whole, and to a lesser extent for the non-OECD countries.

The documents prepared for these purposes, together with much of the Department's other economic work, appear in published form in the *OECD Economic Outlook, OECD Economic Surveys, OECD Economic Studies* and the Department's *Working Papers* series.

The Department maintains a world econometric model, INTERLINK, which plays an important role in the preparation of the policy analyses and twice-yearly projections. The availability of extensive cross-country data bases and good computer resources facilitates comparative empirical analysis, much of which is incorporated into the model.

The Department is made up of about 80 professional economists from a variety of backgrounds and Member countries. Most projects are carried out by small teams and last from four to eighteen months. Within the Department, ideas and points of view are widely discussed; there is a lively professional interchange, and all professional staff have the opportunity to contribute actively to the programme of work.

Skills the Economics Department is looking for:

a) Solid competence in using the tools of both microeconomic and macroeconomic theory to answer policy questions. Experience indicates that this normally requires the equivalent of a Ph.D. in economics or substantial relevant professional experience to compensate for a lower degree.

b) Solid knowledge of economic statistics and quantitative methods; this includes how to identify data, estimate structural relationships, apply basic techniques of time series analysis, and test hypotheses. It is essential to be able to interpret results sensibly in an economic policy context.

c) A keen interest in and extensive knowledge of policy issues, economic developments and their political/social contexts.

d) Interest and experience in analysing questions posed by policy-makers and presenting the results to them effectively and judiciously. Thus, work experience in government agencies or policy research institutions is an advantage.

e) The ability to write clearly, effectively, and to the point. The OECD is a bilingual organisation with French and English as the official languages. Candidates must have excellent knowledge of one of these languages, and some knowledge of the other. Knowledge of other languages might also be an advantage for certain posts.

f) For some posts, expertise in a particular area may be important, but a successful candidate is expected to be able to work on a broader range of topics relevant to the work of the Department. Thus, except in rare cases, the Department does not recruit narrow specialists.

g) The Department works on a tight time schedule with strict deadlines. Moreover, much of the work in the Department is carried out in small groups. Thus, the ability to work with other economists from a variety of cultural and professional backgrounds, to supervise junior staff, and to produce work on time is important.

General information

The salary for recruits depends on educational and professional background. Positions carry a basic salary from FF 318 660 or FF 393 192 for Administrators (economists) and from FF 456 924 for Principal Administrators (senior economists). This may be supplemented by expatriation and/or family allowances, depending on nationality, residence and family situation. Initial appointments are for a fixed term of two to three years.

Vacancies are open to candidates from OECD Member countries. The Organisation seeks to maintain an appropriate balance between female and male staff and among nationals from Member countries.

For further information on employment opportunities in the Economics Department, contact:

Management Support Unit
Economics Department
OECD
2, rue André-Pascal
75775 PARIS CEDEX 16
FRANCE

E-Mail: eco.contact@oecd.org

Applications citing ''ECSUR'', together with a detailed *curriculum vitae* in English or French, should be sent to the Head of Personnel at the above address.

The Electronic Advantage
Ask for our free Catalogue

The Fast and Easy way to work with statistics and graphs!

- Cut and paste capabilities
- Quick search & find functions
- Zoom for magnifying graphics
- Uses ACROBAT software
  (included free of charge)
- Works on Windows

OECD on the WEB: www.oecd.org

- ✂

Please **FAX** or **MAIL** this page to the OECD Paris,
—— or to one of the four OECD Centres *(see overleaf)* ——

○ I wish to receive the OECD Electronic Publications Catalogue **FREE OF CHARGE**

Name _____ Profession _____

Address _____

_____

City _____ E-mail _____

Country _____

Area of interest _____

Where to send your request:

In Austria, Germany and Switzerland

OECD CENTRE BONN
August-Bebel-Allee 6,
D-53175 Bonn
Tel.: (49-228) 959 1215
Fax: (49-228) 959 1218
E-mail: bonn.contact@oecd.org
Internet: www.oecd.org/bonn

In Latin America

OECD CENTRE MEXICO
Edificio INFOTEC
Av. San Fernando No. 37
Col. Toriello Guerra
Tlalpan C.P. 14050,
Mexico D.F.
Tel.: (52-5) 528 10 38
Fax: (52-5) 606 13 07
E-mail: mexico.contact@oecd.org
Internet: rtn.net.mx/ocde/

In the United States

OECD CENTER WASHINGTON
2001 L Street N.W., Suite 650
Washington, DC 20036-4922
Tel.: (202) 785 6323
Toll free: (1 800) 456-6323
Fax: (202) 785 0350
E-mail: washington.contact@oecd.org
Internet: www.oecdwash.org

In Asia

OECD CENTRE TOKYO
Landic Akasaka Bldg.
2-3-4 Akasaka, Minato-ku,
Tokyo 107-0052
Tel.: (81-3) 3586 2016
Fax: (81-3) 3584 7929
E-mail : center@oecdtokyo.org
Internet: www.oecdtokyo.org

In the rest of the world

OECD PARIS CENTRE
2 rue André-Pascal, 75775 Paris Cedex 16, France
Fax: 33 (0)1 49 10 42 76 **Tel:** 33 (0)1 49 10 42 35
E-mail : sales@oecd.org
Internet : www.oecd.org
ONLINE ORDERS: www.oecd.org/publications *(secure payment with credit card)*

OECD PUBLICATIONS, 2, rue André-Pascal, 75775 PARIS CEDEX 16
PRINTED IN FRANCE
(10 2000 41 1 P) ISBN 92-64-17541-5 – No. 51081 2000
ISSN 0376-6438